JOYCE M. LOVELY

Ice Cream
GASMASKS
AND GOD

A YOUNG GIRL GROWS UP IN THE WAR YEARS

MEREO
Cirencester

Mereo Books

1A The Wool Market Dyer Street Cirencester Gloucestershire GL7 2PR
An imprint of Memoirs Publishing www.mereobooks.com

Ice Cream, Gasmasks and God: 978-1-86151-445-5

First published in Great Britain in 2015
by Mereo Books, an imprint of Memoirs Publishing

The address for Memoirs Publishing Group Limited can be found at
www.memoirspublishing.com

The Memoirs Publishing Group Ltd Reg. No. 7834348

The Memoirs Publishing Group supports both The Forest Stewardship Council® (FSC®) and
the PEFC® leading international forest-certification organisations. Our books carrying both the
FSC label and the PEFC® and are printed on FSC®-certified paper. FSC® is the only
forest-certification scheme supported by the leading environmental organisations including
Greenpeace. Our paper procurement policy can be found at
www.memoirspublishing.com/environment

Typeset in 10/15pt Bembo
by Wiltshire Associates Publisher Services Ltd. Printed and bound in Great Britain by
Marston Book Services Ltd, Oxfordshire

CONTENTS

❈

To all those who made this story possible

PROLOGUE

When Jean, my sister in Liverpool, England, called me up to say she had something special for me on our next visit, it came as a complete surprise. Upon my arrival in the conventional semi-detached family home where she and my brother-in-law still live, she presented me with a small cardboard box which had been buried in the cockloft above the bedrooms, amongst the bags and cartons left by our mum.

I sat down at the kitchen table, carefully undid the string and opened the flap. I sat stunned. First I felt the pricking of tears, and then I began to laugh. There lay my ancient, despised, childhood World War II gasmask. It rested there staring at me eerily, the eyepiece still displaying the oval sickly-brown cellophane, which wasn't even cracked.

I carefully lifted out the heavy snout, still intact, with its perforated metal base. The black rubber had all but perished away and crumbled in the corners of the box, but the eyeshield, the snout and the tape straps that held it in place had stayed complete.

I placed the snout part back and next lifted out the wide tapes that allowed for the growth of a small child, with the safety pins still in place where Mum had pinned them during that last year of the war, seventy years before. I sat back. My eyes closed, and the memories streamed back.

World War II and the post-war years that followed in England were grim, especially for the adults. As a young child, however, I knew no other life. It was my mother, grandmother and their friends who would reminisce about cream teas at Reeces', silk stockings and knickerbocker glories, which my mother told me were large tall glasses filled with bananas, ice cream and chocolate sauce, topped with real cream. I had no idea what she was talking about, though ice cream stirred a half-buried memory. All I knew were air-raids, gasmasks, standing in queues with my mum, barbed wire, barrage balloons, and complaints about rations.

The evacuation of Dunkirk, the Battle of Britain, dog fights and North African defeats and victories meant nothing to us. We lived our lives, as children do, centred upon ourselves, and so long as my mum and dad and grandparents were around me and our home stood solid, all was well with my world. We experienced fear only when something went untoward with our individual lives.

Admittedly I did not like the air-raid siren, or the way the earth shuddered when bombs fell, or the crackle of anti-aircraft flak. Sometimes I did have nightmares about a bomb falling through my bedroom ceiling, but then I was also afraid of thunderstorms.

Everyone had adequate food. In fact malnutrition had disappeared in Britain, because everyone had the same rations. As children we heard about such luxuries as chocolate, ice cream, bananas, fresh peaches and real cream, but because we couldn't remember life with such treats and only knew what we had, we were content, so long as we had sufficient food in our tummies. We ate what was in season, most of which was grown locally, which meant enjoying food such as lettuce and tomatoes only in summer.

I remember that in 1947, when Queen Elizabeth was getting married, she reportedly did not have sufficient clothing coupons for the material for her wedding dress, and ordinary housewives sent her their own coupons to be sure she should be married in a gown to befit a future queen. Austerity therefore continued after the war, at least for a few years, before it gradually eased. Chocolate, as late as 1949, was still a special treat. In fact rationing stayed in place from January 1940 until the final ration coupons were dispensed with in 1953, the year the Queen was crowned.

It might seem strange to say this, but despite all this we enjoyed life as children. Girls played with dolls, whilst boys rolled marbles. We skipped (jumped rope) and bounced balls against the brick walls of our homes to rhymes and songs, specifically challenging us to do more and better twists and turns, all the while catching the ball. We imagined ourselves as grown-ups, dressing the part with old clothes; we listened to *Children's Hour* on the wireless; we looked forward to tea, and we had occasional treats, such as lining up outside the headmistress's study for a crisp red apple from a large box that had been sent to our school from generous Canadians. Other times we received a handful of cocoa that we made last by wetting and dipping our forefinger into the powdery mix then licking it clean.

I used to try to imagine how street lights looked. The lamp posts stood tall, but they remained unlit for six years. I loved books, but they were so scarce that a book had to be ordered weeks in advance for a child for Christmas, if it was available, and there was the inevitable queue to collect it (more on this later). Telephones were only for the rich, and cars, except for an occasional taxi, were up on blocks, or had been dispensed with altogether. Coal, garbage and even the rag-and-bone men's carts were pulled by horses.

Blackened ruins did get cleared of rubble, and cheap utilitarian housing sprang up for the homeless, but bombed-out city shops continued business from makeshift warehouse buildings even into the sixties, while McDonald's Golden Arches remained a feast that would not be sampled for another forty years.

Humour, tenacity, sharing and resourcefulness, especially by the women on the home front, kept life normal for us children. We laughed, cried, hoped and dreamed, but we never asked for more than what we knew was around us.

In writing this memoir I relived memories of childhood, teenage years and life as a young adult, including many snatches of conversation. In one instance I have changed the names to prevent the embarrassment of living family members. Otherwise all the events and happenings are true, with supportive dialogue – if not actual, authentic.

I hope that through the pages that follow the reader will taste the flavour and catch the spirit of those momentous years.

PART I
THE WAR YEARS

CHAPTER I

THE LAST LICK (1939)

When wilt Thou save the people? O God of mercy when?
Ebenezer Elliott, 1781-1849

Strawberry ice cream, pink, cool, sweet and sticky, dripped through the mouse-sized bitten-off hole at the bottom of my crispy cornet and rivuletted down my arm and on to my clean smocked yellow frock.

"Joyce! How many times do I have to tell you not to eat off the bottom of your ice cream cornet?" Exasperated, Mum raised her voice. "That's the last time I will ever buy you an ice cream."

And it was. However, Mum had nothing to do with the fulfilment of that ultimatum, for a few weeks later on September 3rd 1939, England declared war on Germany. Chocolate, ice cream, bananas and unrestricted food disappeared, or at least they did for us and the vast majority of people. Of course, as Dad used to comment, "Someone is always on the diddle," and somehow that meant they had more than we did.

Consequently, the flavour of ice cream sank into an almost bottomless pit of memory. Instead more immediate happenings caught my attention.

First, Dad and Daddy Thompson from next door showed up in our small triangular back garden, spades in hand. (Mrs Thompson always referred to her husband as 'Daddy', so everyone called him, 'Daddy Thompson'.) I sat on Horsey, my wooden toy on wheels, waiting to see what would happen next. Dad pulled out a big ball of string from his pocket while Daddy Thompson knelt on our green spiky grass with a long skinny tape measure. This was interesting. First they cordoned off a large square, then stood back talking quietly. Soon the dirt began to fly. Big spadefuls of brown soil flew up in the air, landing in a heap to the side of the string. I climbed off Horsey and pushed him over to the gaping brown scar in our nice green grass.

"Stand back, young lady!" shouted Daddy Thompson. Sweat ran down his red face. As he bent over to scoop more dirt from the hole, I could see that his bald head shone wet in the late September sun. Reluctantly I turned around and pushed my red padded horse to the back door.

"Mummy, Mummy! Why are Daddy and Daddy Thompson digging up our grass?" I stopped for a moment. "And can I have a treacle butty?"

Mum turned from washing up the breakfast dishes in the stoneware sink, placing a couple of wet plates on the wooden draining board. "You're still hungry?" she said. She brought the white loaf and a small dish of margarine out from the pantry and placed them on her round breadboard. Next she picked up the sharp bread knife I wasn't allowed to touch and began slicing.

"Now don't you go near that hole they are digging," she warned me, scraping a smear of margarine on the bread. "If you bother them, you'll have to come inside and play." She twirled a knife covered in black, gooey treacle and spread it over the thick slice. Then she folded it over and gave it to me. "Did you hear what I said?" She threw me a warning look.

"I promise, Mummy. I won't go near them. I will sit on Horsey and just watch and eat my butty. I'll be a good girl."

Mum was always telling me to be a good girl. I'd learned that if I wasn't I'd get a wallop on my bottom, and that would make me cry. I pushed Horsey to and fro with my feet while sitting on the seat, and watched, munching happily on my treacle butty, being careful not to allow the treacle to trickle down on to my freshly-ironed frock.

After midday dinner they met together again and dug and dug. They stopped at teatime, and it was then my bedtime. The next day, Sunday, the hole was huge and neatly square before Dad and Daddy Thompson stopped. Both stood back, nodding at their work, then shook hands.

Dad laughed shortly. "That's the first step to keeping us safe from old Jerry," he said. "The shelter should be here at the end of the week." They both stopped smiling.

"Thanks for helping with my hole too," said Daddy Thompson. He took off for home.

The wooden slatted fence was too high for me to peer over, though Mummy and Mrs Thompson could see each other as they talked sometimes. I could just see Mrs Thompson's head with her thin white hair, bobbing, and the cigarette always hanging out of her mouth. I wondered if she went to sleep with it at night, but I didn't like to ask.

"What is a shelter?" I asked Dad as we had our tea that evening.

"It's a place for us to go in case it isn't safe to stay in our house." He ruffled my blonde curls. "Don't you worry, Snooks. We're going to be okay. No one will harm us." But he glanced at Mum, and for some reason I felt it wasn't all right.

Daddy was true to his word. From the living room window a few days later I watched two men haul in big sheets of what looked like wavy, heavy walls and laid it by the gaping hole. As they left I ran to the front window and watched the two men rush back to their lorry, where more rippled sheets were stacked up on the back to be delivered to other homes. Huffing and puffing, and with the help of another neighbour, Dad and Daddy Thompson pushed the wavy walls into the hole. The two side walls curved and met at the top. The front and back pieces were straight, but they all fitted together, just like the big wooden jigsaw Dad helped me put together that Grandpa Bibby had made me. It took them quite some time to do this, and then to my surprise they began shovelling all the soil from the big pile back on to the top of the shelter, so it looked like a hill of dirt until I peeked in the front and saw the dark emptiness inside, like a big mouth, ready to eat me.

"A stout wooden door on the front and a couple of bunks inside, and it will be as cosy as anything." Dad put his arm around me. "You wait and see."

I soon found out. That night I snuggled down between chilled cotton sheets, searching for the hot water bottle Mum had placed there earlier. I held Teddy tight and closed my eyes.

A strange wailing pierced the inky darkness, waking me up and Mum rushed into my bedroom.

"Come on, upsee-daisy. We have to go into the shelter."

"But I want to stay in bed. It's nice and warm. I don't want to go into that horrid shelter!" I protested loudly. "It will squeeze me inside." I placed my hand on my chest.

"Look, you have a nice warm siren suit we got for you. See, your feet go in the bottom." Mum pushed my reluctant legs into the green fleece one-piece, zipped it up, right to my chin, and pulled the hood over my head. She lifted me on to her shoulder and ran down the stairs, out of the back door to the air-raid shelter.

I gazed up at the sky. Searchlights ran across the clouds, but it was quiet that night. Mum bent over to climb down the wooden steps into the musty damp evilness of the shelter. She had just placed me on a bunk when another wailing shrieked across our city,

"That's the all-clear," Mum said. She sighed. "A false alarm." She pushed open the door.

"Where's Daddy?" I suddenly asked as she unlocked the back door with her large key, glad to be outside again, away from the squeezing air-raid shelter.

"He's joined the National Fire Service, so he's on duty now, ready to fight fires."

I pushed my thumb into my mouth, accepting all she said, as she helped me back up the stairs and into my now cold bed.

Later, after a few more nights of broken sleep, I heard Mum complain to our other next door neighbour, Mrs Dodd, "Another false alarm. Why on earth do they have to put us through that?"

Mrs Dodd shrugged. "Suppose they got to test us. Make sure it works like."

"And get us all riled up!"

I glanced up at Mum. To dig up our soft green grass for that nasty air-raid shelter seemed such a shame. Maybe they would take it down and send it away, and we could have our pretty green lawn back. But they didn't.

Some time later, just after my third birthday, the first bombs fell on Liverpool. And life was changed forever.

CHAPTER 2

CHRISTMAS TRIMMINGS (1940)

Christian children all must be, mild, obedient, good as he.
Cecil Frances Alexander, 1823-1895

The siren yowled through the scary darkness. Waves of planes dropped their bombs over Liverpool, a key port and vital for imported food and materials. They aimed for the docks, often missing, thereby destroying buildings and homes. Deaths mounted.

Night after night, we scurried into the air-raid shelter. Sometimes we simply went straight to the shelter and stayed there all night. Mum would light the paraffin lamp and when it was really cold, even the portable wick-fed paraffin stove to keep us warm. Liverpool suffered 300 raids in 1940, making it the heaviest-hit city next to London. I simply accepted that this was the way life was. The months slipped by. The nights grew longer.

Nana stirred the gooey mixture as I peered at the large blue bowl on her kitchen table. I loved visiting Nana and Poppa's house, Mum's parents. Good smells of soup and home-made rolls seemed to live there. I was even allowed to go to their home by myself now that I was almost four years old. Mum stood at the corner of Alban Road, where we lived, and watched me run up Bentham Drive to where Nana lived and disappear into her front gate. She knew then that I was safe. In summertime, I walked slowly down her gravelly path so I could sniff the sweet-scented, saucer-size, deep-red roses, which just touched my nose as I dawdled by. Then on my tippy toes I reached for the knocker and let it clatter. Nana was always in, and every time she greeted me at the door with a smile.

Today was special. "Now watch how I beat up the egg," she told me. "Then I add the raisins, cut up fine, some sultanas and some currants. I was very lucky to get this fruit because they don't always have it at the Co-op." I watched her carefully as an autumn rain began beating against her kitchen window. But inside the cosiness wrapped itself around me, making me safe, while the coal fire spat, hissed and crackled, throwing heat into the small room, and bread baked in the oven beside the fire.

"Why are you making Christmas pudding so early?" I asked her. After all, nothing had been said about Father Christmas yet.

"Soon it is 'Stir Up' Sunday, and that means it is time to make the Christmas pudding. But this one is for next year." She paused and pointed to her larder, tucked into a corner of the wall. "This year's pudding is in there." She bent down and whispered. "You see, I put lots of brandy into it and that keeps it until the next year." She straightened up. "Now you can help me. You see those two little pieces of greaseproof paper screwed up? Can you throw those into the pudding?"

I did as I was told. "Why are you putting those in? What are they?"

She smiled mysteriously. "You wait and see on Christmas Day."

I thought some more. "Why are you able to have so many raisins and currants? We never have them at home."

"Ah, well, you see…" She paused as she scraped the suet batter into a pudding basin and began tying some greased paper around the rim, then a cotton cloth. "You know we can't get very much food because of the war. But your Mummy saves her sugar ration coupons, and I save mine, then we put them together, so we can buy the fruit for the Christmas pudding. We do the same thing with our meat rations. I've already put in our order at the butcher's for a piece of pork for Christmas." She sighed, then half to herself she added, "But it means we will have no meat for several weeks, and who knows if we'll get the pork roast even. Ah, well, at least we can have apples from our tree for stewed apples."

She placed the heavy basin in a pot of boiling water on the electric stove in the small scullery off the kitchen. I hated going in there as it was always cold. Usually Nana closed the door to save the heat.

"Now we have that done, how about a glass of ginger ale?"

"Oh, yes please." I sat down on the comfortable chair after Nana put three cushions underneath, so I could sit at the well-scrubbed kitchen table. She poured out two glasses of sparkly, home-made ginger ale. The bubbles tickled my nose as I took my first swallow. "Mmmm, that's really good."

"Now let's see if I can find a ginger nut to go with it," said Nana.

I watched as she brought out the square tin, with a picture of an old-fashioned lady on it. She took out two ginger biscuits. One she gave to me, and she took the other one. Biscuits were rationed too, so I enjoyed nibbling the treat to make it last. In fact I couldn't think of anything that wasn't rationed.

As I crunched on the crispy biscuit, I realized that Nana had put an egg into the pudding. Mum had told me that we were only allowed one egg each a week. That meant she or Poppa would have to do without their egg that week. I sighed this time, as well as Nana, as my favourite food was a runny boiled egg for my tea, and I couldn't have it very often. Powdered eggs didn't taste so good, even when scrambled.

All too soon, Nana said, "Well, Joyce, I think your Mummy will be wanting you home now."

Reluctantly I let her help me on with my mac, then she walked me out to the gate, and leaned over it watching as I jumped over the cracks in the pavement and into the

puddles and back down Bentham Drive to Alban Road, where I lived, just around the corner.

A few weeks after the Christmas pudding had been made, Mum began talking about Christmas. I watched excitedly as she brought in holly cut from a hedge and arranged sprigs of it on the pictures and mirror.

"Okay," said Dad, as I watched Mum. "I think it's time for the Christmas tree and decorations."

I jumped up and down. "Can I help? Can I help, Daddy?"

"Of course, Snooks. Let me get the boxes and tree down out of the cockloft first."

I ran up the stairs to observe Dad carefully setting up the ladder into the trap door in the upstairs landing and bringing out the Christmas decorations stored under the roof. The dust flew off the boxes and I sneezed.

"Easy as we go," he said, balancing the boxes as he trod down the stairs. Under his arm he'd tucked a small artificial tree. "I had this tree when I was little just like you," he told me as he pushed the base of the tree into its small red square block, setting it on top of the piano. "And all these decorations we used to hang on the tree too." He pulled each branch down ready to display the ornaments.

"Really?" I thought a moment. "They must be really old."

Dad laughed. "Not as old as you think. Now, you hold this little silver trumpet while I rearrange the branches right." He lifted me up so I could place the delicate glass ornament on a branch. It took a long time for us to hang all the sparkly, delicate glass decorations on the tree.

"Oh, it's lovely, Daddy," I exclaimed after standing back and admiring it.

Next he placed the curly, multi-coloured paper chains around the picture railing, then the best part of all – the many coloured fairy lights above the fireplace. He tested each bulb, because if one didn't work, they all blinked out. Mum always complained about them being 'dust gatherers', but I loved the whole atmosphere.

A couple of days later Mum announced, "Tomorrow we are going to visit Father Christmas."

I bounced around happily. "Are we really going to see Father Christmas?" I stopped and frowned. "But he lives at the North Pole. How can we get there?"

Mum laughed. "He is paying a special visit to Owen Owens'

to meet all the little boys and girls. You'll be able to tell him what you want for Christmas."

I ran to the living room window and stared at the sad winter grass where a few sparrows hopped around. The air-raid shelter stood, like a sore thumb, near the fence, but I didn't look there. Then I began to think of what I wanted most for Christmas. Immediately, it danced in my head. It was a Donald Duck gasmask. My friend Colin had one, so did his brother Derek, and as soon as I saw them, I told Mummy that I wanted one. I hated my black gasmask. The oval eyepiece stared round and nasty, as if it had bad secrets hidden lurking behind it. The black rubbery mask went right over my face with cloth taped straps at the back that I couldn't get off, and everything seemed out of shape when I looked through the smudgy yellowish mask across my eyes. The snout part weighed heavy, pulling my face down. It felt like I was suffocating. I always jumped up and down, crying for Mum to take it off whenever she pulled it on. Every night these masks were carried into the air-raid shelter with us. Now if I had a Donald Duck one, perhaps it wouldn't feel so bad.

The other present I wanted was a book, my very own book. We had a couple in the house, but they had belonged to other people whose children were now all grown up. I loved Dad to read to me, and every day he would pull me up on to his knee and read out loud the adventures of Rupert Bear in the *Daily Express*. That was my favourite. I sometimes used to imagine I could play with Rupert Bear and his friends, Bill Badger and Tiger Lily, then disappear into a land where I could float on lily pads and find Sam the Sailor, who could take us anywhere we wanted to go, and Rupert would be my special friend.

I couldn't wait until the next day, but that night, as always, I had to recite my prayers after Mummy, although I'd memorised them almost by heart now, as I'd been saying them forever. I climbed into bed that night. "God bless Mummy, God bless Daddy, God bless Nana and Poppa and all those whom we love, and please make Joyce a good girl tomorrow." Then I added one more petition, "And please God, help us win the war."

Mum patted my arm. "There's a good girl now. Time to go to sleep."

She clicked off the light and as I closed my eyes, I added yet another request. "Please, please, God. Make Father Christmas bring me a Donald Duck gasmask."

That night, the all-too-familiar wailing of the siren woke me up. As usual I pulled my siren suit up and, with Mum, scurried outside. This time the whistles, explosions and blasts of gunfire sounded louder than ever. I put my hands over my ears. Searchlights overhead caught a small speck flying high in the sky as flak shook the damp earth beneath my feet.

"Don't worry," Mum assured me. "That's one of our planes up there. It's on its way to fight the Germans and help keep us safe."

I glanced up, but I wasn't so sure, as I had already seen some of the damage the bombs had done in our neighbourhood. Sharp smoke made me wrinkle my nose. I felt better when Mum ducked into the shelter, pushing me in before her, then closed the door. Despite the shuddering blasts, I soon fell asleep on the hard bunk bed, and the next thing I knew was Mum shaking me to wake up.

"That's the all-clear," she said with a smile.

"Can we still go and see Father Christmas?" I asked sleepily, pushing my thumb in my mouth as I always did to make me feel better. At the same time though, I looked at our small semi-detached house, to be sure it was still standing. I'd seen too many houses like ours black and hollow from the bombs. Assured that it stood familiar and safe, I heard Mum say that we would indeed, she hoped, go and see Father Christmas.

The next morning, I woke in a breath of excitement. I opened my mouth for the spoonful of cod liver oil I had every morning, then picked up my spoon to eat my porridge, as quickly as I could, then ran in to the hall to wait for Mum to gather my coat, pixie-hood and leggings from the hall hook by the front door. Once dressed ready for the winter chill, we set off.

Hopping, skipping, running and jumping, I raced ahead down Christopher Way, along Bowland Avenue, right to the number 6a tram stop. I heard it rattling up towards the bridge before I could see it. Suddenly, there it was at the tram shelter, big, green and cream, the outside staircase winding up to the top deck. Overhead the trolley snapped and sparks flew as it manoeuvred the junction in the wires. Mum helped me climb the steep steps and I searched for a space on the slatted seats lining both sides of the tram. I wiggled into one whilst Mum sat beside me.

I gazed out of the window. Every so often, we passed new large mounds of black rubble where a bomb had hit, with wisps of smoke curling upwards. We stopped at the dismal tenements where the old shawl women lived. They heaved their bulk on to spare seats, their black dresses, aprons, headscarves and shawls making them look like oversized crows that visited our back garden. A funny smell drifted by me as they eased themselves onto the hard seats. Then I looked for the familiar large barrage balloons that skirted the corner at Old Swan. There they floated, huge, silver and ominous in the heavy winter sky.

We trundled along some more.

"We get off at the next stop," Mum announced, getting up and holding on to the overhead strap as the tram swayed from side to side. I took hold of her hand as we dodged our way down the crowded tram, two steps down and on to Church Street. Now we wound our way up Clayton Square to Owen Owens shop. A couple of sparsely-clad forms in the large paned windows, criss-crossed with brown strips like those we had on our windows at home, sported some basic utility coats. We made our way inside, my heart beating fast with the thrill of actually going to see Father Christmas. We climbed up a couple of flights of stairs and walked between high counters and into a cordoned-off section where there was a long queue of other children and their mums.

"How long will we have to wait?" I asked.

"Just be patient. It won't be too long."

I jiggled on one foot, then the other, and gradually the line grew shorter until I was next.

"Go on - up you go," said Mum giving me a push.

Shyly I walked up to where a very, very old man with a long white beard sat on some kind of throne-like chair. He wore a red velvet coat right down to the floor, with white furry pieces, dotted with black spots around his cuffs and skirting the coat hem. His hood, pulled over his head, was edged with the spotted fur too. On each side stood a pretty lady, dressed in a long fancy dress. One helped me up on to his knee.

Father Christmas put his arm around me. "Well, little girl. What do you want for Christmas?"

I hardly dared look at him. "Please," I whispered, as he put his ear closer to my mouth to hear me, "I would really, really like a

Donald Duck gasmask." I paused, took another breath and added, "And also, if you could possibly manage it, I'd really, really like a book of my very own."

He lifted his head back up. "Well, now. Have you been a good girl? You know that only good little girls get presents. If you've been naughty, you get a lump of coal."

Mum had told me this many times, and I truly tried hard to be good. Tears came to my eyes and I tried not to sniff.

"I'm sure you have. Right you are, off you go. Next one."

So I was helped off his knee by the second pretty lady and walked back to Mum. She spoke aloud to herself. "Oh, this used to be so beautiful before the war. There would be a grotto with moving animals, and elves, and fairy lights. It was so pretty." She stopped. "Right now though, I have to get you a new pair of shoes. You just can't wear the ones you have."

We walked a little way to the shoe department. Mum pulled out her ration book from her handbag and counted the coupons to be sure she had enough for my shoes. I looked down at hers, and suddenly noticed that despite the polish they looked a little scuffed and they weren't so shiny any more. But the lady pulled off my shoes and slipped on a pair of brown button-over shoes, smelling new, and shining in the overhead bulb that made me focus on my feet. Delighted with my new purchase, I chattered all the way back home about Father Christmas.

That evening, Daddy told me that Father Christmas came down the chimney to deliver toys for good boys and girls and filled their stockings. "Will I have a stocking, Daddy? I asked.

"Of course you will."

Satisfied, I then had to wait for Christmas Eve. I wanted

bedtime to come quickly, but first I'd make sure that Mum poured a half-full glass of milk, along with one biscuit from the biscuit tin on a plate, set on the table ready for Father Christmas to eat when he visited us. Dad found me one of his socks, and helped me hang it on the bed corner.

I thought I'd never go to sleep, but I did, and no air-raids awakened us that night. Darkness cloaked the room when I awoke, but then it was December and it was always dark in the early morning. Tentatively I pushed my feet down into a cold part of the bed and wiggled them around. I felt something move.

"Father Christmas did come!" Wide awake now, I moved my feet some more. I could feel something heavy on my toes, and there was a rustling. "Mummy, Daddy," I shouted, "Father Christmas did come!"

Dad came into my bedroom, after he'd brought Mum a cup of tea in bed for her to enjoy. "Merry Christmas, Snooks," he said. "Let's put your dressing gown on and you can open your stocking."

Impatiently I allowed him to help put my arms into my faded green dressing gown, cut down from Nana's old one, and tie the silky cord around my waist. Then I dug into Dad's sock. First I pulled out a tracing book and a pencil. "Mmm. That's good. I like to trace pictures," I said out loud. Then came a savings card with two sixpenny savings stamps. I pulled a face. That wasn't so good. But then a rubber ball fell out. My face lit up. I loved to play ball and wanted so badly to be able to throw it against the wall outside as my big friend Joan did and be able to catch it.

I dug further. A rosy, round apple came next. "Oh, good. I love apples." We couldn't always get apples, especially in winter. Then I exclaimed loudly. "An orange! Oh, Mummy, Father Christmas brought me a whole real orange." We seldom saw real oranges, just the thick, concentrated, dirty orange-coloured liquid in a bottle that Mum poured out into a glass, adding water to it, then stirred it up and made me drink it. Now this was the real thing.

Happy with my gifts, I took them downstairs and straightaway began to trace around the first picture in my tracing book, a motor car. Only then did I look on the table to be sure the milk and biscuit had gone. With a smile of satisfaction, I saw that an empty glass and plate sat there, without a crumb.

After breakfast, we set off for Nana and Poppa's house. I took Mummy's and Dad's hands and held tight as they swung me up over the pavement cracks. After a while they grew tired, and anyway we were at their house by then. I ran ahead and raised the knocker. Nana opened the door, her face red, a few streaks on the pinafore wrapped around her generous middle, and all kinds of delicious smells wafting to my nose from the kitchen.

"Hello there everyone," said Poppa right behind her. "Merry Christmas to you."

I opened my arms wide. "Merry Christmas Poppa." He hugged me and I clung to his tweedy jacket, breathing in the warm comfort of his lingering pipe tobacco.

Nana bustled up to me. "See what we have here for you," she said, and handed me a present. The paper had pretty holly on it and I was reluctant to tear it off.

"Here, let me help," offered Mum. "We can used this paper again next year." She carefully removed it and smoothed it flat, then folded it up and put it in the large bag she had brought with her.

I sat on the couch. "Oh, I wanted one of these. I forgot to tell Father Christmas." I opened the book of paper dolls and their numerous outfits, one for every season, complete with hats and muffs. "Can you help me cut these out?" I asked the grown-ups, hoping someone would help me.

"Let's eat our dinner first," said Nana, bustling in with a mouth-watering joint of roasted pork. "I queued up for almost an hour yesterday to get this joint, but Tom had put it away for me, so here we have it."

After filling ourselves with crispy potatoes roasted in pork drippings and roast pork, complete with the crackling that Nana heaped on my plate, because she knew I especially liked it, home-grown carrots and apple sauce, she went back to the kitchen with the dirty plates and returned carrying a round, brown, luscious pudding surrounded by fiery-like blue flames.

I clapped my hands. "Christmas pudding, Christmas pudding!" I shouted.

"Now just be careful eating the pudding," Nana warned me. "Remember those two scraps of paper? Well there are two in here also. Don't you go and swallow them."

I shook my head emphatically. "Oh, no Nana, I won't do that."

A dish of soft sweet sticky Christmas pud was placed before me, topped with a dollop of custard. I began eating, eager to find one of the scraps of paper. But I didn't get one. So of course, I had to have a second helping, and this time I found a small wrapping.

"See, I have one!" I shouted. Quickly I undid the sticky brown scrap of paper and inside was a rubber button. I wanted to cry.

"Oh, that doesn't count," assured Nana. "It is said that if you find the button you will be an old maid. But that won't happen to you."

"You promise?" I asked. I wasn't too sure what an old maid was right then, but the way it was said convinced me it wasn't good.

"Now where is the silver threepenny piece, I wonder?" she said.

I knew what that was! I had learned about money, and could already count pennies. So I asked for a third helping, as I badly wanted the silver threepenny piece. By now I was so full I thought I'd burst, and what was more, the pudding plate now lay on the table, empty. Everyone wondered where the silver threepenny piece had gone, and looked at me.

Then Poppa gave a wide grin. "Och, my goodness," he said in his Scots brogue, "Just look at yon. It was under my plate all the time."

Nana exploded. "Jim, how could you do that! This child has had three helpings to try and find that coin. Now she will probably be sick, all because you went and hid it under your plate."

I wasn't sure whether to laugh or cry. Then Poppa patted my hand. "Here y'are Chuckles. Take this and keep it, and it will bring ye good luck down through the years."

I took it from him and placed it in my frock pocket. "Thank you, Poppa," I said. I decided at that moment that I would keep that silver threepenny piece for ever.

As Nana opened her mouth to reprimand Poppa again, Mum broke in, "Oh, my! Just look at the time. It's almost three o'clock. It's time for the King's speech."

With dishes and the silver threepenny piece forgotten, we gathered around the brightly burning coal fire, while Poppa fiddled with the knobs of the wireless and Dad piled another shovelful of coal on to the fire. Finally after whistling and static, the BBC programme came in clear. I could tell it was a solemn occasion, so

I climbed on to Poppa's knee and became perfectly still.

The national anthem, *God Save the King,* was played, then there was silence. A man's voice came over the air waves. I couldn't understand most of what he said, but he did say something about children leaving their homes and going to some other place called America. I was glad it wasn't me! Then it was over, and again I heard the music to *God Save the King.* Dad clicked the wireless off.

At that moment I noticed Mum and Nana had been sitting on the edge of their chairs, and Nana now sat back against the cushions. She spoke first, "Oh, he did such a good job, didn't he? I don't think he stuttered more than once or twice."

Mum sat back further in her chair too. "He did do well. I'm sure it's the Queen who helps him. And he must be glad that that's over for this Christmas."

I hadn't noticed anything special. Besides I wanted someone to help me cut out my paper dolls so I could dress them in their winter clothes.

On the way back, we stopped at Grandpa and Grandma Bibby's house, my Dad's parents. I didn't like going there so much, as Grandma Bibby scared me a little with her clacking teeth and her raspy, cackling laugh and hands that kept touching me. But Grandpa Bibby was different. I liked him a lot and when he gave me his gift of a dancing wooden doll, I was so happy. "Thank you, thank you," I told him, and gave him a kiss. His walrus moustache tickled my cheek, and made me giggle.

That night, tired from all the excitement and too much Christmas pudding, I rolled into bed, but I had to recite my prayers first. It was only as I took Teddy into my arms that I realised I hadn't got my Donald Duck gasmask after all, and I hadn't got my very own book to read. But there was always next Christmas. And I did get the silver threepenny piece, now safe on my bedside stand.

CHAPTER 3

SHARDS OF DREAMS (1941)

Thou art my castle and defence, in my necessity.
Thomas Sternhold, 1500-1549

Dr Canter strode into our living room, big and important. He and Mum talked quietly, then he came over to me where I lay in a bed in the corner and felt my head.

"You're not feeling too well, are you?"

I whooped and coughed and shook my head.

He took my temperature and pulled up my nightie. The round silvery circle he put on my chest was cold and I coughed again. He stood tall and turned to Mum.

"I'm sorry to tell you Mrs Bibby, but Joyce has definitely got whooping cough" he said. He paused, then added, "This is a serious bout, and I'm not sure if she'll make it."

I whooped and coughed some more. My throat hurt, my

stomach hurt and I felt hot and sweaty all over. He sounded serious and I was scared. I became even more scared as he took out a large syringe, made of shiny metal. I turned to face the wall. He took hold of my arm and rubbed something on it, then jabbed the needle into my arm. I cried, "That hurt!" I sobbed, then coughed some more, hardly able to get my breath.

"Sorry about that. But you needed that injection to help you get better." He handed a piece of paper to Mum, just as Dad came in. "Get this medicine for her as soon as you can, and I'll be back tomorrow."

He snapped his black Gladstone bag shut, while Mum rummaged in her handbag for her purse. She handed him two half crowns.

Dr Canter gently pushed her hand away. "That's all right, Mrs Bibby," he said. "The medicine for your daughter is expensive, put the money towards that." She saw him to the door.

"Don't worry, Snooks," said Dad. "I'll go to Murray's right now and get that medicine for you. Then you'll soon be better."

I nodded, afraid to speak in case the coughing hacked and hurt me again. I closed my eyes, tired of everything.

The next thing I knew was Mum touching my shoulder. "Come on, sit up," she urged, helping me. As soon as I moved, the coughing broke out and I held my stomach. "Here is your medicine." She held a spoonful of brown liquid to my mouth. Obediently I opened it up and swallowed, making a face. It was horrible.

Dr Canter returned the next day, and the next, and gradually the coughing subsided a little.

It was the following week, while I was still in bed downstairs, with Mum sleeping on the sofa so she could watch me during the night, that the wailing crescendo broke the night stillness. Dad sped off on his bike to his fire duties, but I was still too sick to be taken to the shelter. I lay awake, listening to the anti-aircraft gunfire. Flickers of searchlights probed any chink in the blackout curtain where it pulled tight across the rail at the top. Crashes, then suddenly a deafening explosion rocked our house. I cried out, trying not to cough. Mum threw herself on top of me, as bombs continued to fall. Glass shattered and I caught a glimpse of a red glow through torn blackout curtains, while the acrid smoke tickled my nostrils, making me cough harder than ever.

Mum whispered in my ear, between my sobs, "It's okay. We're going to be all right." She stopped. "See, it's quieter now."

I listened. The explosions had stopped except for small ones, then the big brass bells of the fire engines clanged, closer and closer. I peered over her shoulder and saw sharp pieces of glass all over us and I could even see right through the now glassless windows.

"Mummy, Mummy!" I cried. We don't have any windows!" The criss-crossed brown sticky tape that had made neat diamonds across our living room windows had done nothing to prevent the blast from shattering them completely.

Slowly Mum climbed off the bed, shaking glass from her clothing. She found a torch on the table and searched my face. "Why, all you have is a little cut above your eye." She smiled. "You're right as rain!" Then she lit some candles.

"Can I get up?" I was allowed up for short periods of time and I wanted desperately to see what had happened.

"No, you just stay there. I will see how we are." The glass crunched beneath her feet and I heard her exclaim as she went in the kitchen, "Oh, no!"

"What is it, Mummy?" I called anxiously.

She came back in, shook off the glass on the bed cover and sat down, her face in her hands. "Everything, everything, smashed to smithereens. All my willow pattern china, my basins, dishes, everything. Even the back door is somewhere, ripped off and..." She put her hands down and tried to smile, but I could see she'd been crying.

I touched her arm. "But *we're* here, Mum."

She hugged me a little. "Now I'd better see about sweeping this lot up. Jerry hasn't got us yet," she declared.

Somehow I got back to sleep and when I woke up, the living room was clear of glass, cushions from the chairs had been placed against the windows to keep the chilled air out and Dad was just coming in.

"Oh, thank God you're both safe," he declared, removing his smoky helmet. "We were fighting fires down town. Lewis's got it bad last night, and Blacklers' too."

I knew those shops. Mum sometimes took me to them when she needed to buy something. What would happen now?

Dad continued after sitting down. "We saw the explosions, and one of my mates said, 'Well, Childwall's got it tonight.'"

I knew that where we lived was called Childwall, so I listened intently.

"I thought you'd all be goners" he went on. He took a deep breath. "But we got hit bad here. Houses on Bentham Drive are flattened."

"But, Nana and Poppa, they live on Bentham Drive!" I cried. I couldn't bear it if their house had been bombed.

"They're fine," Dad assured us. "I just rode past their house on my bike. They think it was a landmine that hit homes around the corner from us, going down towards the shops."

I breathed easier. That was the other direction.

"Jerry made one heck of a mess here, didn't he?" said Dad.

"And all my best willow pattern china has been smashed" Mum sniffed, trying not to cry again. Dad put his arm around her. "Don't worry, love. We'll get through this."

And we did, even though I heard a few days later that eight people had been killed in their air-raid shelters, along with many others, including some in the public shelters. And I wondered what good those shelters did after all. Much later I learned that 2000 Liverpudlians had been killed in just that week, with thousands more injured and homeless.

Once I was better I was curious to go and see the bombed-out houses. On our way to the shops at the bottom of Bentham Drive to buy our weekly rations, I stopped to gaze at the blackened ruins. I tugged Mum's hand to stay so I could see more, but Mum pulled me away. "Come on now," she said, "We've shopping to do and by the time I wait in all the queues it'll be time for dinner."

But I couldn't get the piles of rubble, with chimneys and posts sticking out like broken blackened teeth, out of my mind. It seemed strange to see this smoky, sooty heap of bricks when the last time I'd walked down there there had been houses, just like ours. Yet in time, it became familiar and was our favourite place to play. Hide and seek, dens, hunts for hidden treasure and secret places under the debris brightened our days and created a place for imaginative young minds.

Shrapnel often rained down on our streets, and after another bombing raid I pleaded with Mum to let me go outside and play. The street was, for the most part, our playground.

"Please let me go outside. See, Ronnie and Terry and Margaret and Irene are all there." I ran to the front window. "Please!"

"Very well then, but don't get into trouble!"

I pulled my coat on while Mum helped me with the buttons, then flew outside. The neighbourhood children were already bending down picking up pieces of shrapnel. I hoped there were some left. I wasn't even sure where it all came from. It was just there some mornings, and I desperately wanted to find a nice big piece to keep for myself.

"Look at mine," Norman, one of our neighbourhood friends, shouted out, waving a large chunk of shrapnel. We crowded round to admire his new-found treasure.

"Mine's bigger," argued Terry, one of the eight-year old twins from Christopher Way, next to our street, as he thrust out his hand.

"'Tis not." His brother stuck out his chin. "Mine's huger than that back at the house."

I looked at the fragments in their hands, and then peered into the gutter to see if I could find one larger still. I picked up a piece. I threw it back. No, no, it wasn't as big as theirs. I picked up another, then stared at the bronze metallized jagged chunk in my hand, fascinated by it. There were fine ridges embedded into the metal. "How do we get all this in our road?" I asked.

The bigger boys laughed at me. Norman explained. "They're from Jerry's bombs. What they dropped last night. When the bombs hit the ground they explode and the outside of the bomb breaks up and falls all over the place, like now."

The twins' mother yelled. "Ronnie, Terry! Where is youse lot? Yer dinner's ready, and there won't be none if you don't come, NOW!"

No one lingered where food was concerned. The argument stopped dead, and the twins scurried off round the corner to Christopher Way and their dinner. Then the others were called in, but I hung around.

"Ah, there's a really big piece," I cried. It was right beside the pig-bin tied to the street light that was never lit any more, like all the other streets lights. I dropped the fragment I had and picked this up instead, disappointed that I couldn't show it off to the big boys. Instead I ran inside to show Mum and Dad my newest treasure.

"That's a very big piece of shrapnel," commented Mum, as she examined it. "May I put it on the mantelpiece so we can all see it?" She then placed it on the wooden mantle above the fireplace next to the clock and added, "I wonder which poor souls died because of that."

But I stood beaming, so proud of myself. It never crossed my mind to consider the ramifications of my precious find in the road. The shrapnel remained on display for many years, a sharp reminder for us all of death and devastation.

Bombs fell and air-raids continued. My friend Margaret and I played air-raids under the piano, along with hairdressers, and school. Then there were the telegrams. The Moores lived three doors up from us, and one day Peter, Jeffrey and Delia were crying. We tried to play tick around the lamp post and pig bin, but no one seemed to want to play. I nudged Margaret and said, "Ask them why they're crying."

Margaret spoke up. "What's the matter?"

"Mum got a telegram. Our Dad's died in the war." Peter wiped his sleeve across his nose.

We stood around awkwardly. "Has he gone to heaven?" I asked. Mum took me to Sunday school now, and my teacher had told us that when we die, if we are good, of course, we go to heaven.

"Dunno. Suppose so," he sniffed doubtfully.

Gradually we drifted back to our homes. Somehow we didn't want to play outside any more that day.

On Sunday afternoons, after I had returned from Sunday school, we always visited Grandma and Grandpa Bibby across the road for tea. On this day when Grandma Bibby opened the door I ran past her to where Grandpa Bibby sat in his big armchair beside the flickering coal fireplace. I gave him a big hug. He took my hand.

"Come and see what I have for you today" he said. I climbed up on to on his knee as he placed in my hands a wooden ladder with a clown attached. "See, this is how it works," he explained. He pulled the string and the clown climbed the ladder, right to the top, then he pulled the other string, and down he came, one rung at a time.

"Can I try?" I pleaded.

"Of course, it's for you."

I pulled one string, then the other, and laughed delightedly as the clown wiggled his way up, then down. Up and down, up and down, until Grandma Bibby told us it was time for tea.

"Thank you, Grandpa Bibby," I told him. "This is now my bestest toy. And did Daddy tell you I can do that jigsaw puzzle you made me all by myself? I really like that picture of the woods."

He chuckled. "I always knew you were a clever little girl," he said, and chuffed me under the chin. I warmed under his praise.

Now that tea was ready, I took the clown with me to the table and laid him beside my plate. We had white bread and butter, a sponge cake with a smear of jam in it and cups of tea. Mum always said that the way Grandma Bibby cooked she'd kill them both one day, but she didn't say it in front of her. The sponge cake had a bitter taste and Mum told me that this was because it was a bought one, but that was after we got home. Soon after tea we put on our coats, and Dad switched on the big, heavy, silvery torch and shone the way across the blacked-out street to our home.

A couple of days later, I knew something bad had happened the way Mum and Dad spoke in whispers. Then Dad called me and sat me on his knee.

"I'm sorry to tell you this," he said, his face sad, "but your Grandpa Bibby died last night."

I stared at him. "But he can't be dead. I just saw him! He made me this." I ran to find my clown ladder toy, climbed up on his lap again, and pushed it up to his face. "He can't be dead." I knew what dead meant. There was so much talk about people dying and so many dead from the raids that all of us children were familiar with its meaning, but dead didn't happen to any of us.

"Why is he dead? No bombs fell here last night. We didn't even have to go to the shelter."

"He had a heart attack. That means his heart stopped working." Dad pointed to his chest. "If your heart stops working, then you die. But he is safe in heaven now." He looked upward.

There was that word 'heaven' again, which I'd heard in Sunday school. I promised myself that I would ask my Sunday teacher exactly where heaven was.

Then the tears came. I loved Grandpa Bibby. "Why couldn't it have been Grandma Bibby instead?" I asked between my tears.

"That's not the way it works, love, I'm afraid."

I was upset all that day. Mum drew the front window curtains and covered the mirrors. "Why do we have to be in the dark? I asked.

"Because it's out of respect for the person who died," Dad explained.

I knew something else was going on because Aunty Bunty, the grown-up daughter of Daddy and Mrs Thompson, took care of me a couple of days later. I heard the word 'funeral' but was told that they weren't for children.

"Why can't I go?" I demanded of Dad and Mum. "I loved Grandpa Bibby. I have to go."

"Funerals aren't for little girls," said Mum. "You're far too young to go to any funeral."

I cried, but it made no difference. I even tried to ask God about it, but I didn't know what to say.

The following Sunday I asked my Sunday school teacher. She was young and pretty and wore a lovely blue hat with a little veil.

"What is heaven?" I asked.

"It is where God lives," came the reply.

"But people go there when they die."

"Yes, Joyce. That is right, but only good people go there."

"But where is heaven? Is it up there?" I pointed upward.

"Yes, that's right. Now, boys and girls." She smiled brightly and pointed to a picture book. "Let me tell you about this person who was sick and asked Jesus to heal him."

"Can we ask Jesus anything?" inquired the boy next to me.

Feeling on safer ground, my teacher replied, "Of course, Peter. You can ask God about anything at all."

"I'd like a cowboy outfit for my birthday. Can I ask Him for that?"

Our teacher smiled again. "Of course, you can. But you may want to let your Mummy know too."

I thought about this. Such information might be useful for the future. I had already asked about the Donald Duck gasmask. But maybe God had been asleep when I put in my request. Nevertheless I still thought about heaven. No matter how much I strained my neck looking upward. I couldn't see heaven or God, just blue arched sky, some clouds and maybe the sun. Perhaps it was just too far away to see.

CHAPTER 4

VISITORS, UNEXPECTED

When shadows haunt the quiet room; Help us to understand, that there art others
through the gloom; To hold us by the hand.

Anne Matheson 1853-1924

Not long after Grandpa Bibby's funeral, Great Aunt Sarah and her husband, Uncle Tom, came to stay with Grandma Bibby. Great Aunt Sarah was Grandma Bibby's sister, Mum told me. They came over to visit us one afternoon, and I decided I didn't like them.

"Do you have bombs in London?" I asked them politely.

Great Aunt Sarah was very old and skinny with squinty eyes and she just ignored me. Uncle Tom stayed quiet and heavy. His wispy hair, the colour of Nana's ginger nuts, lay 'strap and buckled' across his bald freckled head and his waistcoat, the colour of dirt, had dribbles of food down it.

Great Aunt Sarah instead turned to Mummy. "You wouldn't believe the air raids we have had. The house right next to ours was demolished and ours still stood."

"Were you all right?" I asked, again, politely.

"Those poor people, all killed, except for the oldest child. She was seen wandering the streets. The destruction was terrible, far worse than you've had," continued Great Aunt Sarah, still looking at Mummy. Then I noticed Uncle Tom staring at me, and I shivered. He didn't say anything, just looked, and I picked up Mary, my doll, and played with her hair, until Mum said they were going back to Grandma Bibby's, just for a few minutes, but they would be back.

"Uncle Tom will stay with you," said Dad. I looked down at Mary and pretended not to hear. They closed the front door behind them.

Uncle Tom sat in the other chair. "Look what I have here," he said.

I looked up, interested. He pulled out a round gold disk, then clicked it open. I crept nearer to see what it was. Inside sat a large gold-circled watch.

"Do you want to hear it tick?" he asked. I nodded, curiosity overcoming my fear.

He pulled me on to his knee and held the watch to my ear. I smiled and nodded. "I can hear the ticking" I said. Then put my ear against it again. He had his arm around me, then he slipped his gold, shiny watch, on the looped gold chain, back into his dark brown waistcoat pocket and his thick hand with pudgy fingers slid between my legs. "No, no. I don't like that" I protested, wriggling wildly.

"Shush. Just be quiet and everything will be all right," he said, breathing heavily in my ear. I swallowed hard and shook my head. I started to cry. "No, Please. You're hurting me. Stop it, stop it." I struggled harder to escape, but I couldn't. He was too strong.

"Be quiet, you little vixen!" he whispered hoarsely.

I cried louder, then heard the click of the key in the front door and Mum and Dad's voices. They rushed into the room.

Mum let out a gasp, marched over, and scooped me up. "How dare you touch my child!" she screamed. She shouted and yelled other things as she held my heaving body. Over her shoulder she yelled at Dad. "You deal with them. They're your relatives. Make sure they never, ever come to this house ever again!"

Mum whisked me up the stairs to my bedroom. Then she ran downstairs and reappeared with the old white enamel bowl, with the chipped red rim, in her hands. She took a flannel and washed me with the warm Dettol water. I stopped crying as the soothing warm disinfectant solution washed my hurt away, then Mum gently dried me.

"Come on. Let's put your nightie on. It's almost bedtime anyway." She put the bowl to the side and then pulled my nightgown over my head. "Joyce, there is something you have to promise me."

I lifted my tearstained face to her. "What, Mummy?" My heart turned over. I must have done something wrong. She sometimes told me she didn't love me when I was naughty.

"You have to promise me that you will forget this ever happened."

I nodded. I always wanted Mummy to love me, so I asked her, "Do you still love me, Mummy?" I was afraid it was my fault. But she smiled and kissed my cheek.

"Of course I love you. Now remember what you promised." She left the room and even forgot to remind me to say my prayers. Instead I kept saying to myself, "I promise to forget. I promise to forget." Somehow I fell asleep. I did forget, just as I promised; at least I thought I had. But I was glad that we never saw Great Aunt Sarah or Uncle Tom again. In fact I never even heard their names mentioned. I assumed that they had, in some way, just disappeared.

The rat-a-tat at the door a couple of days later made me scamper out to see who was there.

"Why, hello, Meg," said Mum, opening wide the door, as I peered around her skirt. "Come along in. It's pouring down, and you look like a drowned rat. Here, sit beside the fire while I make a cup of tea." She bustled into the kitchen, calling out, "It's ages since I've seen you. How have you been?"

Meg laid a large bundle on the floor and undid her sodden headscarf from her head, draping it over the fireguard, then loosened her coat. I sat on the tuffet, watching. She smiled at me, an almost toothless smile, and I wondered how she ate her sausages. I smiled back, then Mum came in carrying a tray with a pot of tea, some milk, and even some sugar.

"So, how have you been?" asked Mum again, pouring milk into the two cups.

"Oh, not so good Mrs Bibby. I've been sick, yer knows, so I don't got too many clothes in this 'ere." She pointed to the large bundle. "Youse got any old clothes for me?"

Mum shook her head and grimaced. "These are hard times, Meg," she said. "Any clothes we have we patch or cut them down and I make dresses for Joyce here." She then looked down at Meg's feet. "Oh, look at your shoes. Here, take them off and let them dry a while by the fire."

Meg slipped off her shoes, and I saw newspaper inside.

"You have newspaper in your shoes," I said in wonder, as if I'd made an important discovery.

"'fraid so." Meg turned one shoe over and I could see newspaper showing through a round hole in the sole of her shoe. "That's something we's got to do to get by. Yer knows what I mean? I just ain't got no money to get them mended these days, and the coupons I keep for me little 'uns."

Mum always took all our shoes to Mr Merrigan, the shoemender, whenever the soles in our shoes wore thin. To my amazement, Mum, whose shoes had just been mended, took them off her feet. "Here, Meg," she said, "I think we are about the same size. Try these on, and if they fit you, take them."

"But, I can't do that, Mrs Bibby. I just can't. Youse need them yerself."

"I have another pair upstairs I can wear. They are perfectly good, so I will be fine."

I stared at one and then the other, in amazement that Mum would do this. I knew that Mum's old shoes were all cracked and had been mended lots of times. Meg slipped Mum's shoes on and tied up the laces – a perfect fit.

"Youse is too good for the likes of me," she whispered, tears running down her face. "I doesn't know what to say."

"That's all right," assured Mum in her thick lisle stockings, with well darned toes. "I don't have any old clothes, not today, but maybe the shoes will help instead."

Meg nodded gratefully, finished her tea, then tied her damp grey headscarf around her head, picked up her bundle of old clothes and headed to the door. "Ta-ra for now," she called as she walked down the rain-splattered puddled path. I stayed where I was, gazing at the fire, thinking over what Mum had done.

Summer arrived, but it still rained almost every day, so I couldn't play outside. However Mum said I could go to my friend Irene's house, which was just around the corner, next to the twins' house on Christopher Way, and it looked exactly like ours. We nearly always played dress-up, something we both loved. Today we gathered together a couple of her mother's dresses, a pair of high heeled shoes and two rubber bathing hats we'd found at the back of the cupboard in Irene's bedroom. We took our dressing-up outfits downstairs, where we pulled on the long dresses, then fiddled with the bathing hats. If we pushed the straps in and placed the ballooned headwear on our heads at just the right angle we looked quite stylish.

"You look just like Mrs Moffat," I giggled, as Irene pranced around the living room, tottering on her Mum's best high heels. Mrs Moffat always wore fancy clothes and lots of make-up. Mum called her a 'totty', which I thought meant very smart.

I then hoisted up a skirt, all twirly and flowery, and took a headscarf to wind around my head like a hat.

"Now you look like Mrs Moffat," laughed Irene.

Suddenly a loud knocking at the front door broke up our giggles. Irene rushed to answer it, me close behind. She could just reach the knob, being a year older than me. She stared, dumbstruck. Her dad stood there, tall and handsome, in khaki army uniform, his kitbag slung on his back. He stepped in, closing the door behind him, and Irene yelled at the top of her voice.

"Mum, Dad's here!"

Mrs Griffiths padded around upstairs. "Don't tell fibs," she shouted down. "You girls behave yerselves, or there will be no tea for you."

"It is me luv," shouted the gruff voice.

There was a shriek and a flurry of steps as Mrs Griffiths ran down the stairs two at a time, into his arms, a pair of knickers in her hand, as she'd been getting changed, and they kissed, a long, long kiss, something I'd never seen my parents do. We watched in wonder. This was interesting, and we girls waited to see what would happen next. Alas, I was hustled out of my dress-up clothes and told to go home, while Irene was instructed to play quietly with her dolls downstairs, and not to bother them.

CHAPTER 5

THE OTHER SIDE OF SWEETNESS (1941)

When I am tempted to do wrong, make me steadfast, wise and strong.
John Page Hopps, 1834–1912

I'd been attending Sunday school now for a while, and had learned about God and that Jesus was his son, and knew about heaven where God lived, but I wasn't sure why I had to go to Sunday school. After all, Mum made me say my prayer each night. I had hoped I'd learn to read and write there, but I hadn't. All I did was listen to stories about God and Jesus and sing some songs. The one I liked was "Hear the pennies dropping, listen as they fall. Every one for Jesus and He shall have them all." I would drop my penny in, but wondered how Jesus would get them, as I knew he wasn't around any more.

So one sunny Sunday afternoon, I decided to ask Mum. I held her hand going up across Childwall Valley Road, then just before we got to the top of the hill, I asked, "Mum, why do I have to go to Sunday school? I haven't even learned to read yet."

Mum laughed kindly. "You have to go to proper school to learn to read. You will be going there next year, when you are five. Little girls go to Sunday school, and little boys too, to learn how to be good."

I waited, hopefully for something else, but that was it. My heart sank. I knew all about being good. If I'd been naughty, after I'd cried and said I was sorry, and pleaded with Mummy to love me again, she'd say, 'Well, I'll think about it' and everything would be all right, until the next time. I bit my lip. This wasn't good. Not only would I have to try and not be naughty because of Mum, but because our teacher had said that God loves little children, I'd have to be good all the time, otherwise God wouldn't love me either. I sighed, kicking a stray stone with my shoe.

"Don't do that," Mum reprimanded me. "You'll scuff your shoes, and I don't have any coupons for new ones. Here we are now. Off you go, and here's your penny for the collection."

I skipped in through the heavy oak door into the smell of dust, old wood and lingering cabbage. Today, though, was different.

"Here you are, Joyce. There is a seat here for you," said one of the teachers.

Instead of the big wooden spindle-back chairs today, there were long wooden benches set up. All the children faced the front of the room, where there sat a big machine. I squeezed into a spot between two other children and gazed around with interest. Blackout curtains hugged the frosted windows and the electric light threw a waxy yellow glow into the room.

Just then a man dressed in black with his collar back to front stood up. He smiled, showing long yellow teeth and his nose kind of hung over them. "Welcome, little children," he boomed. I wriggled some more. "Today I am going to show you some lantern slides about a place a long, long way away from here called Africa. I will tell you all about it as you see the pictures."

The room snapped dark and a couple of boys began making rude noises.

"Shush, shush!" we girls told them.

Suddenly a very large coloured photograph flashed on to the wall. Lots of children were shown, but they were black and they weren't dressed properly like us. They had nothing on. I tried not to giggle.

"Boys and girls," said the echoey voice. "These boys and girls live in Africa. They don't know about Jesus the way we do, and people like me, who are called missionaries, go and tell them all about God and how much He loves them. You see they worship idols and don't know the real God, so we tell them and their parents that they need to become Christians so they can go to heaven when they die." There was that heaven place again.

He dropped the next plate down. Now some mud huts appeared on the wall and we were told that this was where they lived. Then followed a wooden church, where all the people went to know about God. Other pictures followed. He showed a little girl who was sick. "Here we prayed by her bed that God would heal her and God did," declared the man happily.

By the end of the show I was leaning forward, fascinated by Africa. The electric light switched back on, the collection was taken, and Mum had arrived to walk me home. I told her about the lantern show and announced, "One day, I want to go there too."

She smiled. "We'll have to see about that."

We arrived home, but I was still thinking about the little African children who had no clothes, who lived in muddy huts and didn't know God.

A few days later Mum stood at the kitchen table stirring a mixture in her big blue bowl. "What are you making, Mum?" I asked.

"A Victoria sponge," she said, then let out a big sigh. "How I wish we had enough butter to put in it."

I tried to be sympathetic, because I knew Mum did her best with the butter we had with our rations. Mum said she got two ounces for each of us and four ounces of margarine. All I knew was that every Friday she would beat the butter and margarine together, with a wooden spoon, to make it go further.

"Never mind about that," she said, cheering her voice up a bit, "Now why don't you be a good girl and take those potato peelings to the pig bin for me. Then I'll make a nice Woolton Pie for our dinner once I've got this sponge in the oven."

I put on my coat, as the chill wind off the River Mersey was blowing drizzle, and ran outside with the bit tin full of potato peelings. The pig bin, attached to the concrete lamppost was not far from our front gate. I placed the bit tin on the pavement, then used both hands to lift the heavy rusting metal lid off the smelly bin. Once I'd placed that on the pavement I lifted the bit tin of peelings with my right hand and held my nose with my left hand. A few lethargic flies buzzed out as I stood on tiptoe to cast in the peelings.

Suddenly I saw something deep down in the pig bin. I stopped, the smell forgotten, and tipped myself up to reach down into the bin. My small hand grasped the treasure I had seen and pulled it out. I even forgot the bit tin as I ran as fast as I could to our house.

"Mummy, Mummy!" I shrieked. "You'll never guess what I found in the pig bin!" I danced on the worn green and white patterned lino floor of the kitchen, jiggling my whole body with excitement. "Look, look!" I placed the precious package on the kitchen table and waited for Mum's reaction.

"What on earth...?" She stopped, then picked up my find. It was a whole pound of wrapped butter, labelled 'National Butter'. She stared at me. "You found this in the pig bin?"

I danced some more. "Yes, yes. Now you can have real butter for your cake."

As she began to unwrap it, Dad strode in, his helmet dangling from its strap in his hand, and stopped short. "Lil, what on earth do you have there?"

"I found it in the pig bin!" I shouted with glee. "It's real butter!"

Mum and Dad smelled it, and their noses wrinkled as their faces turned to dismay.

I stopped dancing, gazing at one and then the other.

Mum shook her head and in a broken voice explained, "I'm so sorry, Pet. But this butter is rancid. That means it's bad. We can't eat it. You'll have to take it and put it back in the pig bin."

Tears pricked my eyes and a couple trickled down my cheeks. "But why?"

Dad took a deep breath and banged his fist on the table. "Someone round here is on the diddle. I wonder who?"

Slowly I picked up the butter and took a quick whiff, then made a face in distaste. It smelled funny, like sour milk, though Mum always saved that for her scones. Reluctantly, hating to let it go, I walked back to the pig bin and dropped it in, then remembered to replace the lid and pick up Mum's bit tin. As I pushed open the door to the kitchen Mum and Dad were talking about the different neighbours. They had decided it must have come from Daddy Thompson's son-in-law, who, Dad said, 'dabbled in the black market', and Mum agreed. Then we all sat down to Woolton Pie, made from left over vegetables with crispy potato on top, and no more was said about the butter.

Margaret was coming to play. That promised excitement. Mrs Robertson and Mum often wheeled Margaret and me in our prams to the Children's Clinic on Rathbone Road, but now we were bigger we walked and didn't have to go as often. Sometimes Mum dropped me off at Margaret's house on Christopher Way, round the corner from where I lived further down from Irene's house, where we played all kinds of make-believe games. Today, Mrs Robertson was leaving Margaret at our home while she went to the shops. Margaret was six months younger than me and the envy of my life. She bounced along with blonde curls, blue eyes, and above all, she had a birthday on 21st June, Midsummer's Day, whereas I was born in cold, wintry, dark January and although I sported blonde curls I had brown eyes.

"Let's play air-raids," I suggested. "We can pretend the siren goes, and we take our dolls under the piano, which is the air-raid shelter and stay there while the bombs drop all round us."

"Oh, yes. And does your mum have any sweets? We should have something to eat."

I thought for a while. Then I crawled out from under the upright piano that hugged the wall. "Mum bought some special sweets and they're in the robin tin" I said. I pulled a chair from the dining table and pushed it against the sideboard, climbed up on tippy toes, and just managed to grasp the round 'robin tin', with the rhyme printed on it, '*Who killed cock robin? I said the sparrow, with my bow and arrow*'. I always felt sad when I read it, but now I pulled it back to the edge, climbed down off the chair and pushed open the lid. Inside lay blue, pink, green and yellow gooey, sticky sugary soft sweets that melted all squishy in my mouth. Mum had given me one and was saving the others for Christmas. But the temptation was overpowering. I brought the tin over and offered it to Margaret.

"Mmm. These are so good," she said, stuffing one and then another into her mouth. I took my share too. "Oh dear. They're all gone!" I said. Quickly I pushed down the lid on the top of the tin and climbed up the chair again and slid it to the very back of the sideboard. Maybe Mummy would think Daddy had eaten them all.

"Let's play hairdressers," suggested Margaret next, her mouth all sticky from the sweets.

"I dunno. We may get into trouble. Mum doesn't like me touching scissors."

"You can put them back after and she won't know." Margaret smiled, with a glint of mischief in her eyes. A little reluctantly I pulled the drawer open, while still on the chair, and grasped the big scissors. Very carefully, I climbed down again and handed them to Margaret.

"Here, you sit on the floor like this, facing the window," she instructed. "We'll stay under the piano because this can be the hairdresser's shop."

I sat down obediently. "Now give me a nice haircut won't you," I said in a grown-up voice, like Mum did when she visited the hairdresser's. Not only did she have her hair cut but sometimes the hairdresser put funny shiny things in her hair, then made her sit under a big machine.

Margaret giggled and began her work. 'Snip, snip, snip,' snapped the scissors. I squirmed trying to turn around .

"Sit still now," my friend said sternly. "There, now it's all done."

Still feeling uneasy, I took the scissors, and yet again, climbed the chair, dropped the scissors back in the drawer, closed it, climbed down and dragged the chair towards the table. I turned around and gasped. "Look at all the hair. When Mum comes in she'll see it and we'll both in be big trouble." Together we stared at the golden curls. "I know," I said suddenly, "Let's put the hair under the carpet, then she'll never know."

Together, we pulled the edge of the Axminster carpet up at the corner, and picked up as much hair as we could and shoved it under the carpet and the pad underneath.

I sat back. "There. Now she'll never know."

The knocker on the front door banged a couple of times.

"Get your doll, quick," I whispered. "Let's look like we're playing with our dolls."

Mum and Mrs Robertson entered the living room. Immediately Mum's hand went to her mouth and she made a sort of cry.

We tried to look innocent.

"Oh no! Just look at your hair," she cried. "All your lovely curls gone."

Mrs Robertson grabbed Margaret by the arm. "You naughty girl. What have you been up to now? Just look at your friend's hair. You wait until I get you home." Without any more ado, except for cries from Margaret, she was lifted up sideways under her mum's arm and carted out.

Mum was really upset. It was only when I looked in the mirror that I could see why. No more curls, only jagged chunks around my cheeks. I cried and cried. Even a visit to the hairdresser the next day couldn't put my curls back, and they never did grow back, until decades later when my hair turned grey, and they reappeared.

That night I received a hard smacked bottom because Mum had also discovered the empty sweet tin and Dad swore he hadn't touched her sweets. So I had no tea and was sent to bed. Mum came into the bedroom, still upset, and I shrank down beneath the cold sheets. No hot water bottle tonight!

"Now say your prayers," instructed Mummy, "And remember to tell God that you've been a really naughty girl today. Not only did you empty the sweet tin, but you let Margaret cut all your curls off."

So I told God, with Mum telling me what to say, and I had to promise God that I would be a good girl for Mummy for ever and ever. The problem was, I wasn't sure that I could keep that promise.

CHAPTER 6

AN AUSPICIOUS YEAR (1942)

Take my hand - ever keep me; Close to Thee
Walter John Mathams, 1853-1931

Nana sat in her usual chair at our kitchen table, her shopping bag bulging with potatoes, carrots and other rations. Her familiar maroon felt hat, slightly ruched to one side, sat firmly attached to her head with the aid of a bulbous pearly hat pin.

Sometimes she brought me an ounce of dolly mixtures, scraped from her own meagre ration for sweets. But not today.

"Lilian, how would it be if I took Joyce with me to Birkenhead on Wednesday? I have to see Mrs Bush to fit her with a new corset, and thought she'd like the ferry ride. It will give you a break, especially as you are so close." She smiled down at me. "After all, she is five years old now, so she's a big girl."

I perked up from combing my doll's hair. Mary had been given to me by Mrs Bush, as her daughter was too big for dolls now. I glanced from one to the other.

Mum nodded gratefully. "That would be very welcome," she replied, patting her big tummy. "I have some things to get done, you know, to get ready, so that would give me a chance to catch up on some odds and ends. What time will you pick her up?"

A time was agreed upon and I was on pins and needles with excitement. To get to Birkenhead we not only got the tram but travelled across the River Mersey on the ferry boat, which I loved doing.

Eventually the day arrived, and holding Nana's hand we set off together.

"If you are a good girl, I'll buy you a meat pie on the way back from the butcher in Grange Road," she said. I nodded enthusiastically. Pork pies were my favourite food, along with sausages. On the boat I ran upstairs and leaned over the rail, my head up into the wind, relishing the sea breeze blowing through my hair. "Be careful now," warned Nana, holding on to the bottom on my coat.

After the tooting of the horn, we set sail. That was the best part. After the ferry ride we caught a bus for a short ways, then alighted at a very grand looking house. It wasn't even attached to other homes.

Nana had her attaché suitcase with her and she knocked at the door. A pleasant, tall lady with a big quishy bun at the back of her head invited us in. "Joyce, it's nice to meet you" she said. "Would you like to play on the swing in the back garden, seeing it is such a nice spring day while your grandmother and I see, er, to the business we need to attend to?"

"Yes please," I whispered. This was even better. A swing all to myself to play on!

She hustled me into the back garden, to where the roped wooden swing swung in the breeze. Mrs Bush hurried inside. I gazed around in wonder. It was a huge garden, even bigger than Nana and Poppa's, and that was bigger than ours. Gnarled trees dressed in pink and white blossoms wafted gently, sharing their fragrant perfume with me. For a few moments I stood still and sniffed, wanting to capture it and take it home. But quickly I turned to the swing and managed to hoist myself up, though it was a bit wobbly and it took a couple of tries, as I wasn't quite tall enough to jump on.

Now I was on, and the world was mine. My legs pushed forward, then my knees bent back as I flung myself higher and higher, holding tight to the ropes hanging down from the sturdy frame. With the wind in my face, as I surged ever higher I could see over the fence at neighbours' gardens. The one next door had a real fancy slide – oh, just imagine having my very own slide as well as a swing in my back garden! Mum wouldn't have to take me to Northway playground then, but at the playground, as well as swings and a slide there were monkey bars, which I could already climb and hang from, and a roundabout, that I always jumped on, even though it made me feel sick.

On the other side of the fence lay an outsize allotment, with the soil rich and dark. Someone bent over the furrow as if planting something. Then he straightened up and waved to me. I smiled, but didn't dare wave back because I knew what would happen. I'd tried that once at Northway swings, and got a bumped head.

Nana and Mrs Bush emerged from the house. Reluctantly I

allowed myself to gradually slow down, but not too quickly. Nana helped me off the swing and I found my legs feeling a little like jelly, but not for long.

We stepped down from the bus at Grange Road so Nana could buy me my meat pie. After walking down to the dockside we walked up the gangway on to the ferry boat, then settled ourselves on the upper deck. Now she finally brought out the meat pie and I began munching.

"Nana…" I asked, my mouth full of meat pie.

"Wait until you've finished that mouthful," remonstrated my grandmother.

I swallowed hard. "Nana what do you do? What have you got in your case?"

Nana patted her small brown, beaten carrier. "Well, this is where I carry the corsets. Some ladies have problems. Something you will know about soon enough about when you are grown up. And to help them, I fit these ladies with special corsets which make them feel much better. I am called a Spirella Corsetier."

I licked some of the pork jelly off my fingers. Its salty slipperiness felt good in my mouth.

"Have you always done this?" I asked next, curious to know more.

Nana settled herself back. "Well now, it began during World War One, when your Poppa was fighting in the trenches overseas. The government didn't always have the money to send us their wages to pay for food and our house, so I had to go to work, and this is what I decided to do."

"Do you like doing that?" was my next question.

She shifted her weight on the wooden bench. "Oh yes. Indeed I do." She whispered to me. "I will tell you a secret."

My eyes lit up.

"I like earning my own money. And what is more, you never ever let a man know how much money you have." She sat back smug. "If your Poppa knew what I had, he'd spend it on whisky!"

I examined my grandmother anew. I knew Poppa liked what he called 'a wee dram' now and then, but he never acted strange like some men who'd visited the pubs on Saturday nights.

"What do you mean, you never let a man know about money?" I liked counting money, and I received sixpence a week pocket money. Dad gave it to me, so I wasn't sure how I could keep that from him.

"When you grow up, you will be earning your own money. Always put some away for a rainy day, and never let even your husband know how much you have salted away." She humphed, satisfied, then turned back to me and smiled. "But I am sure you don't really understand what I mean."

I sat against the hard backing of the bench, swinging my legs and chewing on the last morsels of pie. I had a pretty good idea what she meant. I must have done, because I never forgot her advice and followed it myself. That was the first of many outings we had together over the years.

Not long after that Aunty Peggy came to tea with Angela, her little girl, about my age. We played hopscotch on the pavement outside, then we went in to get warm and played school. I wanted to be the teacher, but agreed reluctantly that Angela could have a turn. Then it was time for tea.

My eyes had already fastened on the six buns filled with imitation cream sitting right in the middle of the table. As Mum poured the tea from the teapot into the cups she and Aunty Peggy chatted, while Angela and I talked too.

"When do you start school?" I asked her primly, knowing full well that I was beginning very soon, just after Easter.

"Oh, I don't know," she replied, spooning the red jelly into her mouth. She looked at her mother, spoon in mid-air, "Mum, when am I starting school?"

"At the end of summer," she told her. "Now, Aunty Lil and I are busy talking." She turned away and Mum passed the cream buns to her. I watched as they gradually disappeared, though I'd make sure I'd had one first. Now there were two left. Aunty Peggy had a second one, then took her last swallow of her tea.

Mum shifted on her chair, as if she was uncomfortable.

Aunty Peggy scrutinised her knowingly. "I think you're getting ready, Lil." She stood up. "Come on Angela. It's time for us to leave. Hurry up, get your coat on. We've got to get home to get your Dad's tea." Casting a lingering eye on the last cream bun, I trailed behind them to the front door. As soon as they departed, I blurted out, "Mum, can I have that cream bun, please?" pointing at the solitary bun.

Mum shook her head, took it, and ate it. Amazement took hold of me. Mum would never do anything like that normally. Then Dad appeared home, from his fire duty, and told me I'd have to go to bed.

"But it is too early," I protested loudly.

He placated me. "I promise to read you a story, in bed,"

"Can you read from the garden book," I implored, "Two stories?"

"Okay. Two stories." Quickly I ran up the stairs, pulled off my jumper and skirt, my vest, bodice, knickers, socks and shoes, and snuggled into my nightie. Prayers were skipped that night, as Dad wasn't so bothered about my asking God to help me be a good girl as Mum was. He read me the two stories, and we gazed at the brightly-coloured shiny photos as he pointed out the different names of the flowers illustrated on the page. I liked the droopy heads of the forget-me-knots, and the tall ramrod-red tulips. Satisfied, I settled down to sleep.

I woke up with a start. No siren, not this time, but a yowling and screeching reached my ears. Bother those cats, I muttered to myself, and drifted off. Then more cat screams startled me awake. Off and on it seemed, all through the night. Local cat fights had woken me up before with their meows and squawking as they sat on the neighbour's fence and fought with each other, but they'd never yowled this loudly or for so long. Eventually, sleep won out once again.

"Wake up, wake up!" My dad was shaking me awake. Rubbing the sleep from my eyes, I asked, "Is it morning already. Dad, did you hear all those moggies fighting last night?"

He shook his head. "No, Snooks. I never heard any moggies." Puzzled, I told him again, "But you must have. They were meowing and squawking all night long." I stopped sudden, realizing how unusual it was that Dad and not Mum had woken me up.

"Where's Mum? She always wakes me up."

"Come and see," he answered, with a mysterious smile.

Wrapping my warm, comfy green dressing gown around me, I traipsed behind Dad down the steep carpeted stairs one at a time. He pushed open the living room door. There, against the wall by the dining room table, stood a straw-coloured wicker cradle. Dad smiled. "Come and meet your baby sister." He nudged me encouragingly.

I tiptoed forward, uncertain, and touched the minute pink hand.

And so I was introduced to my baby sister, Jean.

As for the cats, it was years later, when in labour with my own daughter, that I realized who the phantom moggies were!

CHAPTER 7

EDUCATION FOR MIND AND SOUL (1942)

There's a Friend for little children, above the bright blue sky.
Albert Midlane 1825-1909

I thought the day would never arrive. Finally It was the night before I started school. After Easter, and following the birth of my baby sister, Jean, I snuggled into bed in a flurry of excitement, longing for morning to arrive. It was even more thrilling than Christmas.

Darkness hung about the bedroom when I awoke, but in April and with blackout curtains, that was usual. I wanted to be sure I wasn't late for my first day, so I struggled to get dressed in the dark, getting as far as my liberty bodice, fumbling with the rubbery buttons. My prickly, apple-green Welsh wool knitted jumper lay on the chair, along with a checked pleated skirt attached to a bodice, both home-made. Mum entered the bedroom in her tired dressing gown, slippers slapping on the linoleum floor, with a flickering candle stick in hand.

"What on earth are you doing?" she asked, exasperated.

"But, Mummy, I'm getting ready for school. I mustn't be late," I explained patiently, doing my utmost to quell the excitement bubbling within.

"But it's only one o'clock in the morning. Come on. I'll help you get undressed and back into bed. I promise I'll wake you up in plenty of time." She sighed.

Reluctantly I undressed and crawled back under the still warm sheets. Miraculously, I rolled back to sleep and at eight o'clock, true to her word, Mum woke me up, helping me dress in the cold, shivery air of spring. Downstairs the gas oven popped – the coal fire in the living room only being lit later in the day – spreading its warm infusion into the chilliness. I opened my mouth for the spoonful of cod-liver oil and gulped down half a cup of watered-down concentrated orange juice, issued by the government for children only. I hurriedly ate my cornflakes and milk, the latter having been left on the step that morning, though sometimes the cheeky sparrows pecked through the cardboard centre to have an early morning taste of the cream settled at the top of the glass bottle. With impatience now spilling over, Mum helped me tie my brand new brown lace-up shoes having outgrown my old button over ones. Then we set off. Dad was off duty, so he stayed behind to take care of baby Jean.

Mum's hand clasped mine tightly as I skipped and walked down Bentham Drive, past the bombed-out houses, along Francis Way and on to Rudston Road Primary School. A dull sooty-coloured, child-sized gasmask snug in a mottled maroon cylinder of tin bumped against my side. At the playground crowds of children played and shouted. To my right I noticed the squat, brick, foreboding air-raid shelter. I hated the closed-in feeling it gave me and hoped I wouldn't have to go in there. Mum strode past it without noticing, straight into the first grade classroom where I met Mrs Shemeny. She wore a pretty flowered overall, and had a gentle voice, so I liked her immediately and quickly settled into the fluid routine of Grade One.

At the end of my first day of school I rushed outside to where Mum was waiting by the school gates. "Mum!" I cried breathlessly. "I am going to be a teacher when I grow up."

She smiled. "Oh, really," came the absent-minded response. I didn't know at that time that everyone in our family had left school by the time they were fourteen. Nana had left at twelve.

In my classroom, letters of the alphabet were introduced. These were posted on the fatigued green wall, each side of the grey-tinged blackboard. With her long pointer, Mrs Shemeny tapped the vowels first, and we chorused the correct sound. She then added consonants, and slowly we began to string vowels and consonants together. Quickly I learned my letter sounds. Soon some basic words were introduced. After our lesson we all copied down carefully each letter of each word on to our slippery, charcoal coloured slates, taking care not to break the precious piece of white chalk we'd been assigned. At the end of the lesson, we erased our letters with a rag we'd brought from home, sometimes accompanied by a bit of spit, though the boys took the excuse to use more than a bit. Alongside the daily instruction we were each given a well-worn reading card, with pictures in red, black and white of Mother, Father, Ruth, John and Rover the dog, as well as Kitty the cat. Every day our teacher would introduce us to new words that we had to learn by sight, and gradually I moved from card one to two, to three.

60

After a couple of more weeks a word appeared on my more advanced card that I did not recognize, nor could I say it. I tried to say quietly 'a' and 'i', determined not to be defeated yet hating to ask for help.

Finally I succumbed. I stood beside the teacher's big desk. Mrs Shemeny tried to assist me. She gave me a clue, "When you have a and i together, what sound does it make?"

"a," I replied first, pronouncing the short 'a' sound

She shook her head and tried again,

"i," I tried again.

"Joyce, How do you feel when you hear the siren?"

"A-f-r-a-i-d" I burst out.

She laughed warmly. "Remember, a and i together make the long 'a' sound."

Once I got over 'afraid' nothing could stop me. I was hooked on reading.

On Friday mornings though, 'afraid' resurfaced. We all had to pull our gasmasks over our faces, stand in line and wait for the teacher to place a piece of cardboard under each snout cylinder to be sure they were working properly. Then, worse still, we processed into the horrible air-raid shelter. Flat slatted benches hugged the sides of the dank reinforced brick and concrete walls. The smooth cement floor greeted us with a cold, damp aura as if trying to pull us down. Even the air closed its clammy fingers around us, making me shiver. The only fun part was when the boys blew 'raspberries' into the snouts of the gas-masks and all of us girls giggled, nodding at each other, billowing out hollow, ghost-muffled sounds. The teachers kept shouting, "Stop it, children. Stop it at once!" but the boys sat smug, anonymous behind their black, rubbery masks, so no one could be made to sit in the corner at the back in the classrooms later. Despite the boys' mischief, I was always anxious to leave the shelter and get back to the comfortable safety of my classroom, where I pulled off my gasmask, placed it in my canister and settled back to the reassurance of lessons.

At home, books were scarce because of the shortage of paper during the war years, but along with the couple of old books that Dad had as a boy, I had a secondhand book with stories and pictures, given to me by Mrs Bush. Dad used to read it to me.

"What is that little boy eating?" I pointed to a small boy with a pointed cornet in his hand.

"He's eating an ice cream," replied Dad in amusement.

"Ice cream," I repeated. "What is that like?"

Dad tried to explain, and suddenly I thought that I had once tasted it a long, long time ago. "I think I remember" I said. I was also going to mention that I seemed to recollect too getting into trouble because I ate the bottom off the cornet, but decided it might be better to stay quiet. However, now that I was in school and beginning to read, although I struggled, I was determined to learn a small prayer at the back of the book with Dad's help:

School is over for the day, ended has my evening play. Soon a voice to me will say, time to go to bed. Supper on my little tray, then I clasp my hands and pray, thank you God for this good day and guard me in my bed, Amen.

That became my evening prayer of choice from then on after the obligatory recitation my mother insisted upon.

Twice every day at school, we received a small bottle of milk. First we all stood beside our desks, and upon the given sign from our teacher we sang the grace in which all obedient children in school participated:

Thank you for the world so sweet. Thank you for the food we eat. Thank you for the birds that sing. Thank you God for everything.

Only in school did I ever remember saying a blessing before food, until much later in life, after I was married.

As the summer holidays arrived, Jean began sitting up and making noises. I loved my baby sister, but she was still too little to be of much interest to me. However, she took up a lot of Mum's time, with bathing, feeding, changing her nappies and holding her, especially when she cried, so Dad spent more time with me. The five weeks off from school meant more time for playing outside, much as I loved school, and in the evenings, when Dad was home, he brought out the large coloured boxes.

"How about a game of snakes and ladders, Snooks?"

In a trice I'd climb up on a dining chair. "Oh, yes. Can we play Tiddlywinks too?"

Mum shook her head, tutting, because Dad would rather play games with me than assist her with the dishes. Some nights he watched me fit the wooden pieces of the jigsaw together that Grandpa Bibby had made me before he died. However, I loved it when he brought out the big atlas.

"Look," Dad said one evening, pointing to lots of red drawings. "These are all the countries that England rules. Here is England."

I couldn't believe our country was so small. It took us a long time to ride the tram even into the city. I pondered his words, gazing at the small island of our country. Then I looked across a large amount of blue. "What is this country?" I pointed to a large area across from England.

"Ah, that's the United States of America, and all this blue is called the Atlantic Ocean."

"Have you ever been there, Dad?"

He laughed. "No, no. But some day you may even go there." He said it in such a way that I knew he didn't really mean it.

From that introduction I became fascinated with the large atlas and together we poured over the various countries waiting to be explored. Sometimes he turned on our radio. One evening both of us listened intently to the shortwave station. Foreign voices bounced around our living room. "That's French," Dad said.

I gazed into the oblong Bakelite cover that shielded the different wavelength markers and the pointed dial as Dad twiddled the knob on the side.

"I think that's German."

"German! How come we can hear German?" I frowned. "We are at war with Germany."

"It's probably a propaganda station," he answered. He turned the dial again. Now the static noise ricocheted through the room and Mum yelled from the kitchen, "I can't stand that racket! For goodness sake, turn that thing off, or get a proper station."

Dad winked at me and set the dial to the Light Programme station to keep Mum happy. Vera Lynn warbled her latest song, "We'll meet again..." and calmness returned.

One clear Sunday morning, he said, "Well, love, how about a bike ride today?"

My heart leaped with joy at what lay ahead. 'I'll get the cushion, Dad," I offered, and grabbed the faded brown velour square off the couch. I watched anxiously as he wrapped the cushion around his crossbar, then encircled it tight with twine, tying it securely. His sinewy arms hoisted me up, sideways, so my frock wouldn't blow over my head, of course. Then Dad wheeled his bike down the front path, through the framed wooden gate, cocked his leg over to sit on the seat and we were off, on our way up to Childwall Church. Just past the church the sloping hill of Gateacre Brow melted before me and whoosh, down we sped, wind blowing my hair, air brushing my face, as a wave of exhilaration swept through me.

Dad slowed and braked to a stop. I jumped down and ran to the old market stone cross, embraced by a semicircle of ancient stone seats. Dad always stopped here first. Immediately I climbed up to gaze over the wall. I pointed to Jackson's Pond. "That's where the big boys go and get tadpoles," I told Dad. "When I'm bigger, I'm going to go there too." Then off we cycled again. Woolton Park, another favourite haunt, loomed into view. Off I hopped once more. On the side of a grassy slope lay the outline of a flowered cuckoo clock, now silent because of the war.

"Dad, tell me about the cuckoo clock and how it looked." I always asked the same question and never grew tired of hearing the description.

"It was a big, big circle," he explained, "shaped just like our clock at home, but made of flowers. Different coloured flowers made up the numbers and other colours circled the outside. Then marigolds, carnations and alyssium grew in the middle. On the hour a clockwork cuckoo would come out of a little box at the top of the circle, and say cuckoo each time for the number of hours shown."

I tried to imagine what it might look like. I knew how a cuckoo sounded. Each morning in summer I'd hear one outside my bedroom window. I gazed at the large circle wistfully, trying to imagine the myriad colours.

All too soon it was home again, for boiled cabbage, boiled potatoes, and perhaps, if we were really lucky, a small portion of meat. Rice pudding made with powdered milk always seemed to be served for afters. I liked the skin part best, which I saved until last. I definitely did not like the boiled cabbage, but I had to eat it anyway.

The long summery days shortened as the autumn coolness brought the tang of frost. October arrived, and Dad asked me, "How would you like to go to Harvest Festival?"

"What's that?" I asked, puzzled.

"We'll go on Sunday morning, and you'll find out."

Sunday morning finally arrived. Dad and I walked sedately hand in hand along Score Lane up to the church on the hill overlooking Childwall Valley. Instead of passing by, as we did when bike riding, we stopped, leaving the church hall on the other side of the road where I attended Sunday school. A Roman arch, sooted by centuries of coal smoke blown over from smokestacks in the city as well as from chimneys of surrounding farms and houses, framed the heavy iron-studded doors. We carefully stepped down two foot-worn sloped stone stairs into the cool darkness of the church. Enticing smells of fruit, vegetables and the dry warm fragrance of cut wheat, woven into a large sheaf, greeted me immediately. The abundance of food overwhelmed me.

"Why is there so much food here?" I whispered.

"Well," Dad whispered back, "At this time of the year, because it's harvest time, people give some of their home-grown vegetables from their allotments and gardens, and fruit, if they have fruit trees, to the church. Then we give thanks to God that we have enough food to eat. It goes to Olive Mount Orphanage to help feed the children there."

I'd seen Olive Mount Orphanage from the number 4a tram when going to Wavertree Road with Mum. It stood high and lonely on an empty hill, surrounded by nothing much but scrubby grass and bushes. Mum had pointed it out to me. I felt glad that those boys and girls without mums and dads would have good food to eat.

By this time we'd opened the catch of a narrow swing door, stepping up into a tall dark pew. All the pews had doors, I noticed, and I wanted to play with ours, swinging it in and out, but Dad shook his head, so I shut the door quietly. Then Dad knelt down on a dim, red, musty-smelling cushion on the floor in front, so I copied him, kneeling on the padded kneeler in front of me, peeking through my fingers to be sure I didn't miss anything. After a few seconds Dad got up and sat back on the pew, so I scrambled back up on to the hard wooden seat, scratched and grooved over the years. Organ music intensified whilst a red-robed choir slowly sang its way down the hollowed-out stone slabs between the rows of blackened pews. The minister, draped in snowy surplice and green stole, brought up the rear, his bald head shining in the flickering candlelight and slanted rays of sun struggling through the stained glass windows. The hymn rang out: *"We plough the fields and scatter."* I joined in excitedly. "I learned that hymn in school," I whispered loudly to Dad. He nodded as he joined in with his fine baritone voice, *"For it is fed and watered by His Almighty Hand."*

The vicar's voice echoed in the hallowed eleventh century church, and I didn't really know what words of wisdom were imparted, except we got to sit down a while whilst the vicar climbed way up into the high wood-carved pulpit.

Finally the last hymn burst forth in all its fullness. I didn't know it, but liked the tune enormously. I pretended to sing, "*Come ye thankful people come. Raise the song of harvest home. All is safely gathered in, ere the winter storms begin. First the blade and then the ear, then the full corn shall appear. Come ye thankful people come. Raise the song of harvest home.*" I decided that was going to be my best hymn. Dad explained that Harvest Festival took place every autumn, and if I liked, we could go again the next year. I nodded wholeheartedly in agreement. And we did. Somehow, saying grace before our milk each day took on a new meaning for me. I also found Dad's old hymnal, *Hymns Ancient and Modern,* and he helped me learn my new best hymn.

Some months after starting school, I switched Sunday schools. St David's Church was different to All Saints Childwall, where we had attended the Harvest Festival. For one thing it was nearer, and more importantly it was modern. The gloomy, dark stones of the interior, with stained glass scary pictures watching my every move were replaced by pale brick walls with shiny, blonde woodwork framing the plain frosted glass windows. This was much more to my liking. Besides a children's corner set up with an altar rail, a cross, tables and lots of books, near the vestry, attracted me immediately, a place in church, just for children. On the wall, near the corner, a list was posted where children could sign up to clean (which meant dust) and tidy this special area of God's house.

"Mum, can I sign up to help clean the children's corner?" I pleaded, on the way home from my first Sunday there, hoping she'd say, 'Yes'.

"Are you sure you are big enough to walk there by yourself?" She looked dubious. "I don't know about your crossing Rocky Lane."

"I promise I will look both ways just like I do on the way to school. Please, can I go?" I hopped from one leg to the other. "After all, I'm almost six."

She smiled at me. "All right then." I printed my name proudly on the sheet the following Sunday.

Thereafter, usually about once a month on a Saturday morning, my short legs ran up Bentham Drive to the red pillar box, then across Rocky Lane, after looking both ways, and down to the church. I pushed open the heavy oak door timidly and crept in. Everything stood hushed. I stayed for a moment in front of the altar and bowed, just as I'd seen grown-ups do, then walked on tiptoe to the corner. Clutching a handful of daisies from Mum's garden, wrapped in newspaper, I knelt down on the small kneeler before a cross, laying the flowers on the table first. I folded my hands together, with elbows resting on the rail, and closed my eyes.

I remembered that you could ask God anything, and took advantage of His beneficence often. Sometimes He had given me a sunshiney day when we visited Calderstones Park to feed the ducks, but He still hadn't given me a Donald Duck gas-mask, even though I'd asked Him for one every time I saw a friend at school wearing one on Friday mornings. I sighed as I thought about my petitions. We still had air-raids too.

Despite these setbacks I knew that I would continue to ask Him for special things as I thought about them, like my very own book, which had now crept up the list to number one. But this hushed space quieted my thoughts and created a stillness inside me as nothing else did. It puzzled me. What made me feel like this? I shook my head, perplexed.

After a minute or two I busied myself, throwing the old flowers away in the bin beside the vestry door and placing the smiley daisy blossoms in fresh water. Then I dusted the small altar and table, while rearranging the books. Usually I selected one, and sat in a small my-size chair placed by the table and read for a while. After fifteen or twenty minutes, I reluctantly left this small sacred space, closed the heavy knotted door behind me again, and skipped my way home.

It was at St David's I met fellow schoolmates. Here I also admired fashionable young Sunday school teachers in refashioned frocks and hand-sponged coats, with hats trimmed with bits of veil and worn at a jaunty angle. I wondered how they did it. After all, Mum had told me that a new coat took a whole year's worth of clothing coupons. Even wool was rationed. I learned to knit in school, but the yarn there hung heavy, made of oily cotton, and once we had knitted our square of garter, stocking or ribbed stitches, without dropping one, it was yanked off the wooden needles, unravelled and rewound, ready for the next stitch to be learned. Many of us had woollen sweaters recreated from washed jumpers belonging to our mothers or grandmothers, who had unravelled their own clothing, rewound it into balls, then knitted fancy warm jumpers for us children to wear during the damp, bone-chilled days of winter when we shivered in front of smoky coal fires.

Coal was essential and the coal wagons, filled with bulging sacks of coal, were pulled by huge Clydesdale horses. That was what Dad called them. I watched the coalman heave a hundredweight of coal on his back and dump it into our coal bunker out back. He was always as black as the coal he delivered. Another favourite visitor to our neighbourhood was the rag-and-bone man. "Rags and bones!" he shouted, as he dragged his plodding nag and wooden-wheeled rickety wagon around the streets. All of us neighbourhood children dashed out as he dangled balloons or a rubber ball tantalizingly in front of us in exchange for a handful of rags, jam jars or tattered cast-offs from our parents.

Then of course, the bin-men came too, tossing dented metal bins of coal ash, cinders and old cans into the back of the cart. The same big horses pulled those wagons, sacks of grain hanging about their noses, so they could eat and work at the same time. We never saw cars, unless it was the ambulance or fire engine. Very occasionally someone ordered a taxi, but that was all. All the petrol was saved for the war effort. However, whenever these horse-drawn carts appeared, I knew what would happen. Mum would yell, "Joyce, where are you? Come on. The bin men are here. You get to that pile of manure before someone else does."

Reluctantly I'd take the smelly pail and shovel from her. Into the street I'd plod, to scoop up the nasty-stinky droppings from the horses as they stood waiting patiently for the next bin to be emptied in the cart behind them. I'd carefully scrape the shovel under the straw-streaked brown clumps, trying to hold my breath, but never quite managing it. I'd struggle with both hands, carrying the once-white tin pail, now half-filled, to the back door.

"Here you are, Mum." The smell clung to my clothes as prickly burrs did when walking through a field. Quickly she'd grab the pail, making a face herself, and spread the smelly trove on her rhubarb, next to the air-raid shelter, in the small triangular back yard. We had the best rhubarb in Childwall, I believe. And despite the awful smell, it never stopped me from eating rhubarb pie and custard.

During Sunday school I heard even more Bible stories. I also earned a book for perfect attendance. Within its pages I learned about John Pound, a cobbler who himself lived in poverty, but taught the poor children in his neighbourhood. Seeing that I already knew I was going to be a teacher, I determined that I too would one day teach poor children their lessons. Gradually my understanding of God developed as I struggled with questions. I knew Jesus loved me, but couldn't quite figure out how Jesus was all mixed up with God.

Mum and Aunty Peggy visited each other every week. I looked forward to these visits, at least when I was home from school, as Angela and I could play together. One afternoon, we had a discussion about God. Angela had just started Sunday school.

"What do you think God is like?" Angela asked me, whilst our mums were busy drinking tea together.

I thought hard. "I think He is very old. After all He made the world, and that's even older than Nana and Poppa. So he must have a very, very long white beard. And maybe long white hair too." I could see God in my imagination quite clearly now. "God has to be even older than Father Christmas, if He made the world."

Angela nodded. "I think so too."

Then I pondered. "He's supposed to live in heaven, which is up there." I pointed skywards. "Mum told me that that is where heaven is when she told me that thunder is only when they empty the bins in heaven. Also Dad said that that was where Grandpa Bibby went to when he died."

I thought some more. "So perhaps he sits on a big white cloud way, way up, and looks down on us to be sure we are good."

Angela pouted upon hearing this. She wasn't too sure she liked that part. So we asked our mothers, "What is God like?" But they just laughed and one of them said, "You'll just have to wait to find out." And so it was left, but I continued to wonder.

CHAPTER 8

HOLIDAY TIMES
(1943-44)

Come ye yourselves apart and rest awhile
Edward H. Bickersteth, Jr. 1825-1906

St George's Day in May meant a Bank Holiday. "Mum, can't we go on a picnic on St. George's Day? I have a holiday from school."

Mum looked at Dad. "You said you're off this Bank Holiday. You can give me a hand with the Tan Sad on the tram and boat so we can take Jean."

Dad scratched his chin. "I don't see why not. So long as Jerry doesn't nix it for us."

I was thrilled, but the night before, the siren screeched its warning. Mum hustled me out of bed and as I pushed my legs into my siren suit, Mum placed my baby sister, well wrapped up in a blanket, in the wicker clothes basket, usually reserved for wet wrung-out clothes and pegs. Dad was already at the Fire Station that night. Mum manoeuvred the basket through the back door, then locked it behind her, giving me the big key. I opened the air-raid shelter door and once she'd placed the basket on the floor, she securely closed the door behind us and lit the small oil lamp. I knew the routine too well and climbed up on my bunk, closed my eyes and continued my night's sleep.

"Joyce, Joyce, wake up. The all-clear is going." Mum shook my arm.

"Did any bombs fall?" I asked eyes still sleepy.

"There was plenty of flak and I heard a few blasts but none close by," replied Mum matter-of-factly as she hoisted Jean still sound asleep in her basket up the steps, through the door I'd opened and out into the starlit night. I immediately looked at our house, as I always did. All was well. It stood strong and silent. We'd have our picnic.

"I may as well leave your sister in the basket to sleep out the last couple of hours" said Mum. She closed the back door then turned around and put the kettle on the gas stove. Thank goodness we still have the gas," she commented, mainly to herself.

I wondered why she'd say that. After all we always had gas to boil the kettle for tea.

"Do you want to go back to bed or would you like a cup of tea with me?" asked Mum. "It will be light in another hour or so."

"I'd like a cup of tea," I said, feeling very grown-up. Usually my tea had more milk than real tea, but already it was what I liked most to drink. I climbed up on to a chair and settled myself at the kitchen table and waited. Just as we began drinking our tea, Dad pushed open the back door. I sniffed. "You smell very smoky," I commented. Dad almost always smelled of smoke but today it was very strong.

He took off his shiny fireman's helmet, undid his silvery jacket buttons and sat down on the nearest kitchen chair. "Boy, I could certainly go a hot cuppa." He stretched out his legs. "Docks in Bootle got hit last night. Couple of the lads got hurt – rushed to the Infirmary. We fought it for hours. I'm bone tired."

Immediately I became alarmed. "But Daddy, don't forget we're going on a picnic."

Mum gazed at his weary face. "Maybe we shouldn't go."

I felt my face crumple. I'd been so looking forward to this, and besides, Dad had to go to help with baby Jean.

Dad drained his tea and leaned over to ruffle my hair. "I'll just go and take a kip for an hour or two, then I'll be as right as rain to go on the picnic." He pushed back his empty cup and I heard his feet dragging up the stairs.

I breathed a sigh of relief. "I think I will play with Mary," I told Mum. "She needs to have her frock changed." I trod the stairs softly, so as not to wake Dad and jumped on to my bed to get Mary and began brushing her hair.

Dad was true to his word, and by the middle of the morning Mum had the thermos flask full of fresh hot tea and some sandwiches made ready for our special day, Dad was washed and shaved and I had my coat on ready. Jean was placed in the Tan Sad pram that folded up, now fed and happy, and Mum fastened the soft, velvety brown hat secured with a hat pin on her head. Bursting with happiness, we made our way to the tram stop, then on to the boat at the Pier Head.

"See, over there," said Mum pointing in the direction of a very big ship anchored from us up the river a short way. I gazed at the ship. It overflowed with men in brown uniforms, cheering and waving to us. I waved back vigorously. The young men whistled, and

I laughed. Then I heard Mum say to Dad, "Just look at those young men ready to set sail. I wonder how many will make it home."

Dad looked at the crowded ship and shook his head. "What a waste of young life," he said.

I looked from one to the other, puzzled, then I knew it had to do with the war and people being killed. I stared at the troop ship. Suddenly I realized that Mum and Dad meant that many of those men that I could see laughing and whistling would die. The shine of the picnic had dimmed a little for me. As our ferry boat chugged across the Mersey to Birkenhead I twisted my head around to stare at the men who might not come back.

After a short bus ride, we arrived at Raby Mere. The sun shone warm that May day as Mum laid out the washed-out patched blanket on the spring grass, ready for our picnic lunch. She instructed me to go and play. "But don't go too far," she added.

"I won't, I promise, Mummy," I told her and skipped into the nearby woods to gather bluebells. The blossoms sprang blue with sprinkles of white whilst the sweet fragrance invited me to bury my face into the delicate cool flowers. I gathered my bouquet and became engrossed in my task.

Suddenly I heard a tramping of feet and barking voices. Curious, still holding on to my flowers, I ran towards the edge of the woods by the far road and stopped. Mesmerized, I gazed down upon a long procession of men with hands on their heads marching just below me where I stood on the embankment. Some soldiers in uniform holding large guns marched alongside them. I'd never seen so many men like that before, and especially men with hands on their heads. They marched three or four abreast in a long orderly line down the leafy lane. Who were these men, and why did they have their hands on their heads? The only time I'd seen anyone with hands on their heads was when some of the boys in my class might be naughty, like Victor Cowan, who'd tried to peek up a girl's frock when she stood on a chair. Then he had to stand in the corner, facing the wall with his hands on his head for ever so long before the teacher let him come back and sit down.

I watched the men, all wearing overalls like Mr Croxford, a neighbour, who also wore overalls when he went to work each morning. Mum said he was a plumber. Were all these men plumbers?

One glanced at me, briefly. I half raised my hand to wave, but something made me lower it again. Maybe it was the sight of the soldiers with guns. These men with hands on their heads all stepped together, clump, clump, clump, clump! I watched until the procession had disappeared round the corner of the country lane. Then, still carrying my large fistful of bluebells, I ran back through the woods. "Mum, Dad, do you know what I just saw?" I caught my breath. "There were a lot of men, all with hands on their heads, and some soldiers with big guns seemed to be telling them what to do. I've never seen that before."

Mum and Dad looked at each other. "They were probably German prisoners of war," Dad explained. The soldiers were guarding them, making sure no one escaped." He patted my shoulder.

I felt perplexed. "But they looked just like us. They really did! One even looked at me, a little. They can't be Germans." I'd always imagined Germans looked different and scary.

Mum smiled and brought out the tomato and cheese sandwiches. "Yes, they are young men sent to fight by Hitler" she said. She added, almost to herself, "And I bet half of them are glad they are now prisoners and safe."

By now I was more interested in having my lunch, and I forgot, for a while, about the German prisoners of war. But in bed that night I thought about the troop ship and the Germans who looked like us and wondered if there were any children in Germany.

Nerves were stretched to breaking point. Nights were constantly disrupted. Mum complained about monotonous food and different new recipes to try. It all contributed to Mum saying one day, "I think it's time for us to have a holiday."

"Really, where will we go? Can we go to the seaside? Will there be Punch and Judy?" I couldn't contain myself. "Will Dad come too?"

"Your Dad has arranged it all," Mum replied with a happy smile. "Uncle Arthur and Aunty Em live in Hoylake. Uncle Arthur works with your Daddy in the fire service, but his home is over the water, and they have invited us there for ten days.

Even the air-raid siren that night couldn't dampen my excitement, but I still had my nightmares. I'd dream that a bomb fell right through my bedroom ceiling. Invariably I'd wake up with a jolt, then as I'd search upwards the jagged hole stayed, sinister, hollow, foreboding, and I'd scream with fear. Mum always came running in with a candle light, then flicked on the electric light to show that the hole with dripping plaster and broken laths was gone and the bedroom ceiling appeared whole again. No bomb had fallen that night, at least not through my bedroom.

My other recurrent nightmare began with a walk through my house after emerging from the air-raid shelter. I'd climb the rickety stairs, which were all twisted and broken, and knew we'd been hit. At the top of the stairs I would step into the bathroom, to see the overhead toilet tank sideways, ready to fall, and debris surrounding me. Again, my sobs would disturb my mother's sleep, and she, once more, would console and reassure me that all was well. So, a holiday was 'just the ticket', as my Dad said.

Dad hauled down the battered family suitcase from the cockloft above the bedrooms and Mum packed a couple of dresses for me, some clothes for her and Dad, who would join us on his days off, and my cream woollen bathing suit, knitted for me by Mum.

At last the day came. We walked to the tram that took us into town, Dad carrying the suitcase, Jean in the Tan Sad pram, which folded up when we boarded the tram, and me skipping with sheer joy. At Central Station we stepped off the tram and caught the train to Hoylake. As soon as we alighted, I began. "Can we go to the sands now? Will you buy me a bucket and spade? I can't wait any longer."

Dad took hold of my hand. "I promise we'll get you a bucket and spade, but first we have to go to Uncle Arthur's and Aunty Em's."

Reluctantly I grasped his hand and with backward glances towards the beckoning sea, with tantalizing crisp little strips of foam rising and falling, we turned a corner, and I wondered what the house might be like.

"Here we are." Dad knocked on the door of a red-bricked terraced house. Immediately the door opened and a grey-haired lady with a bobbed hair-do and wearing bright lipstick smiled and welcomed us in. It was the first time I'd seen her, though I'd met Uncle Arthur several times when he'd come back with Dad for a cup of tea at our home when they were off duty.

He stood right behind her, big and burly. He said in a booming voice, "Hello, hello. It's so nice to see you all. Come along in."

I climbed the stairs behind Aunty Em. "Here, this is your room.

I hope you like it." Her voice warmed me. "There are some children's books here for you to look at, and if you look really hard you can see the sea from your window."

"Thank you," I said and smiled to try and show how much I liked everything. Then she was gone.

I knelt on a chair close to the window and gazed out. Aunty Em was right. There in the distance was the promise of sandcastles, paddles in the sea and maybe a Punch and Judy puppet show.

Although blackout was still observed, no sirens screamed that night, or the next night, or the night after. I suddenly realized that bombs did not usually fall here, but I did hope that our home in Liverpool stayed safe.

The next morning I woke early, and pushed the lamp at the side of the bed to one side to see the room better. It was then I noticed a fancy gold-framed picture hanging on the wall opposite my bed. It captured me. I sat up and stared hard. *That's Jesus,* I said to myself. I recognized Him from the pictures I'd seen in Sunday school. *And who are all those children?* I focused on the children. There were hundreds of them, streaming across the picture right under the frame even. One was sitting on His knee. "Oh, how I wish I could be that little girl," I whispered out loud. Then I peered closer. There were all kinds of children, big, small, black, white, and others I didn't know. But I could see clearly that there was a very, very long queue, all waiting for their turn to sit on His knee. I slid out of bed and moved forward. Was I there, I wondered? I examined each one, and as my eyes moved toward the end, the children seemed to merge together and I couldn't see who they were any more. Maybe I was at the very end. My heart sank. I knew all about queues. We queued for everything, potatoes, bread, sugar, tea, and if oranges had come in at Waterworth's the queue was extra long, because oranges were also rationed, and were only given for children, one each, and often by the time Mum and I had gradually moved closer, they were all gone. If I was at the very end, would Jesus be so tired he would have left and gone home by the time I got there? The thought saddened me.

Each evening and each morning I gazed at the picture, and by the end of the ten days, I decided after a while that it didn't really matter because my Sunday school teacher told us that Jesus loves all the children and that meant He loved me, even if I wasn't in the picture. The memory of that painting stayed imprinted on me and brought a warm feeling whenever I thought about it, even after I arrived home.

However, with the morning sun and the sweeping away of the blackout curtain, I squirrelled over breakfast, until we finally put on our coats, and with Jean safely ensconced in her pram pushed by Mum, and me holding on to the bar at the side, we crossed the road to the sands. A shiny new blue metal bucket and a wooden spade dangled in my left hand, while I held on to the pram with the other. But now we were there. I let go of the pram's safety and jumped on to the sand, trying to undo my sandals at the same time, longing for the trickling, satiny feel of warm sand between my toes. Then I ran to the water's edge, anxious for the lapping wavelets to wash my feet.

"Oh, oh!" I shrieked, "It's cold!" But it didn't stop me.

Dad joined me, his pants rolled up to his knees. He shivered, "Maybe it is too cold," he joked.

"Nah!" I said laughing at him. Then daringly, I splashed him.

"Come on, Snooks. Let's get your bathing costume on, then you can get really wet."

I rushed back to where Mum had spread the same old moth-eaten blanket on the beach and where Jean sat beside her letting the soft sand run between her fingers. Mum wrapped a towel about me and discreetly removed my clothes while pulling up my woolly costume. Off I raced again, back and forth, sometimes bringing pails of water back with me. I poured one pailful over Jean's toes, thinking she'd like it, but she howled, so that was that.

"How about a sandcastle?" asked Dad.

I clapped my hands. "Yes, yes! But how do we make a castle?"

With his hankie knotted at four corners over his head to protect him from the sun, like the other few dads or granddads around, he began digging with my spade in the firmer sand. I tried to help, but messed up some of his digging. So he instructed me, "Why don't you fill the bucket with sand? Here, take the spade, and I'll show you how we make the fancy turrets on the castle."

At first I filled the bucket with loose sand because it was easier to dig, but then it spilled and the sand pie didn't come out right.

"You need to use wet sand," instructed Dad, "That way it will keep its shape."

It was harder to dig into wet sand, but in order to make my castle look real, it was the only way. So I learned that sometimes you have to work harder to get things the way you want them. But I didn't mind. My only problem was that the weight of the water, once it soaked my hand-made woolly bathing costume, pulled it down, so Mum had to keep squeezing the water out while it was on me, to prevent it falling around my knees.

Late in the morning a man appeared, dragging some long poles, a case and some red striped sheeting. I watched, curious as to what might happen next. I asked Dad.

"Wait and see," he said with his wink.

So I waited. Then to my delight I saw a puppet theatre booth emerge from the poles and the cloth. A small dog with a ruffle around his neck and a box attached at the front wagged his tail happily as he walked around his owner. Other children began to gather, and we all sat on the sand in front of the closed curtains above us to see what would happen.

"A Punch and Judy Show!" I suddenly exclaimed, while the other children cheered. The curtains pulled back with a jerk, and a funny-looking puppet with a red curled hat popped up.

"Hello boys and girls," he said in a gruff voice.

"Hello, Punch," we all echoed back.

Then began the fun. Punch began arguing with Judy, a fellow puppet. Then he brought up, from somewhere underneath the stage, a big bat.

"Oh, no!" we shouted, then "Boo, boo, boo!" we yelled as Punch began to hit Judy. Judy disappeared quickly, but then to our delight a big-toothed crocodile appeared. He was looking for something to eat. He looked for Punch, and asked for our help. "He's over there." We pointed to the corner. But by the time the crocodile looked in the corner, Punch had gone. "No, no, he's over there!" we shouted. Again, alas Punch had ducked down out of sight. But in the end the crocodile chased Punch away so we didn't see him again. Then finally the crocodile appeared again, smiling.

Suddenly the crocodile came forward towards us, and out flew a stream of water from his mouth, spraying those of us in the front row. "Oh, oh!" we squealed with delight.

But the show was over. The man came forward. "Would you please put some pennies in the box when it comes around?" Dad pressed three pence into my hand. Toby the dog, who had been patiently sitting beside the puppet box, got up, wagged his tail and began to circulate among us. Eagerly we placed our pennies in the box around his neck. I asked Dad for more pennies, but he said, "That's enough for today."

One day we had lunch out, a rare treat. Mum pushed Jean in the pram to Red Rocks, not too far away, and with Aunty Em we purchased a meal from a special wartime cafeteria. The food was plain, like at home, and we all sat at long tables. Back at the house Mum and Auntie Em had shared their ration coupons, to make it fair for us all.

Too soon the holiday ended and we packed up our suitcase once more and caught the train back to Liverpool. I sat on the scratchy train seat, kicking my legs, thinking about the beach, the water, and then the painting of Jesus and the children.

Then it was back to school, air-raids and Christmas. Winter breezed in with its wizened hands casting fancy patterns of ice inside my bedroom window. Sometimes I'd look at them and wonder at the intricate geometric patterns, though I didn't know how to express it at the time.

Early in 1944 we had another holiday, this time at a place called Pen-y-ball in North Wales at a summer home belonging to Great Aunt Nell and Uncle Alf, relatives of my dad. It was a grand stone house, standing all by itself with a centre wooden door adorned with a large knocker hanging like a lion's head, waiting for someone to lift it. Immediately around the house a brown stone wall stood, just about my height. Then there were woods which surrounded the whole area, and I longed to go outside and explore.

A lovely hollowed-out dell secretly hidden among some bushes excited me. It was perfect for a fairy home. I loved hearing stories about fairies in school, and often imagined myself going into a secret place like this and being invited to go to fairyland. There I'd see myself taking a special train ride and meeting all kinds of magical fairies with their wands, ready to grant my every wish.

That evening, I watched Aunt Nell instruct my mother on lighting up.

"You, see Lil," she explained, "You must just turn the wick up so high, then light it. Once it has caught, you can turn it higher to give more light."

Mum followed the directions, and flickering gas lights made the living room like Aladdin's Cave, which our teacher had just read to us in school. The only bad part about the house was that we had to go outside to go to the loo. The seat was a long plank, with a hole in the middle, and no chain to pull. I wasn't sure about this at first, but Mum came with me a couple of times until I became used to it. A pile of cut-up newspaper sheets was strung on a nail to the inside door, just like at home. Toilet paper was very scarce because of the war and was only found in the underground public toilets near T. J. Hughes in downtown Liverpool. But that was slippery and no one liked it. I preferred newspaper.

The next day, we caught the local bus and alighted in the small town of Holywell. Dad explained. "Many hundreds of years ago, there was a holy well here, called St. Winifred's well, and people came to be healed."

"Really? And were they healed? Is the well still here? Can people still see it?" My questions came fast and furious.

"Let's see if we can find it," said Mum. "Maybe it will cure my swollen glands."

I glanced up at her face. Every so often the left side of her face near her ear would swell up and hurt. "I do hope it can," I said earnestly.

With Jean toddling beside us we explored the small streets and shops while Mum used some of her ration coupons to buy food for us while on holiday. Suddenly, I stopped and stooped down.

"It's somebody's handbag." I held it up to Mum.

She took it. "My goodness. Someone must have dropped it. Let's look inside and see if we can find out who it belongs to."

Together we looked and found a ration book with clothing coupons as well as a small purse with three shillings and three pence inside. On the ration book was the address: 21 Primrose Hill, Holywell.

"We must find Primrose Hill, Mum, to give it back."

Dad and Jean decided to wait on a bench close by while Mum and I searched for Primrose Hill. After asking several people we were directed to a small alleyway on a steep hill, buried in the town. I gripped Mum's hand.

"Let's see if we can find the house," Mum said, her voice tightening a little.

My tummy jiggled slightly as we began checking the numbers and walking up the dirty, darkened alley. Some women in dirty pinnies with cigarettes drooping from their mouths seemed to hang over the half-doors. I felt a little scared and held Mum's hand tighter. Despite this, we carefully examined each house. Mum bravely asked one lady, "Could you tell us where number twenty-one Primrose Hill is, please?"

"Dunno," came the response.

We search up one side and down the other. There was number

twenty and twenty-two, twenty-three, twenty-four, but no twenty-one.

"That's it," declared Mum. "Let's go back to your Dad and Jean."

Quickly this time, we walked down the cobbly hill, back to the wider streets, cheerful people and safety.

"What are we going to do, Mum?" I asked.

"Well, I think you should have the money in the purse," she said.

"Oh, boy! Thank you." I was thrilled.

"And the clothing coupons." Mum hesitated, then turned to Dad. "Your cousin Alfred is getting married in a couple of months. I think I'll give these to May, and she can get herself a nice suit to get married in." I felt sure that Aunty May would be very happy.

We continued on our way.

A couple of days later, we found the Holy Well of St Winifred. We entered into a place that had a pool with concrete all round. Under a shelter, I discovered crutches, wheelchairs, walking sticks, even leg braces. "Look, look, at all these," I called to Mum and Dad.

They came over. "It seems that even people today are healed here by the looks of it," said Dad.

"Maybe it will heal my swollen gland," offered Mum.

We walked over to the head of the square pool, and I noticed a spring trickling into the pool. "See, that's where you need to get the holy water." I pointed to the sparkling stream, bubbling on the surface of the pool. Mum bent down and dabbed some of the holy water on the side of her face, over the swollen part.

"There. Now you won't have it any more," I said assuredly.

"We'll have to see," she replied.

It was time to go back, and I was introduced to a new surge of excitement through climbing and hiking hills. Mum and Jean stood at the bus stop, anxious to catch the bus back to Pen-y-ball, overlooking the town of Holywell. Dad gave me a quizzical look. "Would you like to try and walk back, up the hill to Pen-y-ball?"

"Oh, I don't think the child can do that," protested Mum.

That was all I needed. "I can do it. I know I can," I pleaded with her.

Dubiously she looked down at me, then at Dad. "Well, she can try, but…"

"I can always give her a piggy back," Dad assured her.

So as Mum and Jean climbed on to the platform of the bus, Dad and I, hand in hand, made our way to the outskirts of the town and to the hill that led near to where we were staying in Pen-y-ball. I pushed my head back to stare at the high hill in front.

"How high is it, Dad?" I asked.

"About eight hundred feet or so," he said with a smile.

"I can do it" I said, and took my first steps. I huffed and puffed a bit, and my legs felt tired in a different way from walking on the flat pavement at home. But my cheeks tingled and I felt a surge of energy. Halfway up, we turned around and I experienced a thrill to see the town down below. I continued to trudge up, getting a little slower as the top loomed into view.

"Do you need a piggyback?" asked Dad, stopping.

"Oh, no," I responded. "I can do it!"

And I did. At the top we turned around. A sense of accomplishment invigorated me as I stared down upon the village below me resembling a toy town, like in story books, and way across I could see our city of Liverpool.

"Look. See way over there." Dad pointed to the far skyline. "That is Liverpool Cathedral. See that tower standing tall above the buildings."

I strained to where his finger pointed. "I see it, I see it!" My voice rose excitedly. I revelled at the sight of the still-unfinished cathedral rising like a beacon over the blackened buildings scratching the sky far, far off. "Can we do this again? Can we do it every time we go into Holywell? Can we walk down the hill and walk back up each time?"

Delighted, he laughed out loud. "I love to hike up hills. And I am so glad you do too," he said, and squeezed my hand.

That night physical tiredness drove me to bed early, just after the lamps had been lit. But the thrill of climbing that hill and looking out miles into the horizon, far above all that was moving and standing still, created a warm contentment deep inside me.

All too soon, it was time to return to the soot, grime and bombs, but I still had my three shillings and threepence to dream about and how I might spend it.

The day came when that three shillings and threepence came due with interest, to the people who now live in twenty-one Primrose Hill, renamed Rose Hill. Through an unexpected coincidence more than six decades later my husband and I stayed at that same address and the money was repaid with interest, as our home exchangers enjoyed some Maine hospitality prior to our stay in their home. What is more, I climbed that same hill to Pen-y-ball several times over, just as exhilarated as I was when I first experienced that thrill as a young child As I climbed the steep hill one bright autumnal day I felt Dad beside me as I turned around to gaze upon the skyline of Liverpool, with the cathedral, now complete, still standing tall in the far-off horizon against the clear fathomless sky. I discovered that the hill was 820 feet in height, and found the house where we had stayed so long ago, still standing and lived in.

CHAPTER 9

SURPRISE! (1944)

We are little children, weak and apt to stray
Harriet Burn McKeever, 1807-80

Each morning at 8:15, before school, my mum would remind me, "Be quiet now. Joyce, take care of your baby sister while I listen to the Recipe for Today." Then she sat with her ear to the radio, a newly-sharpened pencil and a dog-eared half-filled exercise book at the ready as she wrote down the speciality of the day.

"Okay, Mum." As I kept an eye on Jean, now toddling all over the floor and trying to pull open the sideboard cupboard, I tried to listen too, hoping it might be a new recipe for a cake. To my disappointment it usually offered something like "oatmeal soup" or "Woolton Pie", made with all root vegetables. But occasionally an eggless Victoria sponge made with dried egg, flour, a little sugar, milk powder and water, with mock cream (usually involving flavoured, cooked cornflour) was offered. Now that was more to my liking. (From *We'll Eat Again,* a collection of recipes from the war years by Marguerite Patten.)

No one had a party because there was barely enough food to feed one's own family, so when Irene announced she was going to have a party for her eighth birthday, everyone wanted to be her special chum. In the end seven of us were invited, including me, and I was beside myself with anticipation. Maybe there would be a real birthday cake. I longed for a new dress, but knew better than to ask. No one else had a new dress for anything, unless it was someone else's made over.

I arrived bursting with excitement. But when Irene opened the door, I almost stopped breathing. A beautiful, shimmering, crimson silky dress swished around her slight form. As she turned, it swung out.

An envious sigh escaped me. "Oh, I love your dress. Is it new?" I had to know where her mum had bought it. Maybe I could get one too.

She laughed, twirling round again to show it off. "Oh, this is from parachute silk. My Dad brought it home when he was on leave, and my Mum made it into a party frock for me on her sewing machine. Do you like it?"

"Oh, yes," I breathed. "It's lovely." And she spun around once more.

I sighed deeply. My dad was a plain old fireman, and there was no chance of him bringing home a gorgeous red silky parachute. (I found out later that red parachutes didn't stand out at night, when men were dropped into enemy territory.) I glanced down at the dark green secondhand frock that Mrs Bush had given to Nana for me.

When Irene closed the door behind me I presented my present, two sixpenny National Savings Stamps, worth a shilling. I apologised to Irene. "I'm sorry that it's only savings stamps, but Mum said you'd be glad of it one day."

"Oh, that's all right," responded Irene graciously. "You should see what I did get."

I didn't think it much of a gift, but then I usually ended up getting these myself at Christmas and birthdays, besides the sixpence I took to school each Monday to purchase an additional stamp. When my card was full, Mum deposited it into a Post Office savings account for me, and whenever I complained she reminded me how I'd be glad of it one day.

While such thoughts scampered through my head, Irene danced into the living room and held out a book. Not just any old book, but one by Enid Blyton, who was every child's favourite writer. It was entitled *Mystery of the Spiteful Letters*. I wasn't sure she could even read it, but my envy increased tenfold. To scrape back my green twinges, I asked her if I might borrow it, after she'd read it of course. I wanted her to think that I could read it too. She nodded.

But now there were games to play. After Blindman's Buff and Oranges and Lemons, Mrs Griffiths told us we had a surprise game. "Children," she announced, "you are going to go up in an aeroplane."

We all gasped. She smiled. "Now then, you must all leave the room, only Irene's aunties and I will stay here."

We stood outside the living room door, giggling and wondering how they would ever get an aeroplane into the living room. Auntie Rhona came out. "Come on, Irene. It is your birthday, so you can be first. But we must blindfold you as we are going to a secret destination." Despite Irene jumping up and down, they managed to blindfolded her so she couldn't see anything before she was led into the room. We could hear low voices, then Irene let out a scream, "No, No!" she shouted out. "I can't!" Then there was silence, and we thought we heard her laugh, but that couldn't be.

The same aunt emerged again. "Who's next?" We pushed Margaret to the front. She left us blindfolded and we listened intently. Again there were some cries, then silence with some muffled laughs.

"Right," said the aunt coming out once more. I took a deep breath. I always liked to get scary things out of the way.

"I'll go," I volunteered and bravely stepped forward. A blindfold was tied tight around my eyes, and I was led into the living room. I heard the door click behind me.

Mrs Griffiths said, "Now, Joyce it is your turn for an aeroplane ride."

My tummy somersaulted, but I'd never let them think I was afraid. She led me forward, then told me to sit down and place my hands in my lap.

"You are now on an aeroplane," she explained.

"We are going higher and higher, higher and higher. You're now right up in the sky with the clouds," said her Mum, as if frightened.

I felt the seat wobble a little to one side then the other, as I rose higher and higher. I was afraid I was going to hit the ceiling and half ducked my head.

"Oh dear," came her worried voice, "the plane has a problem, a real problem. I'm sorry but you've got to jump, now!"

Fear and trepidation tingled through me, as imagination swept me way up beyond the ceiling, maybe even into the clouds. I now clung tight to the chair seat.

"Jump!" they urged.

My imagination had soared by this time, along with the seat on the plane, and my heart raced, terrified, but someone gave me a push, and lo and behold I was only a short way from the ground when another aunt caught my arm. I pulled my blindfold off, and laughed, sort of, as I realized I had been duped. But now I sat, waiting on another chair, ready to watch the next victim squirm and shriek, then jump. I observed how the two adults gradually raised and lowered the chair seat, taken out from one of the dining chairs, telling the next guest just how high they were going. I smothered a laugh as one girl began crying, "I can't, I can't!" But, of course she had to, and somewhat chagrined, took her seat with the rest of us, waiting to gloat and smirk as the next unwitting girl was led into the room.

After it was all over, we relaxed and laughed with each other. I also decided that I liked surprise games better than predictable, tame ones.

Now the birthday tea was spread out for us on the small square dining table at the far end of the living room. We sat down, squeezed in together, hungry and hoping secretly for cake. Spam sandwiches were passed around first, which we devoured, followed by red jelly and pink blancmange. Then in walked Mrs Griffiths with a birthday cake complete with eight glowing candles ready for Irene to blow out and make a wish. As we held our breath, Irene blew hard and long until all eight candles were blown out. Now came the best part of all, as we all tucked into a jam sponge cake with icing on top.

All too soon, Mrs Griffiths brought in our coats from the hooks in the hall and we left the warmth behind us. With filled tummies and a tired contentment from the fun and games, we all ran to our homes, shouting, "Ta-ra for now. Ta-ra!" I rushed into my house, eager to tell my parents all about the book that Irene had received and the birthday cake with real icing.

That evening as usual I knelt beside my bed, with Mum hovering over me, and recited my prayers. However, right after I prayed, "And please God, help us win the war," I mumbled to myself, "I'd like a party like that too one day, if it isn't too much trouble." Then I jumped into bed, grabbed Teddy and snuggled down to sleep.

Irene came to play at our house the following week, and we chatted about a film she had seen that had a monster in it. We laughed loudly at the thought of monsters and the idea that they could live under a bed.

Suddenly I had a brilliant idea. "Why don't we play monsters with Jean? She loves for me to tell her stories."

"Yes, let's." Irene's eyes flashed with mischief.

"Why don't you go under the bed," I instructed, "And be the monster. Then I'll bring Jean in and lift her onto the bed, so her legs dangle down. Then I'll tell her the monster story." I grew light with excitement, my imagination soaring into the land of make believe. "When I say that there is a monster living under my bed, I will lift her down and as soon as you see her legs, grab them."

She hooted. "That will be such fun."

I ran downstairs to where my little sister was playing with Flossie, our small dog, who'd joined the Bibby family the previous year. "How would you like to hear a story?" I asked her. She stood up and Flossie escaped into the kitchen, where Mum was preparing tea.

"Come on upstairs, and I'll tell you the story."

Jean stood up and toddled after me, up the stairs into my bedroom. There was no sign of Irene. Good, she was hidden under the bed. I closed the door quietly.

I lifted Jean up and began my tale. "Once upon a time there was a big, bad red monster who was huge with long sharp teeth, and loved to eat little girls." I carried on as Jean's liquid brown eyes grew larger and larger as she became more and more scared. Then I concluded, "And, you know, that monster who loves to eat little girls lives under my bed. And that's the end of the story."

I lifted her down, and right on cue, Irene grabbed both her short legs. I almost collapsed laughing as Jean with her two-and-half- year-old screams shook the whole house. Her mouth was wide open and shaking with pure fear.

Mum bounded up the stairs just as Irene started to crawl out from under the bed. Mum's yells were even louder than Jean's screams and sobs. "You go home, young lady!" she shouted at Irene and pointed to the stairs. "As for you," her ire brimmed over, not only are you going to get a good hard slapped bottom, but you are going to bed without any tea."

As Irene slid out of the room, down the stairs and out of the front door as fast as a slippery snake, I began quaking in my shoes. Mum grabbed me, yanked down my knickers and SLAP, SLAP, SLAP, her hand resounded against my bare bottom. Then she turned me to her and glared right into my eyes as she pronounced, "Let me tell you something, my girl. You are going to be sorry you ever did this to your baby sister. Someone will one day grab your legs from under the bed. You mark my words. You will get paid back for this in the same way you treated your poor little sister. You wait until your father comes in."

Much as I pleaded and expressed how sorry I was, nothing could take back her edict. I cried and cried. Even Teddy couldn't console me. Eventually I fell asleep, but her dire threat burrowed itself deep into my sub-conscious mind and stayed there for years to come. Consequently I always checked under my bed, every night, just in case.

Jean, now more than seventy years old, still remembers that day.

It was about this time that Jean began to use her imagination, and thereby got into trouble herself.

It was a wintry afternoon a few weeks before Christmas when we noticed that Flossie had been whining all afternoon and looking up at the window. We couldn't figure out why. Her dish, an old frying pan without the handle, was licked clean from her dinner. Water slopped over the top of her chipped, discoloured drinking bowl. No one was coming up the front path; no rag-and-bone man was coming round the corner to bark at.

Night arrived and I climbed the stairs to bed. During the darkness the siren screamed its warning, and we all rushed downstairs, Jean in Mum's arms and Flossie leading the way, down into the air-raid shelter. This night there was a crowd as Mr and Mrs Chambers who had moved in next door, where Mrs Dodd used to live, didn't have a shelter, so they joined us. Mrs Dodd had gone to live with her daughter in another part of Liverpool.

Part way through the night I saw flashes and noticed the air-raid shelter door open. Silhouetted against the sweeping searchlights stood Mr Chambers with his back to us, balanced with his legs apart and his hands in front. I stared over the top of my prickly blanket. Why was he standing there like that? What was he doing?

Then he turned around and I saw him doing something with the buttons on his trousers. It was a mystery. But just then the all-clear wailed the good news. The air-raid was over. No bombs had fallen nearby that night and Mr and Mrs Chambers walked back to their house while we trooped back into ours, Flossie running out in front.

The following afternoon, as I sat looking through the window, I idly pushed my mother's favourite jade vase to one side so that I could see Mrs Lunt better as she swept her front path. I realized that the vase seemed surprisingly heavy. I peered inside and a strange, stale smell spiralled up from the darkness. Taking great care, I climbed down off the chair, carrying the vase very carefully, well away from my nose, into the kitchen to show my Mum. Shaking her head, she tipped it out, and Flossie jumped wildly. There lay her dinner from yesterday, complete with spoon, spread out in messy brown clumps on the wooden draining board.

Mum turned to me, "Did you do this?"

"No, no, of course not. I wouldn't do that to Flossie."

"Then, it must be Jean!"

Upon hearing this, Jean fled and scrambled upstairs, with Mum right on her heels. I heard a loud wallop, and winced. Cries trembled down the stairs, as Mum yelled. Reluctantly my little sister stumbled back down the stairs after Mum, and into the hallway, and then into the kitchen where Flossie stood beside her empty dish looking up at the draining board where her dinner, from yesterday, sat in tired congealed chunks beside the sink.

"Now, then, you go ahead and do what I told you to do," commanded Mum, her hands on her hips.

I stood at the kitchen door waiting to see what would happen next.

Jean, between sobs, managed to quaver, "I am sorry, Flossie, for hiding your dinner in Mummy's best vase. I promise I won't do it again."

Flossie, hearing her name, looked at Jean and wagged her tail, then Jean knelt down and put her arms around the dog. But Flossie was more interested in getting her dinner back and she broke away and tried to jump up at the draining board. Poor Flossie, I thought – no wonder she was whining so much at the window.

Mum threw the old dinner away, then made her a new meal. Flossie watched her intently, and then slurped and gulped her scraps of bread, soaked in Bisto gravy, immediately, not trusting to leave one scrap for even a minute. I felt sad for Flossie, who had missed her dinner, but I also felt sad for Jean after she had been smacked so hard.

One frosty Saturday morning a few weeks later, I skipped my way with my skipping rope up Bentham Drive to Nana's house, accompanied by Mummy and Jean. I had just bought my four-ounce ration of sweets from Barker's for the week and realized that Christmas was now only three weeks away. Despite buying my sweets I still had my sixpence pocket money left for that week.

I wondered what I could give Mum and Dad for a present. Maybe I'd find something in the bombed site where we sometimes played. Then I remembered I still had two whole shillings left from our holiday in Holywell when I'd found the handbag. I could buy something really special with that. Christmas I knew, from Sunday school, had to do with the birth of Jesus in a stable shed, but then Father Christmas came into it too, and he was the one who brought presents. I did have some doubts now about Father Christmas, but it didn't matter.

I still wanted a Donald Duck gas mask, but at the very top of my list now was a book. - my very own book, and in particular, I wanted *Ten Minute Tales* by Enid Blyton. I'd told Mum, I'd mentioned it to Dad and I'd even shared it with Nana and Poppa. Jesus was given gold, some kind of sense and myrrh, so surely between Father Christmas and God they could help me get *Ten Minute Tales*?

A particular story stood out, one the teacher had read to us in school. It was all about a queen who came to tea. I tried to be extra good too, and hoped that scaring Jean with the monster story wouldn't result in a lump of coal.

We arrived at Nana's house and I clattered the knocker above the letter box. A warm smell of fresh bread cloaked me as I stepped into the hallway. That meant a fresh bap roll with golden syrup slathered over it.

Mum and Nana chatted while Jean and I sat at the kitchen table waiting for our treat. Nana got the milk from the larder for tea and pulled the kettle on the trivet away from the coal fire to make a pot of tea. I sat patiently. Then, still talking, she cut the warm roll, pushed off the lid to the syrup tin and twirled a rich, golden knife-full on to my bread. Oh, such bliss! I tried to make it last as long as I could.

"Thank you, Nana," I told her. After all, I wanted to be sure I could have another one when I came next time.

Then I needed to go to the bathroom. I had a problem, a personal problem. I'd always had difficulty going to the bathroom, and Mum often plied me with nasty tasting medicine to make me go. Off I went up the stairs, hoisted myself on to the seat, did what needed to be done, used the requisite piece of newspaper hanging at the side, then wiggled off the toilet, pulled up my knickers and smoothed down my skirt. Now I was ready to pull the chain, but how? At school I had no problem. They hung low down. Usually my Mum pulled it for me at home, but now I was getting bigger.

I studied the situation thoughtfully. Then I carefully climbed onto the toilet seat, reached up with my hands, grasped the rubberized green mottled ball holding the chain tightly in both hands and yanked it down. The force of it gave way so fast, I slipped, right into the messy toilet bowl. My brown shiny lace-up school shoes were covered with a dull, nasty mess. "Oh, no," I cried out sobbing, mortified and horrified at the sight, the smell and just simply being where I was.

Nana and Mum rushed up the stairs. "Whatever have you done?" exclaimed Mum as she and Nana ran into the bathroom. Mum immediately lifted me up, while Nana wrapped a towel around my legs, so I wouldn't drip the hateful stuff on her carpeted stairs. I was carried downstairs, while Mum tried to hush my distressed cries, then between them they removed my socks and brown shoes, and while Nana washed my feet in warm, soapy water, Mum hastened home to bring another pair of socks and my sandals with the toes cut out.

"Mummy, do I HAVE to wear those brown shoes again?" I whispered, my cheeks tear-stained with my feet finally clean after being thoroughly washed with carbolic soap.

"I'm afraid you do. It's the only pair you have and there aren't any coupons left to get you another pair." Seeing my horrified face, she assured me. "I'll make sure they are absolutely clean for you."

Of course it didn't help when Jean toddled into the kitchen from the living room and announced, her fingers holding her nose, "Ugh, kaaka, kaaka," and pointed to my shoes which Nana was hurriedly wrapping in layers of newspaper, along with my socks, for Mum to take home and clean.

I wrinkled my nose, but I didn't argue. I knew too well how long my Mum had worn her own beaten-up shoes, so my sister could have her first real shoes this winter and how she'd given her better shoes to Old Meg. But even today, seventy years on, I still hate brown shoes.

It was the Saturday before Christmas, 1944. Saturday mornings were always special, as Poppa and I went a walk, just the two of us, to the Rocket pub, about a mile or so away. There he had a pint of beer and bought me a lemonade. After we'd drained our glasses, Poppa picked up the Saturday *Daily Express* at Shuttleworth's, then we'd make our way back. First, was our secret ritual when we'd go to the railings, overlooking the train rails that ran from Lime Street Station to somewhere else. I wasn't sure where the trains actually rushed to, but I always stood on the slatted park bench, gazing down the embankment, waiting for the eleven o'clock train to go whizzing by while Poppa held tight to the back of my coat. The driver always waved to me, and I waved back, before the black monster engine, breathing out clouds of steam, whooshed on its way.

I stayed watching until the last carriage leaned its way around by the signal box. Then we walked to Nana's house for a cup of tea. Nana always got upset with Poppa because he would give me some of his in a saucer with milk. Today, instead of the biscuit to go with the tea, Nana had a treat.

"This is a little piece of taster cake," she announced.

I took the sliver of cake, sprinkled with some raisins. "Why are we having cake?" I asked, amazed at the treat.

"Ah, you see when I made our Christmas cake for next week, I put some of the batter aside and baked a little taster cake, so we could have a taste of it before the big day."

She stood back and smiled at me, her displeasure with Poppa forgotten.

"Mmm, it's good." I swallowed a mouthful of cake. "I can't wait for Christmas," I told her, yet again. "I do hope Father Christmas brings me a book, especially *Ten Minute Tales*." I never lost an opportunity to press my hope.

Nana smiled again. "Who knows what the old gentleman will bring? Now finish your cake." I ate my cake and slurped up my tea, then was on my way back home.

Christmas morning arrived. I knew it was Jesus's birthday, but my attention focused on my own presents. To my dismay there was no book in my stocking, but I did get a paint box and tried to be thankful. I kept quiet and did my best not to let my disappointment show, because I knew books were scarce because of the war. Mum had told me this many times. There simply wasn't any paper available and even if a book was ordered from Philip, Son and Nephew, it didn't mean it would be in print. At least I didn't receive the dreaded lump of coal.

Jean received a big spinning top. She kept asking me to help her push the handle down to make it spin and I soon grew tired of that. But then it was time to leave for Nana and Poppa's. For dinner there would be the traditional roast pork and Christmas pudding. The thought of it made me hungry. After I'd had the slice of taster cake Nana showed me the bigger fruitcake she'd made snug in the big round cake tin. On this one though, small miniature marzipan fruits decorated the top.

"How did you get those fruity sweets for the top?" I asked her.

"Ask no questions and speak no lies," she told me. And that was the end of it. She clamped the lid down firmly on the tin. I knew I wasn't supposed to know, but I had a feeling Mrs Bush might have given them to her.

Now it was Christmas Day, and Mum banged the knocker. Poppa opened the door and hugged me. "Merry Christmas, Chuckles," he said in his rich Scots voice. I hugged him back. We all jostled in and gave our coats to Poppa to hang on the hall-stand. But now the familiar Christmas cooking smells assailed me, and I hoped there was a good amount of crackling over the top of the roast pork that I could have to suck and crunch on, the best part of all.

"Merry Christmas, Merry Christmas!" we all shouted out to Nana in the kitchen as she stood stirring gravy on the stove in the scullery. She put the spoon on the draining board and bustled out, wiping her hands on a well-used pinny. I then ran into the warm living room, where a coal fire crackled its way up the chimney, and huddled in front of it to warm my hands.

Nana followed us in and I noticed two wrapped presents on the couch. "Well, well. What have we got here?" said Nana with a twinkle in her eyes. "I wonder if Father Christmas dropped something off on his way to your house." She picked them up, giving a large package to Jean as I eyed the small square package still in her hands. Could it possibly be? She handed it to me. With hands trembling with excitement, I ripped off the paper, not even gingerly peeling it off carefully to be used for next year.

I jumped with joy. "I've got it, I've got it!" I whooped into the hallway. "I've got *Ten Minute Tales!*"

Poppa leaned toward me and whispered in my ear. "I have to tell you Chuckles, that your Nana ordered this specially for you, months ago, and she had to stand in a long queue to get it last week. So this is a very special book."

I clasped it to my heart. "I will always love this book, and keep it for ever and ever," I promised him earnestly from my heart. I thought it strange that Father Christmas would deliver presents to their house, because they were so old. What Poppa said explained what I'd suspected for a while, that Father Christmas was really for little children. But I went along with it, for Jean's sake.

Then Jean showed off her gift, a new doll that had eyes that opened and closed, and we all admired it

"Dinner time," announced Nana. Once again, we enjoyed the small but sufficient Christmas feast set before us.

While Nana and Mum cleared the table and washed the dishes in the chilled scullery, I lay on the couch with my book. On the front of the purplish cloth cover there was a clock, and inside the name of the book, *Ten Minute Tales.* Underneath it said clearly, ENID BLYTON. At the very bottom, I read slowly, "School Edition". I wasn't sure what that meant, but I did resolve to cover this precious book with brown paper to keep it clean and protect it as soon as I returned home. I turned to the inside where it said, 'Contents' and slowly brought my finger down the names of the stories. There it was, 'When the Queen Came to Tea', and I slowly began reading. 'Elizabeth' was hard to sound out, but I remembered that the little girl who couldn't walk was named Elizabeth, so I continued. I just got to the part where it said, 'Only Elizabeth was left out. Her mother knew that the little girl could not climb down all the stairs to see the queen, and she herself had to go to work as usual,' when Nana said, "Come on, Joyce. Put your book down. It's time for the King's speech."

Reluctantly, I found a piece of newspaper, tore off a corner to use as a bookmark and sat back to listen to our King. It was now 1944, and not so many bombs were falling on Liverpool, but I had heard about the 'doodlebugs' that were hitting another city called London. The King didn't speak for very long, but as usual Nana and Mum commented on how well he'd done. I wanted to get back to 'When the Queen came to Tea'. Some of the words I struggled with like 'carriage' and 'palace', but by the time Nana said tea was ready I'd just read, 'And all because,' she said, 'the dear queen came to tea with me one day!' and I closed the book triumphantly.

"I finished the whole story," I announced, and everyone smiled, pleased with my accomplishment. Then I wanted a piece of cake with the orange marzipan fruit on it, and hoped for more treats of marzipan after everyone else had eaten their piece.

That evening, as Jean slept in the Tan Sad, made into a bed, I curled up on the couch, with a cushion at my head and a warm Scottish plaid blanket covering me. The fire flickered its secret messages in the small fireplace, curling about hot coals and hissing every now and then. The four grown-ups sat around a card table playing whist, talking in low voices. Just the standard lamp glowed gold shining over their heads and on to their cards.

It had been a very good Christmas, and though I wasn't too sure about the whole Father Christmas story any more, it didn't really matter. Whatever I'd done had worked. My lovely book lay tucked under my pillow, safe until tomorrow and I didn't even think of a Donald Duck gasmask.

Decades later when I saw the movie *The King's Speech*, I finally learned why Mum and Nana had been so anxious when King George VI had made his speech each Christmas afternoon. Now I knew the full story.

CHAPTER 10

EASTER PROMISE (1945)

So let us feast this Easter Day
Martin Luther 1483-1546, tr. Richard Massie 1800-1887

My Sunday school teacher told us all about Easter. Even in school we sang "When I Survey the Wondrous Cross" in morning prayers. So I knew about Jesus dying on a cross and that he then rose from the dead and is alive for ever more. I listened hard to the different stories related to Easter, and accepted that this was what happened. In the Children's Corner, I searched for a picture book about Easter and placed it on the small table, then I gazed again at the cross hanging on the wall. It was hard to imagine anyone hanging on that. If Jesus was God's Son, as the teacher said, and could do anything, why didn't he get himself down? When I asked her that, she just said, "He couldn't," and began talking about something else. After kneeling down for a while and simply tasting the sweetness of the silence, I noticed my knees hurting, so I stood up and left the church quietly.

This morning I knocked at Nana and Poppa's door on the way home.

"Well, now. Just look at you," declared Nana opening the door. "Come along in and see what I am doing."

I followed her into the kitchen, leaving my coat over the banister, then down the step into the chilled scullery. On the stove bubbled four real eggs.

"You have four eggs. How did you get so many?"

Nana laughed. "Well, Easter is coming, so Poppa and I saved our eggs these last couple of weeks and I'm going to colour them for Easter."

"How do you do that?" I asked, standing on my toes to watch the eggs gurgling away.

"Ah, that is a secret. You will find out Easter morning." She turned the heat off. "Now why don't you go and see your Poppa."

I ran back through the kitchen into the living room where Poppa's head drooped forward. "Hello, Poppa," I called, not too loudly to frighten him.

"Och, it's you Chuckles! I was just resting my eyes for a wee moment."

I put my elbows on the arm of his chair. "Poppa, will you show me again how you put your legs behind your head?"

He grinned. "Shsh, but don't tell your Nana." He then twisted one leg, then the other at the back of his head. I clapped my hands in delight. "How do you do that? Even I'm not that good."

He unwound his legs. "Well, now, ye ken I am a tailor, and I sit on the floor cross-legged, on a type of platform, so that keeps my legs pretty nimble." He chucked me under the chin. "But when you grow up, you'll no be a tailor."

"No," I told him, yet again. "I am going to be a teacher."

"Och, that ye will," he said approvingly. "Now how about coming into the back garden and we'll see how yon tomatoes are growing in the greenhouse."

I grabbed my coat and followed him out the back door, past their air-raid shelter, down the path between the two rows of brown earth waiting to be planted with leek and cabbage seeds, to where he opened the door to the greenhouse. As he shut the door behind me, I breathed deeply the rich musky smell of growing tomatoes. Several clusters of shiny green fruit hung heavily down, propped up with straight sticks.

"Look," he said, "Here is one beginning to turn already."

I examined the orangey-green tomato. "I don't suppose I can eat it yet?" I asked hopefully.

"Och, no, me lass. Ye'd have a big tummy ache if you ate that. Tell ye what, though. I'll save that one for you. Ye can have the very first tomato on the vine."

Now I glanced up at the grapevine. Tiny green grapes were already forming on the old brown vine crawling overhead, under the glass roof. Nana always gave me a bunch of juicy black grapes when they were ready later in the summer. Being in the greenhouse with its warm growing smells, where tomatoes and grapes grew safe from the storms outside, created in me a sense of hope about summer coming with warm sunshine and not having to wear a coat.

We walked back to the house, where Nana reminded me, "If you don't go home now, your Mummy will be thinking you're lost."

"I suppose so." I reluctantly left her house of lovely smells and walked back down Bentham Drive to Alban Road and home, with Nana still hanging over the gate to watch me and wave each time I turned around.

After school one afternoon, the week before Easter, Margaret, her mum, my mum and I, along with little Jean and Margaret's new baby brother Ian, in his pram, walked to Childwall Fiveways so Mum and Mrs Robertson could change their library books. As we passed the bread shop, I pulled up sharp. "Just look at those Easter eggs!" I cried, pointing to the large plate glass window.

Margaret stopped too, and then so did our mothers. Sitting on little holders squatted ten prettily-decorated real chocolate Easter eggs. I couldn't believe my eyes. Some were big, decorated with pink and green squiggles and flowers. Some were medium size and some smaller, but all had delicate decorations painted all over them. Our eyes goggled at the sight. Chocolate eggs had only been dreamed of, and vaguely described by nostalgic parents. We hadn't even tasted chocolate. Four ounces of pear drops or dolly mixtures, and even sticky lice, a twig stick that we sucked on then put in our pockets to suck again later, which my Mum hated, somehow paled in the sight of real, brown, rich chocolate Easter eggs. I'd asked my Mum to describe what chocolate tasted like, but I couldn't really imagine how good it must be.

Margaret and I stood riveted, our noses pressed against the zig-zagged fortified glass window with its diamond-shaped crossed tape. I read the notice out loud: "These eggs are for sale on Saturday morning at 9:00 am."

I pulled Mum's well-worn coat sleeve. "Can we come and get one? Please, please!" I begged. Margaret chimed in too. "Please, Mum, can we?"

"We can come by ourselves to buy one each," I suggested. "After all we are big now, then you won't have to bother coming with us." I added the last bit, thinking that she might be happy not to get Jean ready and leave the house again.

Margaret jumped up and down, her blonde curls bobbing and her blue eyes sparkling. We even agreed to share one, if we had to, because after all it was wartime, and we wanted to leave some eggs for other boys and girls.

Mum and Mrs Robertson agreed, and while they continued around the corner to the library, Margaret and I tried to decide which one we each wanted, or which one we would share, if necessary. On the way home, all we could talk about were the chocolate Easter eggs, and how we might even give just a small piece each to our little sister and brother.

That night, I prayed under my mother's eagle eye, then added, "Please Jesus, you can do all kinds of miracles, could you please save two of the chocolate Easter eggs for Margaret and me. I'll even let her have the largest one." I figured that such a generous offer would be irresistible for the Almighty Powerful One, as I pulled my hot water bottle up to my chest along with my knees to try and get warm.

Finally Saturday morning arrived. I bundled up in my coat and pixie hood, took the half a crown Mum gave me and rushed out as soon as Margaret appeared at our gate. We ran just about all the way to Childwall Fiveways and were there by half past eight. Already five people were queued up in front of us. But there were ten eggs, so we smiled, full of confidence, at each other. Quickly more women, with cow-brown canvas shopping bags or frayed baskets hooked on shabby coat sleeves, quietly lined up behind us. I gazed at the tantalizing eggs, still trying to decide which one I like best. I whispered to Margaret. "Do you still want that one with the pink squiggles on it? I think I like that middle one to the right best now. The one with the green and white icing."

"I still like that big one with the pink icing," said my friend, pointing to the middle, largest one.

"Mmm. That's a good one too," I agreed longingly. "But if we can't get one each, which one shall we get to share?" I thought briefly of how I really would like one just to myself, but knew that Jesus wants us to share. After all, I'd learned that in Sunday school, and felt quite self-righteous in thinking about it.

"We'll share the biggest one."

"Shush, here she comes!" I whispered with excitement. We stood rigid, with bated breath, as the shopkeeper came to the door and unlocked it. My heart beat faster. "Please God, please God, let us get that egg," I prayed fervently. The half-crown in my hand became hot and sweaty.

Another shopkeeper, a streaky apron tied loosely around her skinny waist, stood behind the counter, hands on hips, waiting for the first customer. The first shopkeeper came to the queue squinting in the pale spring sun, and beckoned to a lady in front of us. She hustled in, basket over her arm, and a minute later, a scrawny hand grabbed the middle large pink-iced egg. A hollow gap remained. That was the one we had planned to share!

The customer scurried out, eyes downcast, and on her way. A wave of disappointment washed over me. Our first choice was gone. Still, there were nine eggs left and only four people in front of us. My hope winged upward. Another woman with a bleak, wool-stretched pork pie hat pulled over her ears, right in front of us, was ushered by the same shopkeeper into the shop. The same scrawny hand appeared, with another egg disappearing from the window. "Please, God, please God. I'll be happy with even just the little one, if only you'll let me get it." I kept my eyes open, two feet on the ground, and hands clenched with anticipation.

The first shopkeeper, without a word, slid out yet again from the door. This time she passed by us and whispered something to a woman looming tall behind us. Almost furtively, the hopeful buyer, still in her long-stained pinny wrapped about by a shorter baggy coat slunk by us, eyes in front, padding behind the shopkeeper. Another egg disappeared.

"It isn't fair," Margaret whispered. "She was behind us!"

"I know. Sssh, here she comes again."

This time, someone was selected from still even further behind, and so it continued. One small tantalizing chocolate egg remained. I prayed harder than ever. "Dear God, please. Let that one be for us. I promise to be good for ever and ever if only we can have it!"

The solitary egg stood, lonesome, in the almost empty window. Then suddenly it was snatched away.

The first shopkeeper emerged for the last time. She actually spoke with a tight smile, "I'm sorry ladies, but that is all we have." She disappeared inside, defiantly shutting the door. The crowd began to disperse patiently, bearing their disappointment, used to being denied, used to not having. Tears pricked my eyes.

Margaret stamped her foot. "It's not fair!" she shouted, "It's just not fair!"

"Well, God," I muttered to myself, "You certainly didn't help me, and I wanted a chocolate Easter egg so bad." I kicked a stone.

Neither of us said very much on the way home. We were sniffing too hard. Margaret continued on to Christopher Way, while I opened our gate and knocked at the front door.

Mum opened the door and saw my tear-stained face, whereupon I immediately launched into the terrible injustice served upon us. She took me on her knee. "I was afraid that might happen." She sighed as she explained to me. "You see what they did was just sell the eggs to their best customers. Two little girls weren't their best customers, so that is why you didn't get an egg. I am really sorry you didn't get one, not even to share."

I cried some more, then Mum said she had some bangers and mash for dinner and that cheered me up a little. I also heard her say to Mrs Robertson later that she thought it was a shame that the shopkeeper didn't give two little girls a chocolate Easter egg. Mrs Robertson retorted that she wouldn't have let us go if she'd known that was going to happen.

I still had to say my prayers that night. They were recited begrudgingly, as I realized that God doesn't always give us what we want, despite what my Sunday school teacher said.

The following day, Sunday morning, I trotted up the road to Nana's as usual. She smiled as she opened the door. "Come and see what I have for you," she said. She beckoned me to follow her into the kitchen. There, wrapped in a nest of crinkled paper, were four coloured hard-boiled eggs, a blue, a green, a pink and a yellow one.

"Happy Easter. Maybe you'll share these with your baby sister?" Nana raised her eyebrows, waiting.

"Of course, Nana," I assured her. After all hard-boiled coloured eggs were good, maybe not quite so good as chocolate ones, but the grown-ups were saying that they thought the war was coming to an end because of something called D-Day had happened last year, so maybe chocolate was just around the corner after all. I pondered some more. Perhaps there might even be ice cream again. I smiled happily at that thought and cracked open one of my Easter eggs.

CHAPTER 11

CELEBRATE!

O God of love, O King of peace; make wars throughout the world to cease.
Henry Williams Baker, 1821-1877

One leg dangled over the peeling, blistered gate leading to the allotments where our neighbours had vegetable plots. I hovered between street and vegetable patches as Jimmy raced down Christopher Way, yelling and shouting, "We've won the war! We've won the war!"

My leg swung back. I rushed up the hill to my house in Alban Road. "Mum, Mum, is it true? Have we really won the war? Is it truly over? Can we get rid of the air-raid shelter? There won't be any more sirens, or bombs or gasmasks now, will there?"

She laughed happily. "Yes, we have indeed won the war against Germany. And there will be no more air-raids. We'll dismantle the air-raid shelter when we can. And we can throw your gasmask away." She sang one of her favourite wartime tunes as she prepared our tea. I danced around for joy. My gasmask disappeared and I believed that she had indeed thrown it away, but she hadn't.

"Jean, Jean," I said. "Did you hear the news? We've won the war!"

Jean looked up at me, puzzled. "What is war?"

"Humph! You're too little to understand."

She turned away, more interested in combing Flossie's fur with her doll comb.

I thought to myself, *I will remember this day for always, Tuesday, eighth of May, 1945.*

Dad arrived home for tea, and all I wanted to talk about was the war ending. "Will we have ice cream now?" I asked my parents eagerly.

Both laughed. "I doubt it somehow," replied Mum. "The food shortage here isn't going to go away soon, I'm afraid."

"At least no one has starved and gone hungry with everyone having the same rations," pointed out Dad.

"You don't have to do the cooking," snorted Mum, giving Dad one of her looks.

"And no more people are going to be killed," I pointed out, thinking of the newsreel I'd seen when Mum had taken me to see the *Snow White* film. The grainy black and white moving pictures of our soldiers firing guns and men lying on the ground dead, stayed with me, along with the memory of the train full of men in blue clothes with bandages around their heads and arms, waving to us children at Broadgreen Station as they waited for the signals to turn green. The Boardman twins told us that they were wounded soldiers, and that was why they wore blue uniforms. I shook my head sadly, why did we have to have wars?

That night, after Jean was tucked in, I listened to the six o'clock BBC News on the radio telling us all about winning the war. Now

I climbed the stairs to bed. Mum didn't even have to pull the blackout curtain in the little front bedroom where I slept. I knelt by my bed and after my usual prayers were recited, I added, "Thank you God for helping us win the war." I thought briefly about children in Germany as I had before, and figured there had to be some there. I wondered what they might be praying, until I fell asleep.

I awoke suddenly. Was that singing? It was twilight, but I could see shafts of lights outside and hear people cheering and laughing. I crawled down to the end of the bed, pulled the net curtain to one side and stared out of my bedroom window. All the houses had their lights on and curtains wide apart. Front doors stood open as lights streamed out. But what amazed me were the people all dancing and singing. One would start a song, and everyone would join in. I thought I saw some bottles being passed around, but couldn't imagine why. The only bottles I saw were the milk bottles put on the doorstep at night, and then of course, the sherry bottle brought out only at Christmas time.

I opened the window to see and hear everything better, and leaned out. All the neighbours were outside, Mrs Robertson and her husband, who limped badly, Mrs Griffiths, my Dad and Mum, even crotchety Mrs Lunt and my very old Grandma Bibby, as well as the other neighbours. "We'll meet again," drifted up to me, the popular song sung by Vera Lynn, along with "There'll be bluebirds over the white cliffs of Dover." Others I knew echoed down the streets and over the housetops. Someone ran out of their house on Christopher Way, which our house faced, being on the corner, waving a red, white and blue Union Jack flag. People cheered again, and sang *God Save the King*. I knelt there with my elbows on the sill of the wide open window, mesmerized by the scene, allowing the cool May breeze to brush my face. Everyone was so joyful, including me! Finally against my will, sleepiness closed my eyes, as I curled up at the bottom of the bed, the window hanging open, as the merrymaking continued into the night.

The next day during the daily assembly, after the hymn, which was *I Vow to Thee My Country*, and the prayer out of the big thin black book, Miss Pogue, our headmistress, actually smiled.

"Children, as we have won the war, you can all go home for the day." Her teeth whistled on the 's' and clacked a little, as usual, like Grandma Bibby's, but we hardly noticed. " Hooray, hooray!" the boys shouted, while we girls chattered excitedly.

"But first, we will all sing 'God Save the King," said Miss Pogue, which we did, then we raced home.

Parties were organized, parties in the streets, parties in school, parties in Sunday schools, parties everywhere to celebrate the end of the war in Europe. Alban Road had the first party, where mums and dads brought out kitchen doors and laid them on trestles to make tables. Snowy-white sheets covered them, while an assortment of chairs were brought out and a feast of food tantalized us on the makeshift tables. Jean and I, along with the other children, all had new outfits. Somehow our mums had scrounged clothing coupons to buy material in red, white and blue to make new frocks with matching bows for our hair. Jean and I had the same patriotic small check ones. I wasn't happy that my three-year-old sister had the same kind of frock as me, but the excitement of the party overcame any resentment.

We sat down to a rare feast. Jelly and blancmange wobbled and the ubiquitous Spam sandwiches piled up like sandcastles on plates down the middle. We tucked into the luxurious meal, albeit on combined limited rations, while the grown-ups watched, chatted, and did without, but we were too busy eating and talking to notice at that time.

After the meal, there was a contest as to who could sing the best.

"I'm going to sing *You are My Sunshine,*" I whispered to Hilary Jones, who'd come to the party from Christopher Way.

Hilary stood up before me, and opened her mouth and sang my song. I wanted to cry. But I sang it anyway. Then there was a dancing competition, for those who could tap dance, followed by a recitation of poems.

I waited, hoping I'd won the singing competition. Grandma Bibby had brought out pretty grown-up jewellery including necklaces and brooches, all sparkly. A fancy brooch was held up. "This is for the winner of the singing competition," said one of the neighbours. "And the winner is - Hilary Jones."

I bit my lip, trying not to cry as Grandma Bibby pinned the white glinting jewelled prize on her frock.

But then we played games. Higher-and-higher with a long washing line had us jumping the rope, until even the big girls couldn't jump over it sideways. A running race from one end of Alban Road to the other took place, and then another game to see who could jump the farthest. The girls received Grandma Bibby's jewellery as prizes, and the boys got a bag of marbles each. After that the dishes were removed from the tables, the sheets whisked off and taken home to be bleached and washed again and the few men around hauled the doors back to the various kitchens while we children trundled back to our houses and to bed. But as I left the living room to go into the hall, I overheard something interesting from Mum talking to Dad.

"Do you realize, Rich," she was saying as I stood at the bottom of the stairs, ready to make my way up, "That your mother gave away her best jewellery to those young children? I know some of those brooches had diamonds in them. I swear she is going doolally in the head. I always knew she was a little queer."

Dad mumbled, "Well, we can't do anything about it now."

Mum made some noise and began moving to the door. I skiddadled up the stairs fast. I'd always known that there was something not right about Grandma Bibby, and apparently Mum thought so too.

Our next party was in Christopher Way. I think the same kitchen doors and the same white sheets came out, but we were happy to delve into another feast of food.

"What is happening?" I whispered to Dad, as I saw old chairs and firewood and other wooden debris being piled up in the middle of the road.

"We're going to have a big bonfire to celebrate the end of the war," he explained. "You will probably have another one on the fifth of November, Guy Fawkes Night, which I'll tell you about later."

We all cheered as the bonfire was lit and sparks flew high into the sky with crackles and some bangs from old paint on the wood. Then as the fire died down to red ash and low-licking flames, the mothers threw whole potatoes into the embers to bake. Until they were cooked through, we filled in the time playing tic, hide-and-seek and hopscotch on the pavement.

At last the potatoes were cooked. With a piece of newspaper in our hands we each took a freshly-baked potato handed to us by a grown-up, wrapping the paper around it, and feasted on the piping hot, floury-tasting treat, blowing on each piece to cool it down a little.

"That is the best potato I've ever tasted," I declared to everyone around.

With tummies full, and the glorious bonfire, now a faint glow, we turned homeward once more. But the best was yet to come. Our teacher, Miss Cowley announced that we would have a school party to celebrate VE Day, and we didn't even have to take any sandwiches.

"I can't wait until Friday," I announced to Mum and Dad. "We are going to have a party, in our classroom and we don't have to take any food." Usually whenever we went to a Sunday school party we had to take our own food, which we then shared around.

"Can I come too?" asked Jean, jumping up and down.

"Of course not!" I said, somewhat witheringly. "Only children who go to school can be there."

Jean began to cry. "But I want to go too!"

"Don't cry Jean," placated Mum. "We will go to the swings at Northway instead."

My little sister stopped crying and brightened considerably.

I counted the days off until Friday; four, three, two, one. It was the day. After lunch, excitement mounted. Miss Cowley had a hard time keeping us quiet. There were fifty-four children in our class, so we had to be patient. Various sandwiches were laid on our desks, Spam, Marmite, and sardines, all three. Usually we only had one kind at home, so this was special in itself.

Then something magical happened. Something big, important and the most wonderful thrill of all. A strange man struggled in with a large box. What was in the box? We all tried to guess.

"It's a puppy," said one, who really wanted a dog.

"Can't be," commented a boy. "They are toys."

"I think they are apples, like what we got from Canada last year from Miss Pogue's room," I whispered to Margaret next to me, where we shared a desk. And still I squirmed at my desk, like everyone else.

The man cut open the large cardboard box, which had strange steam coming from it. Miss Cowley bent over the package and smiled. Then she turned to us all. Every eye watched her, as a cat fastens on a mouse.

"Well, boys and girls," she said. "Thanks to the generosity of a shop nearby, we have a very special treat for you all." She looked around at us slowly, savouring the moment. We hardly dared to breathe.

"It's ice cream," she announced, now smiling broadly.

"Ice cream! Ice cream!" We yelled in unison. I couldn't believe it. Real ice cream!

Now the class was in uproar. Miss Cowley clapped her hands. "Boys and girls," she said sternly, "If you don't quiet down, you won't get any!"

That was sufficient. Quietness, except for some shuffling, reigned over the room.

The man began at one end, and Miss Cowley helped him as she placed one small rectangular block of blue and white paper on each desk before each pupil.

I watched anxiously as each out-of-this-world treat was handed out by our teacher, and turned to Margaret. "Will there be enough left to reach us do you think?"

"I hope so. Remember the chocolate eggs? Maybe we will be lucky this time."

Her eyes never left the man as he came closer. Keeping my fingers crossed, I nodded, my whole body a-quiver, as I waited my turn. Then there it was, on my desk. I picked it up, my hand shaking slightly. I noted the name, Walls, written on the side of the wrapper. Carefully I peeled back the folded paper at one end. Ooohs and aaaahs echoed around me.

Slowly I raised it to my mouth and bit off a small piece. Oh, what bliss! Creamy, cold, really cold, but smooth and soft, and sweet, not like the ice we used to beg off the fishmonger from his marble slab where he kept the fresh fish at Old Swan. No, this slid down my throat like heavenly nectar, tantalizing every taste bud I had. But I needed to hurry up. It had already melted around my fingers and trickled down my wrist, yet I hated to eat it all at once.

All too soon it was gone. I licked every vestige I could find and was tempted to eat even the paper. Its coolness lingered in my throat and tummy. I then licked each finger, even my wrist, to be sure every morsel was savoured in order to prolong the experience.

"Is there any more?" asked one cheeky boy.

"No, that's it. We must thank the shop that provided it for us," reminded the teacher. "Thank you!" we replied in one voice. The man smiled, touched his cap and left.

I sat back. Wait until I got home and told Mum and Jean that we'd had real ice cream. They would be so envious of me! I smiled with self-righteous satisfaction. It was a day to remember.

That evening, after going into a long explanation of how wonderful ice cream was, I asked Mum, "Now that the war is over, and I have actually had ice cream, does that mean we can now buy ice cream whenever we want it, and maybe chocolate too?"

"I doubt it somehow," said Mum wistfully.

She was right. It took a long time before I tasted ice cream again, and even longer for chocolate. The ration books stayed firmly in place.

PART II
POST-WAR ENGLAND

CHAPTER 12

THE WAY AHEAD
(1945-47)

*Standing on the promises that cannot fail; when the howling storms
of doubt and fear avail*

R. Kelsa Carter, 1886

Not long after the peace celebrations Grandma Bibby died, and we
moved to 2 Alban Road, another corner semi-detached home, but
looking up Bentham Drive this time. Aunty Bunty and Uncle Bill,
Daddy and Mrs Thompson's daughter and new husband moved
into our old home. Consequently Aunty Bunty used to babysit Jean
and me whenever Mum and Dad went to see a film.

Now that my gasmask had disappeared, much to my relief, the
old air-raid shelter was left to Uncle Bill to dismantle. At Grandpa
and Grandma Bibby's house the heavy steel shell that was their
inside air-raid shelter, which jutted out below their back living
room window, had gone. This house was just a little bigger but not

much, with one living room, a kitchen and scullery, whilst upstairs were two bedrooms, three if we included the little 'box room' at the front of the house.

Of course we also had a bathroom. This was painted blue, rather than green like our old home, and always seemed freezing cold, especially for our Saturday night baths, when Mum lit a kerosene heater and placed it near the bath tub to take off the chill. The coal fire in the living room was stoked up to heat the water, and Jean and I shared the same water to save coal and hot water. This was better than when we had lived in our previous house, when Mum had brought in the big zinc bath she always washed clothes in on Monday mornings, and poured hot water into that. This used to be placed before the fire in the living room, and there we had our baths. It was the way life was.

We'd been in our new home for some time when we heard our neighbourhood chums shouting to each other on the street. I dashed to the front door and threw it open to see what the commotion was.

"Barker's have got ice cream!" yelled one of the boys.

"How do you know?" I demanded, shouting back to Norman Croxford running down to his house. "How much does it cost?"

"Just bin there. Youse got to get there fast. Sixpence," he added pushing open his front gate.

"Mum, Mum! Can I go to Barker's and get ice cream?" I hopped on one foot and then the other. It was ages since I tasted that delicious creamy sweet at the school victory party.

"Here's a shilling," said Mum. "That should be more than enough. See if you can bring one back for your little sister too."

Throwing on my gabardine raincoat, I slammed the door

behind me, turned the corner and raced down Bentham Drive. I crossed the street where the bombed blackened ruins still stood, to the red pillar box where we posted our letters, then ran down the rest of the hill. Quite a queue of mothers and children were lined up outside the shop. I sighed, thinking of the chocolate egg experience. Finally, the line shortened and I came up to the counter.

"Yes, Joyce. You want an ice cream?" asked Aunty. Everybody called her Aunty, and no one seemed to know her real name. You could tell she had false teeth because they were all even and yellowish, and rattled. They seemed to match her pale face.

"Yes, please, Aunty," I said politely. She brought out a square piece of greaseproof paper and on it plopped a round white frozen mound accompanied by a small oval wooden scoop to help us eat the ice cream.

"That's sixpence, please."

I wondered about getting another one for Jean, but quickly figured out I couldn't carry it home. Already, as I turned away from the counter it was beginning to slide to one side. A child was crying at the doorway as her treat had already slithered to the floor and she pointed at a very small circle of white pooling out at the edges. Her mother was trying to comfort her. "Don't cry, I'll get you another," said her mum, her arm around her, propelling her into the shop where people and children still waited.

But at that moment Aunty declared in her loudest voice. "I'm sorry. All the ice cream is gone for today."

I was tempted to give her mine, but then it was half gone and had my spit on it, so I didn't think she'd want it. I slurped up the remaining granules. It wasn't anywhere near as good as the Walls ice cream we'd had at our school party. This was gritty, with little bits of ice in it. I sighed again as I slowly, this time, walked back up the hill toward home. I hoped that maybe one day we'd have real ice cream like Walls. At least I could tell Jean it wasn't very good.

Now that I was eight, Mum promised I could take piano lessons. The tinny, upright, brown-mottled piano stood in our living room, where Mum sometimes played old songs. Mrs Whitehead round the corner gave piano lessons, and one Saturday morning I set off high with anticipation. I held an old leather-bound *Beginner's Music Book* tightly under my arm and in my hand a two-shilling piece. Bursting with importance, I sat on the swivel piano stool, with a cushion on top, so I could reach the keys. Now I was ready to play real music.

"I will teach you first the five-finger exercises," instructed my teacher. She looked stern with her air-raid-shelter-grey hair cut short, almost as short as Dad's. "I'll also expect you to learn the notes on the treble and bass clefs for next week."

I nodded, anxious to do everything right. She lifted my right hand so it hovered over the keys, then the left, and showed me how to almost stroke the notes. Ah, such bliss. The notes rang out, and I was playing the piano, at last!

I practised daily, and continued to take lessons. My first tune was *Twinkle Twinkle Little Star*, until I graduated to traditional English songs like *Ramsgate Sands*. Now I could actually play!

It was a long time later when we heard a penetrating bell ringing from outside in the street. Jean, Mum and I all ran to the door wondering what it could be, and opened it wide.

"What is it?" I asked Mum, staring at the man in the white cap climbing off his three-wheeled tricycle. At the back, attached to his trike was a cart with two large lids with the words 'Ice Cream' written across the cart. A painting of an ice cream cornet sloped sideways beside the fancy writing. "Ice cream, ice cream!" I shouted. "See Jean, it says Ice Cream on the side there!" Other local children were running out of various front doors to see what was creating all the excitement.

The man shouted, "Ice cream, ice cream! Only threepence a cornet or sandwich. Come and get it! Ice cream, ice cream, boys and girls!"

Immediately everyone ran back inside to get their threepenny bit. "Mum, Mum. Can we have some?" Jean and I chorused together.

Without any more ado, Mum ran back inside, dug into her handbag and gave us each the required coin, and with our threepenny pieces clutched tight in our hands, we ran across the road to the ice cream cart and lined up behind three other children who'd arrived there before us.

"Yes luv, what d'you want?" asked the ice cream man.

"A cornet please," I said and handed him my damp coin. He ladled me a scoop of slightly drippy vanilla ice cream into the long pointed wafer cone. I gasped it firmly, quickly licking the drips that were already sliding down the sides.

Jean, right behind me, got the same thing. As soon as she took her ice cream, Mum put her hand around Jean's then, with her little finger of her other hand, pushed the ice cream down into the cornet so it wouldn't drip, or spill over the side.

I licked my tongue around the inviting coldness, then closed my eyes. Heavenly! Just as good as Walls. Then I noticed the name on the side of the cart, 'Walls Ice Cream'. I smiled delightedly. "This is the very best ice cream," I told Jean with authority. "And don't bite the end, either, or you'll get into trouble with Mum." A vague memory stirred at the back of my mind.

She looked up at me wonderingly. "'Course I won't," she retorted. "If I do that, it will come running out of that end."

I stayed silent. Then I wondered if we'd ever see chocolate too. Even though the war was over, everything was still rationed, including sweets. Mum complained bitterly one teatime. "Here we are. We're supposed to have won the war, and they've now rationed bread, and even potatoes! It's a real doggle."

I knew the grown-ups were frustrated. Rationing was even more stringent, including eggs, which were back to one per person per week.

"It's this bloody Labour government," retorted Dad. "they're nationalizing everything so everyone's out on strike."

"Don't swear in front of the children," Mum said, as she automatically mixed the meagre rations of butter and margarine together with a splash of milk. She stopped and looked up. "But it is terrible. This country is going to the dogs. I wonder what the government is doing with all that money we are supposed to get from America, something called the Marshall Plan."

Dad shrugged his shoulders. "Goodness knows. Throwing it away on the colonies, according to one paper."

Now that I could read, I sometimes read pieces of Dad's *Daily Express*, so I learned that living conditions were bad from the headlines.

"At least there's no air-raids," I offered, trying to bring some peace into the conversation. No one said anything.

"Well, I've got to get back to work," said Dad eventually. He buttoned up his bus driver's jacket and put on his hat, then clipped up his serge trousers ready to ride his bike to the bus depot. He now worked for Liverpool Corporation and drove a big double-decker 'Green Goddess' number sixty-one bus. It always thrilled me to be on Queens Drive and see a sixty-one bus go by, especially if Dad happened to be driving it.

"Time for your piano practice," Mum reminded me, and began clearing the dishes.

I left the warmth of the small kitchen with its coal fire for the chill of the living room. We only had a fire there at weekends or on special occasions, such as when the boiler at the back of the fireplace heated the hot water for our baths, so I plugged in the single-bar electric fire, placing it as close to the piano as I could. Soon I found myself lost in mastering my first real adult piece of music, *Für Elise,* which I was determined to learn by heart. I repeatedly played one passage over and over, trying to get the rhythm smooth and tranquil.

"Joyce, it's almost bedtime." Mum's voice broke abruptly into my concentration and reluctantly I closed the lid and unplugged the fire.

That evening after tea, we listened to the six o'clock news. "We have just received an important announcement from Buckingham Palace," the announcer proclaimed in his deep voice. "The Princess Elizabeth is engaged to be married to Lieutenant Philip Mountbatten. The wedding will take place on 20th November of this year."

"Oh, how nice," exclaimed Mum happily. "We need a bit of romance to cheer us all up."

I was thrilled. "I'll keep a scrapbook, just like I did of the Royal Tour of South Africa," I said. "I'll ask Nana and Poppa to save me their newspapers too so I can cut out all the pictures and news about them." I had a fat scrapbook, made from old copies of the *Radio Times*, which came out weekly, and in it I had pasted pictures of the Royal Family as they made their first royal tour after the war. Now I'd start another one. Daily I scoured Dad's newspaper for photos and news about the royal couple. I commandeered the Sunday papers from Dad and my grandparents, cutting out pictures of the couple from when they were babies right through to the present day. I also heard that because material and clothes were still rationed, the Princess Elizabeth didn't have enough coupons for the cloth for her wedding dress.

I overheard Mum talking with Mrs Flowers next door over the back fence.

"I see in the paper that a lot of housewives have sent their clothing coupons to the Princess so she can buy the material for her dress," commented Mum.

"Youse don't say," commented Mrs Flowers, balancing her latest baby on her hip. "Well those lot can send their coupons, but I'm keepin' mine."

Mum agreed. "You're right. It's hard enough to clothe two children not to mention ourselves without sending them to anyone else."

Personally I thought it was wonderful that some ladies would send their coupons to help the beautiful Princess. But I knew better than to say anything.

Another milestone took place that year. Margaret invited me to go with her the following week to Dovecot Baths, where she took lifesaving lessons. She could already swim several lengths of the pool, she told me.

"Mum, can I please go?" I asked. After being assured that I would be careful, and that Margaret was already an accomplished swimmer, she agreed. While Mum chose her library books that weekend, I took out a book on learning to swim from the Children's Section. Once home, I dragged out the tuffet in the living room, spread myself over it, with arms and legs outstretched and the book lying before me on the floor, and began practising the breast stroke. Every evening after school, once I'd finished my piano practice, I worked hard at making my arms and legs coordinate together so I could surprise Margaret with my swimming prowess.

Full of confidence, I set off with Margaret on the appointed day. I had my bathing costume wrapped in a towel tucked under my arm as we walked to the baths, some distance away. Hardly able to wait, I changed in the small cubicle, tucking my clothes into the corner of the narrow wooden bench, so no one else would take that cubicle, closed the door to, and walked across the tiles to the large rectangular pool. Margaret stood poised at the six-foot end, arms high above her head as she prepared herself to dive right into the water. She sliced through the water with hardly a splash, then surfaced and swam towards me at the side.

I walked around to where Margaret had dived into the deep end of the pool, and pushed my shoulders back. I couldn't dive yet, but I knew how to swim; after all, I'd practised daily on the tuffet. So taking a deep breath and holding my nose, the way I'd observed other children do, I ran and jumped with a big splash right into the six feet of chlorinated, green, chilled water.

But I wasn't swimming. A nose full of water made me thrash and panic. I couldn't breathe. Green water swirled silently, like a slow motion film, around my head.

Suddenly a hand grabbed the back of my bathing costume and yanked me up out of the water and pulled me to the concrete surround of the pool. Gasping and spluttering, I clutched the hard surface of the edge.

"You shouldn't come into the six foot until you can swim," said my exasperated friend. "You could have drowned!"

I nodded, shivering with fright. Slowly I edged my way to the metal stairs that dipped right into the water and hauled myself up. Still coughing with the chlorine burning my nose and throat, I walked down the side of the bath to the other end. Somehow I knew that I had to get back into the water immediately, or I might never learn to swim.

At the three-foot end, I gingerly walked down the steps carefully, one foot at a time, feeling for the bottom of the bath. There it was, firm beneath my feet. Holding to the side, just to be safe, I walked the width of the three foot end. Then I made myself take my hands off the rail and try to swim. Water sucked over me, and hastily my legs sought the safety of the sold base. Then I tried again. Margaret swam down to where I was and began to give me lessons. I became bolder and even managed to try a couple of strokes without holding on to the side.

By summer I could swim part way across the bath. And, in August we moved up to a new grade at school, where weekly swimming lessons at Picton Baths were part of our curriculum. Before long I was swimming the length of the fifty-foot pool, back and forth. But I never did tell Mum about my episode in the six-foot end. Only later did I realize the enormity of that event, and how Margaret had literally saved my life.

CHAPTER 13

OPEN AND CLOSED DOORS (1947-48)

Be not dismayed, whate'er betide, God will take care of You

Civilla D. Martin, 1886-1948

This year, we all knew, was very important. The Eleven Plus Scholarship Examination would face us in the spring. However, few of us thought about it as we met our new teacher. "Old Ma Willy", also known as Miss Williams, was the teacher for our final year at Rudston Road Primary School. Because the school was overcrowded and classrooms bursting at the seams with children, the boys were siphoned off to Northway School, while we girls were joyfully assigned to 'the Chapel', thanks to the Methodist Church across a couple of fields and on the other side of Childwall Valley Road.

To be precise, fifty-two of us girls were sent to the 'upper room,' whereas downstairs, we vaguely assumed, was the chapel itself. A fire escape leading from the upstairs became our favourite entrance and exit to school, if we could get away with it, despite inside concrete stairs. The windows afforded a wonderful vista across farmland and Jackson's Pond. A large empty area filled with grass, scrub and shrubs surrounded the immediate building.

Miss Williams bobbed like a pigeon as she walked, her black-streaked iron grey hair pulled into the standard sausage roll pinned tightly to her head. She wore horn-rimmed glasses, and a face scrubbed as nature intended. She was always the same. Around her neck hung a cross with 'INRI' inscribed upon it. We had no idea what it meant, but we invented various 'secret' code meanings.

Miss Williams had one impressive feature; she had eyes at the back of her head. At least, that is what we had to believe.

"Joyce Bibby, stop talking to Margaret," she said, continuing to write on the chalkboard, her back to us. "Irene Griffiths, pay attention to what I am writing and don't look out of the window."

It never ceased to amaze us, until I told Nana. "Oh," she declared. "If she wears glasses and looks through them at the right angle, she can probably see you girls reflected in the glass."

I still wasn't convinced, but our teacher was definitely adept at keeping tight control of us all, at least until we had our October break. Excitement rippled through the class on the Friday afternoon at the anticipated week off, and even silent reading, my favourite activity (next to swimming) made me antsy.

Finally we streamed out, laughing and joking, then Margaret, carried away with exuberance, yelled out, "Me no daft, me no silly. Me put whitewash on Ma Willy."

We stopped dead, aghast at her audacity. "Oh, what now?" I muttered under my breath.

Suddenly the door atop the fire escape was flung open and an on-fire small bristly elderly lady stormed out and yelled, "Margaret Robertson. You get in here right this minute," and marched down the fire escape. She grabbed Margaret, now chagrined with her head low, by the scruff of her gabardine raincoat and frog-marched her back up the rattly fire escape and through the open metal door. The door closed with a resounding clang. At the same moment, a dozen or more girls scuttled away instantly like scared rabbits, disappearing behind shrubs and low bushes at the edge of the field and scrunched down with bated breath.

Behind the safety of welcome bushes and shrubs we whispered excitedly, wondering what terrible death threats might be laid upon our friend. Fortunately, like most of us, she didn't have a telephone, so there could be no calls to her mother, and notes usually got lost on the way home.

Eventually Margaret emerged with a smirky smile on her face as she appeared through the lower door. Once she reached the safety of the outer edge of the field and by the road, we besieged her. "What happened?" "Did she wallop you?" "Or cane you?" The questions came fast and furious. To which Margaret shook her head decidedly.

"Or will she tell Miss Pogue?" I asked in horror, thinking of Colin Morley who, the previous year, had played truant to go and see the big boys play footie and how Miss Pogue had marched into our classroom her cane swishing, then made him stand up front and caned him three times on the backs of his legs. (Boys always wore short trousers until they were about fifteen years old.)

But Margaret just grinned and shook her head. "She just told me off for being so rude and not to do it again."

We all breathed a sigh of relief for her and continued on our way home, talking about it, reliving the whole episode and laughing loudly. I told Mum and Jean about it when I arrived home. Jean giggled, but Mum said sternly. "She is a very lucky girl to get off so lightly. I hope you will never do anything like that."

"Oh, of course not, Mummy," I assured her, all the while admiring Margaret for her courage and daring.

That Christmas Nana gave me a 'Letts Schoolgirl's' Diary' for 1948 so I could write all the interesting happenings of each day. But first I read all the information at the front. First were 'Daily Wants' where it listed the different seasonal terms, such as Easter and Michaelmas, bank holidays for the year and basic imperial measurements. The next page was headed, 'Careers for Girls' which I perused carefully. It began with 'Accountants' and ended with 'Youth Leadership'. I was glad to see 'Teaching' listed too. Then followed Latin, French and German verbs with a list of Prime Ministers and even a recommended list of books to read. When I got to logarithms, I skipped to the list of kings and countries.

I was anxious for January 1st to arrive and at the end of the day I wrote: *Very enjoyable day. Nana and Poppa came to tea and dinner. We had turkey,* and on the second day, *Sweep came too early. We played dolls' hospital.* Then on the 7th day I entered, *Went back to school, Aunty Carrie got a baby on Sunday. Nothing much.* However on Saturday the 10th of the month, I wrote with pride, *Exam result. Passed with HONOURS.* I'd changed music teachers, and had begun to climb the ladder of music examinations with the London College of Music.

Now I was ready to begin the next level. However, on my birthday, January 30th, not only did I mention this auspicious day, but I noted, *Gandhi dead*, and drew a small crucifix at the side. I also visited Nana to take her and Poppa's books to be changed at the library, something I did every Saturday morning. Nana liked romances, especially Mills and Boon ones, whilst Poppa enjoyed mysteries. However, while Poppa was busy having a snooze, Nana beckoned to me.

"Wait here in the kitchen. I won't be a moment," she said. She disappeared upstairs. I could hear furniture being moved, or at least what sounded like that, then more scrapes and bumps. Soon she trotted back down stairs, closed the kitchen door and whispered. "Happy birthday. Here is a five-pound note for your present. I know you don't waste your pocket money, and being eleven years of age is very special."

"Oh, thank you so much!' I hugged and kissed her.

"Not a word to your Poppa, now."

We both smiled as fellow conspirators. That was the first of many presents from 'upstairs' during the next several years.

Shortly after my birthday I borrowed a book from our class library, a story that changed the direction of my life. It was called *The Young Pilgrim* and every day I hurried through my music practice and helped Mum with the tea dishes so I could get to read my book. A boy about my age badly treated by his sisters and family, was befriended by a young curate from a nearby church. The hero, sick though he was, had a strong faith in God, and I read how he turned to God, with help from the curate to enable him to deal with his fears and sickness. Every day, as I read the book, I entered in my diary '*YP*' and sometimes additional comments such as '*Reading Young Pilgrim - lovely - giving me good thoughts*'.

Lent was drawing close and my Sunday school teacher had talked to us about it being a special season, so I told Mum on Ash Wednesday, "I've decided to give up sweets for Lent." I had also decided to read the collect, Epistle and Gospel each day. I wasn't terribly certain that I'd be able to do this, but the sweets I was sure of.

"That's nice." My Mum always said that when she disapproved slightly. Later this morphed into teasing and trying to tempt me to break my 'fast' of sweets. She told me that it would mean more for her and Jean because they could now use my sweet coupons. I told them they could, but only until the end of Lent. I persisted and made it through, almost, though I struggled.

Saturday, the day after Good Friday, I wrote in my diary, '*Lord, forgive me*'. I had fallen into the tempter's power and succumbed to my desire for some sweets. That afternoon I'd found a pear drop all by itself on the sideboard by the sweet tin, and before I knew what I was doing, I had popped it into my mouth. During Lent I also managed to read the Lenten Collect each night before I climbed into bed, as I wrote, *LCT* for Lenten Collect for today. Best of all on Easter morning I received not one but two chocolate Cadbury Easter Eggs.

"Mum, Dad. Thank you so much," I said. I knew that chocolate was still very scarce, so for Jean and me to each have two real chocolate eggs made Easter very special that year.

In addition Dad surprised me. "Guess what else we have for you?"

I shook my head, satisfied with my two eggs.

"I have tickets for the Liverpool Philharmonic Hall, to hear Albert Sandler and his orchestra."

I jumped up and hugged him. "Oh, Dad! That is the very best present. I love to hear him play on Saturday nights on the radio. Is he really coming to Liverpool?"

Dad assured me that he was, and I crossed off the days to the concert.

That Saturday evening, Mum, Dad and I took the bus and then walked the rest of the way to the concert hall whilst Aunty Bunty babysat Jean.

The crowd hushed as the lights dimmed, and I held my breath. Then the real live orchestra began tuning their instruments. I sat on the edge of my faded red plush seat. Then Albert Sandler himself strode in, baton in hand and bowed. We all clapped. First we all stood for 'God Save the King,' then sat again, and the concert began.

I found myself transported through the music into a world of wonder. Listening to his music on the radio thrilled me, but to actually see Albert Sandler and the whole Palm Court Orchestra, right there before me, caught me up into an ecstatic experience that rooted a love of classical music in my heart for evermore.

A few weeks later Dad got tickets for a Campoli violin concert. The way Campoli played his instrument amazed me and I jumped up to applaud loudly when he had finished.

When the concert was over I asked Mum and Dad if I could go backstage to get his autograph in my special book, received for my birthday. I shyly asked the great maestro if he would kindly sign my autograph book. Indeed, Campoli signed it with a flourish and spoke kindly to me, encouraging me to practice hard at my piano lessons.

On the way home, I asked Dad, "Do you think if Eileen Joyce comes we could come and see her?" She was my favourite pianist and I always made sure the radio was on whenever she played.

Dad said he would see what he could do, but although she did come to Liverpool, the tickets were always too expensive, so I never did see her, only listened to her music. I did however procure her autograph. Our next door neighbour, Mr Flowers, was a taxi driver and after he'd taxied Ms. Joyce to the Philharmonic on the night of her performance he asked her to sign my autograph book, which she graciously did. That had to suffice.

I told Miss Greenhalgh, the following Saturday, "I want to play like Eileen Joyce. Do you think I ever will?" My voice was wistful with longing.

She patted my hand. "If you practise hard, maybe you can. You play very well for an eleven-year-old and I will do what I can to teach you."

That encouraged me to double my efforts as I tackled Mozart, Beethoven and *Clair de Lune* by Debussy, but the masterpiece that spoke to my heart was Beethoven's *Moonlight Sonata*. I'd heard Eileen Joyce play it, and that was my goal.

At eleven I had reached the age, the magic age, to join the Girl Guides. The idea of a uniform, working for badges and learning the Morse Code appealed to me greatly. Yet perhaps the most important responsibility that filled me with pride was the Sunday Matins services on the first Sunday of each month. I always volunteered to be part of the colour guard, and with heady self-importance I hoisted either the Union Jack or the Girl Guide flag into the holder hanging down from around my neck and led the procession of guides along Queen's Drive from the Parish Hall to St David's Church. Slowly, in step, we walked down the aisle, handed the flags to the vicar and retreated to the light oak polished front pew until the end of the service. Such joy and peace washed over me, especially as the words of the liturgy became familiar to me. It moved me to see the Brownies, Cubs, Girl Guides and Boy Scouts, all in uniform taking part in this grand tradition.

In the meantime the moral message in my now favourite book had taken a hold of me. I had always been afraid of the dark and inevitably looked under my bed every night, in case Mum's fearful threat was lying in store for me. I regretted scaring Jean the way I had years before, though I never mentioned it, in case it made things worse, so I took it to God in prayer.

"*Please, God, help me not to be afraid of the dark,*" I prayed. I thought of the little boy and how brave God helped him to be. "*Make be brave. Let me trust in You to take care of me.*" I tried then to let God lift it from me, but somehow it still buzzed around, like a fly that evaded the fly-swatter, especially if Mum and Dad were out at night, and I was in bed, supposedly asleep, but the fear did dissipate slightly. I was discovering that prayer did make a difference. Yet I still continued to look under the bed, just in case. (Years later, Jean and I both confessed to each other that we continued looking under our respective beds until the day we each of us were married. Then, we presumed, our husbands would protect us!)

However, the major event of our school year had loomed up and was now facing all of us; the Eleven Plus Scholarship exam date had been announced. Miss Williams had been preparing us for it all year. The entrance papers had been filled in by our parents, and all of us children waited in trepidation for the day to arrive. Miss Williams cast dire warnings almost daily. "If you don't work harder, you'll never pass the scholarship" became her mantra.

I knew I had to pass. It was the only way I could be a teacher. We all knew that only the small percentage of eleven-year-olds who passed could go to a prestigious grammar school, take special examinations and one day go on to college or University. Not many actually got to go to a teachers' training college or university, and even then usually it was the boys who were admitted. No one I knew had ever been to university. The vast majority who failed the scholarship exam were routed to a local secondary modern school, where general subjects were taught until at age fifteen you left to get a job in an office, factory or a shop like Woolworth's. Both Mum and Dad had left school at fourteen, so they never had the opportunity to have further education, but I was determined I would pass. I had to pass!

All fifty-two of us sat in our desks on the dreaded day, a new nib pushed on to our wooden pens. Inkwells full of dark blue ink, set into the holes in the front of our desks, waited for the new-nibbed pens, whilst multiple forbidding pages of test questions sat in front of each of us ready to be filled in. I began. Sums, writing, questions, and more questions.

At last the day ended. My booklet was collected. We all scraped back our chairs with relief, stood up noisily, grabbed our gabardines and clattered down the cement stairs to the outside.

"Wasn't it awful," remarked one girl, to which we all readily assented. We dawdled home, rehashing the worst parts and gloomily predicting that none of us would pass. However, it was a Thursday, which meant Girl Guides, so my gloom and doom dissipated as I pulled on my uniform, and my light blue tie with gold trefoil badge. I was now working on my second class badge and anticipated practising the Morse Code, which I had already memorized, with the necessary signal flag,

By the end of May of that same year, we were all anxiously awaiting the scholarship results. On Monday, the seventh of June, Miss Pogue walked into our classroom, ram-rod straight, with her hair pulled even tighter into the usual permanent sausage roll curl that encircled her head from ear to ear. She held a sheaf of papers in hand.

We stood automatically.

"Good afternoon, girls," she said, her voice whistling on the 's'.

"Good afternoon Miss Pogue," we answered automatically.

"You may sit down."

Chairs scraped.

Not a sound; Breath suspended…

"We just have received the results of the scholarship exam." Her papers rustled slightly while she cleared her throat. Slowly in her tinny voice, while continuing to whistle the 'sess' she began. "These children have passed the scholarship exam and can come up and receive their paper. Pat Coleman, Jean Welsh, Helen Hunt, Patricia Neal…" Twelve names were read out and twelve girls shuffled up to the headmistress to receive the good news. Miss Williams stood in the background, her face impassive.

I waited, hardly daring to breathe. There had to be more. I must have passed. But that was it.

"I'm sorry," said our headmistress in a flat voice. "Not as many passed as we had hoped this year. Those of you who have passed can go home right now and show the paper to your mothers and father and tell them the good news."

Once more chairs scoured back on the concrete floor, a smatter of nervous laughter from the chosen few as they threw on their raincoats and left. Miss Pogue departed on their heels. Those of us remaining sat at our desks, stunned. How could this be? I believed I was a good student. I got most of my sums right in tests. I received top marks in reading and writing. There must be some mistake. But there wasn't. Behind me I heard a muffled cry, then another, and another until almost all my fellow classmates were crying. Tears filled my eyes. Intense disappointment claimed my whole being. Now I could never be a teacher.

Miss Williams busied herself with some papers at her desk, then told us, "Why don't you get your reading books out and we'll have silent reading for the last half an hour." There was a clatter of desk lids as we brought out our books and let the lids fall with a bang, out of frustration. Miss Williams looked up, but didn't reprimand us. Eventually at four o'clock I made it home, avoiding my friends on the way. I stumbled through the front door and with a deep catch in my voice told Mum and Dad, who was off duty, that I hadn't passed the scholarship. Then the tears flowed, hot and copious. My dream of being a teacher lay shattered.

However, that night I wrote in my diary, *We heard the scholarship results. Irene didn't pass. All the children were crying. I didn't pass. I am not going to worry.*

Margaret hadn't passed either. At the end I wrote, "YP." A fibre of faith took hold, despite my intense disappointment.

The author with 'Horsey' in the back garden, about 1939

The family on holiday in
Colwyn Bay, 1944 or 1945

In Preston during the war - Colin (left),
the author, Derek and Jill. Dad is in the
background.

Nana and Poppa,
taken about 1935

Jean and the author with Poppa, 1948

On a trip to see Blackpool Lights with Colin (on left), the author,
Jean (a friend) and Gabby

On honeymoon, 1960

Nursing days, 1958

Jean's wedding, with bridesmaids, Mum and baby Kathryn

Jean and Brian, married at last! (1963)

Rev. and Mrs Searle (1962)

The remains of the wartime gasmask

CHAPTER 14

CUPID BENDS HIS BOW (1949-50)

And on eagles' wings of love; to joy's celestial rise

Charles Wesley, 1707-1788

By now, I had accepted my fate. Highfield Secondary Modern School was a couple of miles away, so I walked each day up to 'the prison on the hill' as we called it. My dream of becoming a teacher had all but disappeared, but the prospect of earning money at fifteen consoled me, to a point.

I still enjoyed school, and especially history. We studied the historical events of a nearby old Roman town, Chester, with a field trip promised at the end of the year. Miss Irvine brought the subject alive for me, and as I wandered around the ancient cathedral of St Werburgh and walked the Roman city wall later that year, I almost felt the chink of Roman armour alongside me, especially as I watched some archaeological students dig up a couple of Roman coins. *Imagine*, I thought to myself, *I am the first one to see those coins, since the person who dropped them almost two thousand years ago.* English History especially became a passion of my life.

I gazed through the front window one Saturday afternoon, idly passing the time. Suddenly I jerked to my feet. "Mum! Colin and Derek are here." I rushed from the living room window and to the front door. By this time, Mum had joined me and Jean, and as we opened the door wide, they were both wheeling their bikes down our front path with sloppy grins on their faces, and their knobby knees glowing red from the chill of the day.

"Put your bikes against the house there" Mum pointed to the side wall, "and come along in." She smiled happily.

This was exciting. Colin, Derek and Jill were the children of Aunty Elsie and Uncle Bill. It had only been last year that Uncle Bill had called up Mum and Dad and told them that Aunty Elsie had cancer and wasn't expected to live very long. She had died shortly thereafter, and the family had moved back to Liverpool from down south. She had been my favourite aunt, and I'd shed quite a few tears when I'd heard she'd died. But now Colin, age fourteen, two years older than me, and Derek, a few months younger than me, were here, in our house. Colin had always had a special place in my life, for some reason, though I wasn't sure why. Maybe it was because he, and Derek too, had the coveted Donald Duck gasmasks, not to mention the bright red pedal-car that we used to career around in their back garden when they lived in Liverpool years before.

Mum hugged them both, then Jean asked, "Where's Jill?" Jean and Jill were close in age, and she was hoping for a new playmate.

"She's back home, with Dad and Aunty Alice, who is taking care of us all now." Aunty Alice was Uncle Bill's sister.

"Maybe you could come on the bus next time and bring Jill with you," suggested Mum. Jean nodded enthusiastically.

That was good news for me. My mind had already jumped ahead, hoping that we might see them again soon, particularly Colin!

Of course they had to stay for tea, and Mum rustled up boiled eggs with bread and butter and half a chocolate cake (a special wartime recipe). Uncle Bill was starting a new florist's shop a few miles away, we learned, and Colin was attending Rose Lane Secondary School. We chatted, then played a couple of card games, had tea, then they set off home.

A week or so later, Uncle Bill came with Colin, Derek and Jill and asked Dad if he would help deliver flyers to people in his old neighbourhood, not far from where we lived. "Maybe Colin and Joyce could help us deliver them?" he said. We agreed readily.

In the meantime, Colin and I found we both loved swimming.

"How about us going to Picton Baths on Saturday?" he suggested.

"Then you can come back for tea," I added.

"Well if you two are going to get together this Saturday, maybe we can deliver our flyers Saturday evening, if you aren't working, Rich." Uncle Bill turned to my Dad. He was indeed free.

The days dragged until Saturday finally arrived. Colin was on time, and we walked up to the number 4a tram stop to catch the tram to the baths. Quickly we scooted into the boys' and girls' changing rooms, and met at the six foot end. We jumped in together, then sank to the bottom of the pool, accidentally touching hands. A thrill coursed through me. As we surfaced, we exchanged knowing smiles.

"How about going down again?" Colin shot me a mischievous glance.

Without saying anything, just exchanging matching grins, down we went again, and as we touched bottom, this time we actually held hands. Needing air, we surfaced, then down again, several times. We swam the length of the pool a few times, then back down to the bottom of the six foot end.

Without even talking of our new discovery, we arrived home breathless for tea, where Uncle Bill and Jill were waiting for us. Jill and Jean were playing with their dolls, and Derek had been unable to come. After tea we donned warm coats and scarves, though Colin in his short pants was used to the chill on his knees. We set off for the suburb where the family had once lived before moving south.

As we walked in the dark, Colin and I together, his hand slipped into mine, and I slid in seventh heaven. We glanced at each other, a warm glow between us. Then I noticed Dad and Uncle Bill nod as they saw us and a smile creased Dad's face.

Before they left, Colin hurriedly asked, "How about the pictures next Saturday afternoon?"

"Yes, yes, I'd like that. What's on, do you know?"

It didn't really matter. We saw it as an opportunity to be together by ourselves and to hold hands in the dark. As the film flickered and adjusted itself, we sat back oblivious to all except the warm glow radiating between us. Halfway through, the lights blinked on for the interval and we quickly released hands, embarrassed in case someone we knew might see us.

During the interval, the voice called down the aisle, "Ice cream.

Ice cream for sale." A lady in a short maroon skirt and jaunty matching hat, carrying a large tray of small paper-covered chocolate coated ice cream blocks, minced down on her high heels.

"Would you like to share a choc ice?" asked Colin.

I nodded eagerly. He brought out sixpence and carefully handed it to the usherette, then pulled the paper back, breaking the ice cream into two. I had the paper part so I was able to make mine last a little longer. It became a double thrill, to be at the pictures with Colin, and to savour half a choc ice.

That evening, after tea, I saw him out to where his orange, drop-handlebars sports bike leaned up against the brick wall of our house. As he went to get his bike, he turned.

"I really had a good time today."

"Me too!"

Then, wonder of wonders, he turned to face me, put his arms around me, and kissed me lightly on the lips. Oh, the bliss of that first kiss! Words weren't necessary. We simply held hands tight, and gazed at each other in the sweetness of our discovery.

After that we rode our bikes to all kinds of events, fairs and picnics at Ogden, near Speke Airport, where we always stopped to watch the propeller planes rev up then lumber down the runway to take off for Northern Ireland and the Isle of Man.

"I do so want to go in one of those," I said longingly.

"You'd really like to fly in one of those planes?" Colin asked, surprised.

"Oh, yes. I want to visit all kinds of countries and to fly there." Something had stirred within; an intense desire to travel.

"In the meantime, we'd better get back, or Aunty Lil will be after us," he commented, turning his bike around. We jumped on our bicycles and cycled furiously to be sure we didn't miss tea.

It was a couple of months later that I visited one of Dad's boyhood friends, Sophie, and her husband, Simon. They lived out in Cheshire in a quaint cottage in the country, and I was excited about taking my first weekend away from home. When I arrived, it was Friday evening, and after we'd eaten and listened to the radio I went to bed. The next day Aunty Sophie took me out with her as she grocery shopped, then we spent the afternoon playing cards. After tea we washed the dishes and my aunt settled herself into her armchair to take a nap in front of the fire. She was short and dumpy and not very well. Consequently she slept in her armchair most of the time, while her longish, thin brown hair flowed out like a fan with air holes in it at the back of the high, heather-tweed chair.

Uncle Simon stood tall with a balding head and a trim moustache. He'd also been at Dunkirk, he told me, but was one of the lucky ones to make it back to England. As Aunty Sophie snored gently, he said, "I have mushrooms growing downstairs to sell to the local greengrocer's shop. Would you like to see them?"

"Mushrooms, growing in your cellar?" I asked surprised. "I've never seen mushrooms growing before."

"Come on. I'll show you."

He turned on the light, as we trod down the stone stairs, and I couldn't believe what I saw - dozens of boxes filled with tiny mushrooms, though some were bigger than others. "Gosh, I never realized that mushrooms grew like this," I commented looking around.

Then, without warning, Uncle Simon grabbed me, held me

and squeezed me tight to him, pinning my arms to my side, and tried to kiss me. I turned my head one way and the other, trying to escape. With a loud cry, I managed to push him away, and raced up the stone steps back to the brightly lit room and safety.

"Are you all right, Joyce?" Aunty Sophie suddenly woke up and threw me a concerned look. Then she glanced at her husband.

"I'm fine," I said, gathering myself together hastily. I clenched and unclenched my hands. "I think I'll go to bed," I said, wanting only to escape. Still shaking, I locked the bedroom door and removed the key, placing it on the dressing table. Even so, I slept fitfully.

I couldn't wait to leave the next day, and asked if I could catch an earlier bus than planned. By this time we had a telephone at home, and Aunty Sophie called Mum and Dad to expect me a little earlier. I told them I didn't feel well, which was true. Uncle Simon acted as if nothing had happened. On the bus back I was still mixed up inside, even as I left the place behind where it happened. That evening, I told Mum.

"I'm sorry that happened to you, Joyce," she said, putting her arms around me in a rare show of caring. "Did he try to do anything else?"

I shook my head miserably, not sure what she meant.

Mum sighed deeply. "Come on, let me get you a beaker of Horlicks. That will help you sleep tonight."

I climbed into bed, feeling a little better having shared the experience with Mum, but still shook at the thought of being held so tight, almost like a prisoner.

Apparently she told Dad, because the following evening she told me. "I told your Dad, and he said that Simon would never do anything like that to you. He doesn't believe you."

"But, Mum," I cried. "You know I wouldn't make anything like that up. Honest, he really did try to kiss me!" The tears came, especially at the thought that Dad didn't believe me.

Once again, she gave me a quick hug. "Joyce, there is something you need to know," her face serious and stern, "That is the way men are. They behave like that, and you have to be aware of it, and avoid being alone with any male. You can't trust any man."

I was taught an important lesson that day. Never trust any man. After all, I'd heard Nana talk about 'those damn men' often enough. Was this what she meant? From then on, even though I enjoyed the attention of the opposite sex, I always kept a distance within me emotionally, to avoid major entanglements, as well as without – no more than a chaste kiss!

Above all, I carried the hurt that Dad didn't believe me. Even though I learned to let it go eventually, the relationship thereafter was different, especially as I became busier with my own social circle and Dad became less important in my life.

Not too long after that Mum was talking with Mrs Flowers, who was expecting another baby. I'd just come home from school and, as I was leaning my bike against the wall at the back of our house, I overheard their conversation.

"I like it, yer know," said our neighbour, but he wants it all the time, and it gets a bit much. Yer knows what I mean?"

Slowly I positioned my bike, wanting to hear Mum's response.

Mum pursed his lips and spoke in a righteous type of voice. "Oh, I am very lucky. My husband hasn't bothered me for at least eighteen months."

By now, Mum had seen me, and shooed me inside to put the kettle on, ready for tea.

But I'd heard enough. I wasn't sure exactly what 'it' involved, but knew enough it had to do with what married people did in bed. But other, more interesting opportunities now crowded my life.

In order to achieve my second class badge in Girl Guides, an overnight camping trip was required. "Mum, I've got to have a sleeping bag," I announced one Thursday evening. "We're going camping in two weeks to Arrowe Park, and I've got to go because I need it for my badge."

After humming and hawing for a while, she dragged out a couple of slightly moth-eaten army blankets and a well-patched faded blue sheet. To my silent horror, she pulled off the top to her treadle sewing machine and began stitching sheet and blankets in an oblong shape. I felt sure everyone else would have a real sleeping bag, but realized that Mum didn't have the money to buy one for me, so I accepted it, though perhaps not as graciously as I should have done.

The weekend arrived. On Friday evening we gathered at the Parish Hall, ready to set off on our journey by local bus to the Pier Head, then over the Mersey by ferry, and bus to the park. Excitement overflowed as we scampered up the stairs to the upper deck of the bus. Older women passengers, their heads covered with faded felt hats on prim hair-dos, shook with disapproval, throwing frowns our way as they passed us to get off the bus. But we were not deterred.

With dark ponderous clouds overhead and a sprinkle of rain, we attempted, with much fumbling, to erect our tents. We tripped over ropes and lost tent pegs, until an older, seasoned, hefty Girl Guide stepped through the dusk to assist us. She directed and helped us and soon the tent was secured, standing upright and firm.

"Do you think it will collapse during the night?" Jean, my friend in Girl Guides, asked, still anxious.

"Of course, it won't. It's steady as a house," replied the girl who'd helped us. She marched off to assist a couple of other inexperienced guides.

I threw my sleeping bag into the darkness of the tent. Between the threatening sky and the drizzly rain, night had crept on us. However, a camp fire blazed cheerfully, and I huddled with others around the warmth.

"Stop loitering, guides," came the authoritative voice. "Go and get some more sticks, you guides over there." She pointed to Jean and me. Scurrying into the surrounding woods, we tried to gather an assortment of dry twigs and branches. With twigs sticking into our faces and arms loaded, we dumped them down beside the fire.

"Oh boy, we're having cheese dreams!" I cried happily. My mouth watered as the tantalizing smell teased my nostrils. Bread soaked in pork lard and sandwiching thick chunks of cheese sizzled cheerfully in the outsize blackened aluminium frying-pan. About a dozen of us girls hung over the fire. Baked beans in tomato sauce, straight out of a tin, bubbled on a grate next to the cheese dreams. I eagerly held out my tin plate for the squishy, luxurious treat, and sunk my teeth into the squelchy sandwich, lard dripping down my chin, as melted cheese rolled around my mouth. Even the increased wetness squeezing down the collars of our gabardine raincoats failed to quell our enthusiasm.

Before retiring to our, now, soggy tents, we closed with taps. *Day is done, gone the sun, from the sea, from the hills, from the sky. All is well, safely rest, God is nigh.* We all shouted "Amen", then scurried into our respective tents. Four of us crowded into our very damp propped up shelter. There was chattering of teeth, but little talk as we pulled our sleeping bags up to our chins.

Some time during the night, I woke up. My feet seemed wet, but they couldn't be. The next time, my legs felt wet too, but in the darkness I didn't dare do anything. At the first streak of dawn, I whispered to Jean, my friend, "Are you awake?"

"Yeah, and I'm wet," came the reply

"Me too." I tried to move around, and felt sogginess wrapped around my body.

Rain pelted on the sides of the tent. Eventually, all four of us managed to get dressed in our uniforms, pushing our arms into the damp stickiness of our macs, and stooped to emerge into pouring rain outside. Jean and I were the only ones with wet sleeping bags. For some reason the other two girls' bedding were dry.

The Captain strode around, barking out orders, her distinguished side-brimmed captain's hat firmly planted on her head. "

Please, Captain," I stood hesitantly, afraid to complain, yet not knowing what to do. "Jean's sleeping bag and mine are both wet."

Immediately, her voice rose in disdain. "Well, Guides. I am surprised at two big girls like you wetting their sleeping bags." The other guides grouped around and tittered.

"But, but, we didn't," I explained, close to tears.

"No, no," broke in Jean. "We didn't wet our bags. It was the rain that did it."

'Huh," the Captain retorted. "How about the other girls? Explain to me why their sleeping bags aren't wet!"

We shook our heads miserably.

"Well. You'll just have to go home," she finally said.

"But how about our badge?" I asked quickly.

She lifted up her plain face to the relentless rain, then marched around inspecting the tents, all sagging with rain. The apology for a camp fire flickered, spluttering, despite the encouragement of banned matches. She blew her whistle three times. Everyone clustered around shivering. "This rain has created a major problem," she announced in her foghorn voice. "Therefore we will break camp, and we will all have to go home. However, I will sign the papers so it will count for your badges." A faint cheer erupted.

This captain-in-charge then marched over to our tent and surveyed our soggy sleeping bags. She gave a short sniff, and harrumphed again.

"It would appear that your sleeping bags did get wet due to excess flooding," she announced. A sign of relief escaped me.

We packed up the tents and rolled up the sleeping bags. We were happy to see a special bus put on for us to take us back through the Mersey Tunnel and on to the various parish halls. Somehow I trundled back home, with my soggy sleeping bag weighing me down. My eagerness to tell Mum and Dad about our watery adventure kept me warm, despite the clinging dampness.

Not long after our wash-out camping episode all of us guides, along with other guide troops in Liverpool, were invited to attend a rally in the city. It promised to be a major event. Our uniforms were washed, ties set clean and straight, trefoils polished and badges sewn neatly on to sleeves, ready for the big day. We sat on benches, listened to speeches, then came the biggest thrill of my life - we solemnly paraded by to salute Lady Baden Powell herself, the founder of the Girl Guide movement, following the example of her brother, Lord Baden Powell, who had begun the Boy Scout movement. It was a heady moment when I came face to face with her. She stood tall, with her serious outdoorsy face, wearing her unique, navy blue, side-bonnet replete with white-fringed insignia, and returned my salute. I felt as if I could fly and overflowed with awe and pride.

Halloween that year brought forth fun and games, especially because Colin, Derek and Jill were with us to help us celebrate. Mum had an old zinc bathtub filled with water, complete with bobbing apples. With hands tied behind my back and a blindfold tight around my eyes, I lowered my head into the tepid water, enthusiastically searching for an apple. I caught one, but then it slipped and bobbed away. Deeper I dived, holding my breath into the water trying to wedge one against the side of the tub. I was determined to catch an apple to show Colin just how good I was.

Then I slipped, falling head first into the water. The tub upended, with water cascading over me and the other children, including Jean, my sister, who shrieked, and even Mum and Dad, not to mention our living room carpet. That ended Halloween, at least it did until the people next door (in the house attached to ours) complained that water had seeped into their living room, after Mum told them about our escapade. She didn't believe them, but we couldn't prove otherwise.

Soon after Halloween big excitement swirled around the young people at church. "There is going to be a bus trip to see Blackpool Lights in a couple of weeks" Jean, my chum, told me. "I'm going to go with Gabby. How about you and Colin?"

"Oh, that would be so much fun," I exclaimed. Gabby, short for Gabriel, was Jean's new boyfriend, and of course, she knew all about Colin.

I asked Colin, who was delighted to accept. Dad had told me all about Blackpool Lights, even when I was little and how the whole promenade was lit up with brightly-coloured dancing lights depicting folk tales and fairy stories.

So that autumn when the Blackpool Illuminations were finally switched on, there was tremendous excitement. I booked two seats for Colin and myself on the youth bus trip from our church. With great anticipation we joined the other young people outside the parish hall, then piled into the bus with much jostling and teasing. I sat on the inside seat, smoothing down my warm skirt as Colin seated himself beside me in the aisle seat, now all grown up, wearing his first pair of long trousers. We chattered and laughed, made jokes and giggled all the way to the seaside resort.

Everyone cheered as the bus slowed down and gradually stopped in a bus park. Out we tumbled, running towards the prom dazzled by the intense, overwhelming plethora of multi-coloured lights blinking in and out in unison, as if the characters were moving.

"What shall we do first?" I asked Colin. His smile widened, mischief sparkling in his brown eyes.

"How about fish and chips?"

"You and your fish and chips!" I laughed. I didn't want to admit I fancied some myself, but I didn't want to miss the lights either.

"Let's see some of the lights first," I suggested.

It was agreed. We'd view the lights until we found a fish and chip shop.

Holding hands with our boyfriends, we strolled down the pavement beside the swishing waves, with lighted tableaux shining along the path ahead.

"Just look at this one!" We stopped and gazed at the moving lit bulbs, outlining the characters of Little Red Riding Hood and the Wolf, then on to the next one, which was even better. After the dreariness of wartime, with no lights, not even street lights, and only a modicum of colour in the post-war years amidst the still bombed sites of the city, it appeared like a grown up fairyland. We oohed and aahed, rushing to exclaim at how one bulb-popping display outshone another.

"Like your photo taken, luv?" cut in a voice. "Have a picture taken with your young men to make this a special night?"

The man jerked his head toward an old car, rigged up with a bench in front. "Only a shilling a picture," he said. Meanwhile, he edged us toward the seat, and before we knew what was happening, the four of us, with the boys' arms draped around us, were sitting smiling into a camera on a tripod. A flash, and it was over.

"Come back in thirty minutes and there'll be a picture for each for you," he said. "Remember that's only four bob for the four of you."

We giggled, but then we smelled the tantalizing fragrance of vinegary fish and chips, drifting down the prom, urging us to a nearby chip shop. The queue stood quietly, waiting their turn. Fortunately it was short, so we soon grabbed our newspaper packages, warming our hands on the paper as we uncovered fourpenny worth of chips and a piece of haddock crispy golden, waiting to be eaten, with fingers of course. Revelling in our evening's freedom, and eating fish and chips, we strolled along the brilliantly-lit promenade, wanting life to continue like this for ever. We stopped to pick up our four photos.

I moaned. "Oh no. Look, you can see the Elastoplast on my head."

Everyone looked closer and chuckled. I'd split my head open a couple of weeks earlier playing netball at school, when I slipped against a stone wall, cutting my head on a jagged corner.

"We'd better move," Colin suddenly announced looking at his watch. "After all, it is a little too far to walk home."

Laughing some more, we ran toward the parked bus and clambered aboard. We settled into our seats filled with sensory satisfaction from tummies full of fish and chips and with our minds spilling over with the afterglow of the scintillating lights. Then we sank into a comfortable weariness as the bus spun its wheels over the bumpy main road south, back to St. David's Parish Hall and home.

CHAPTER 15

PROMISES FULFILLED (1950)

O Jesus I have promised to serve Thee to the end
John Ernest Bode, 1816-1872

"Would you like to go to the pantomime with me?" asked Colin that winter, a couple of weeks after Christmas. "My cousin is in it and it's *Cinderella* and it'll be held at the Village Institute Hall." The information spilled out of him, his eyes willing me to say yes.

"Oh, boy! That'll be fun. I love pantomimes. When is it?"

"George, my cousin, gave me a couple of tickets for next Saturday night."

"Mum, it's all right to go, isn't it?"

Mum smiled benevolently. She liked Colin. "Of course. Colin can stay in the box room overnight and you can sleep with Jean, so he won't have to go home late."

I smiled too, delighted with the news.

The following Saturday, after tea, Colin and I, clasping hands, walked along Bentham Drive, then Thingwall Road to the Village Institute, a building that even Dad had gone to for dances and special local events when he was young and had lived in that area. Dust was ingrained into the woodwork and even the chairs, but I wasn't bothered by details like that. We were each given a ticket and told to put it in a safe place ready for a raffle during the interval. We found a chair each and waited for the musty red curtains to loop up and there, up on the stage, stood the dame, the stepmother of Cinderella, played, in the pantomime tradition, by a male. She loped forward telling us about her step-daughter who she complained about loudly in her male voice. Soon he had us all laughing hysterically.

"That's my cousin," Colin whispered. "He's really good."

I became caught up in the humour and applauded when Prince Charming, the 'principal boy', always played by a girl dressed in a very short tunic and tights and a cocked hat with a feather in it on her head, eventually came to the rescue of poor mistreated Cinderella, who was of course in love with him. The two ugly sisters appeared. The older one, with a huge wart on her nose, was also played by a male. He was just as funny as the dame, and I asked Colin who he was.

"Don't know. Have to look in the programme in the interval."

The plot thickened and the traditional fairy tale continued to delight us all.

Then the light flipped on for the interval, dazzling us briefly.

"Please look at your tickets," came a loud voice on the stage. A man stood at the front with a trilby hat in his hand. "We are going to draw for a lucky winner, so please see if you have this number." He placed his hand into his hat and pulled out a ticket. Everyone stayed quiet as he called out three numbers.

I jumped up from my chair. "I've got it. I've got the number!"

The man came down and handed me a quarter-pound box of Cadbury's Milk Tray chocolates. I gasped with delight at the purple box with the squiggly "Cadbury" name scrawled across the front. A small two-ounce chocolate bar, shared between us all at home, was as much chocolate as I had ever tasted. After all, it was still rationed. But a whole quarter pound box of real chocolates all to myself! What was more, I had never had chocolates with different fillings.

I was tempted to open them immediately, but instead I put them under my chair, planning to take them home and show off my prize to Mum, Dad and Jean before opening them, and maybe I would let them have one each, and Colin too, of course, seeing he was the one responsible for helping me win.

On the way home, with my box of chocolates firmly in one hand and the other clasped firmly by Colin, we strolled down Thingwall Road towards home, taking our time, despite the winter nip, and oblivious to any damp chill rolling off from the Mersey. I felt in seventh heaven.

It was the next day when placing my programme in my top dressing table drawer, I glanced to see who had played the older ugly sister. Roger Gardener, I noticed. I smiled in recollection. He was very funny!

St. David's Anglican Church had become an integral part of my life by now. If I couldn't be a real teacher, I figured, perhaps I could be a Sunday school teacher. Miss Harris, the elderly bespectacled superintendent, knew me well. I approached her after Sunday school, near my fourteenth birthday.

"Miss Harris," I enquired in my best voice, "I would really

like to teach Sunday school. Just the little ones. Please, may I?" I waited hoping against hope.

She looked at me kindly. "Well, Joyce. I think I could use you. One of the teachers has just left, so maybe you could teach a small class of five-year olds?"

I wanted to jump for joy. "Yes, oh yes! I'd love to do that. May I start next Sunday?"

Her smile warmed me. "Yes, of course. Here is the book we use." She handed me a well-thumbed book of Bible stories interwoven with tales of special saints. I handled it as if it were gold. I would be a teacher after all!

About the same time, instruction began for those who wanted to be confirmed. Several of us young teenagers joined the Catechism Class for instruction, even though the vicar reminded me that I was supposed to be fifteen years old. The culminating event would be when the Bishop of Liverpool confirmed us in April.

Our instruction was eventually completed and the day arrived. Mum had bought me a new white linen dress, accompanied by a new pair of navy suede shoes, though Mum almost bought me brown ones. The white dress was to be dyed green after the ceremony because, Mum said, "White makes you look like death warmed over." But nothing could detract from the specialness of the day.

My friend, Jean, and I anxiously waited our turn in the vestry to have our spotless freshly-starched white veils pinned around our heads. We giggled as we surveyed each other in our outfits. The adults shushed us, then we filed into the front pews, and the solemnity of the service embraced me.

Oh, good. A favourite hymn, I thought as the service commenced. (Favourite hymns changed frequently!) I sang loudly, "O Jesus, I have promised to serve Thee to the end. Be Thou forever near me, my Master and my Friend." Tears pricked my eyelids as I lifted my commitment to God. I filed forward, kneeling at the altar rail. Bishop Martin raised his hand, laid it on my head, and confirmed me in the Anglican Church. I slowly walked back to my seat, with head bowed. Then the Bishop in all his glory climbed up the steps into the golden oaken pulpit, just above our pew. I listened intently.

"My text is from the book of Jeremiah," he intoned sonorously. "The potter went forth…" As the homily wound on, he stressed, "Remember these words, all of you who are confirmed. Make these your own: 'Take me, break me, remould me and make me Your own…,' remembering the promises you have made this day." He raised his hand in blessing. Suddenly the service was over, the linen headsquares whisked off, and home I walked with Mum and Dad, who had actually come to church for the occasion, as well as my godparents. I clasped a small red prayer book tightly in my hand, presented to us after confirmation, something to savour later, in private.

The following Sunday morning at eight o'clock, I knelt at the altar rail, this time to receive the blessed communion. "Please God," I prayed, "Don't let the wine go down the wrong way." God heard my prayer, at least on that occasion, and kindly answered it. Attendance at communion at least once a month, during the year, and every week during Lent, became embedded into the tissue of my life.

Then scholarship fever swept through our three second-year classes at Highfield School. A new thirteen-plus scholarship had recently been established for 'late bloomers', though we were forewarned that very few passed. I prayed the night before. "You know, Lord, how much I need to pass this exam so I can be a teacher. This is my last chance. If I don't pass, I'll have to stay at Highfield and leave school at fifteen. And I'll never get to be a teacher. " But I had now learned *not my will but Thine be done,* and therefore added that adjunct. Yet I still hoped against hope that God's will and mine coincided.

One hundred and twenty girls from Highfield Secondary Modern School trooped off to various grammar schools in Liverpool to take the day-long test. Calder High School, a short bus ride away, was my destination. The school had originally been an old manor house, complete with stately gardens and a sturdy stone wall, to keep out intruders, along with high iron gates which were usually open, though these were a warning to male students from Quarry Bank, the boys' grammar school next door, to stay out! Additional buildings had been added to house the female students who attended the school.

I arrived in plenty of time, anxious, yet trying not to be. We were assigned to a classroom and soon a quiet intensity filled the room.

During the lunch break I walked around the grounds, admiring the grassy bank and rhododendrons, all in bloom. Beyond lay the playing fields. More tests followed, then the day eventually concluded.

I walked down the wide chalky corridor through the main door and out into the afternoon May sunshine. As I stepped on to the driveway the warmth of sweet-scented wallflowers in the variegated bronze-coloured, well-tended beds on each side wrapped their fragrance about me. I stopped to breathe in the pleasure of relief, as well as the sweet perfume. And at that moment, I had a strong premonition that I would walk this driveway again, between sweet-scented flowers. I belonged here. A euphoric joy lifted me, as I knew beyond all doubt that I had passed the scholarship, and not only that, I would attend this very school. I couldn't explain it, and told no one. However, it became the first of many presentiments that would come to me as I journeyed through life.

In the meantime my life was filled by school lessons, Girl Guides and the heady excitement of seeing Colin at weekends, when we'd go visit local haunts, go bike riding or simply go for a walk. Some foods were still rationed, but not so strictly, and Mum always managed to make a chocolate cake, albeit filled with her 'mock' cream, and sardine sandwiches or a boiled egg, to fill us up when we arrived home, starved from our various outings.

Girl Guides also meant boys; Boy Scouts to be exact. Our Lieutenant and the Scout Master were good friends, and they announced to the patrol leaders of our troop that they would teach ballroom dancing to the leaders of the Guides and the Scouts on Friday evenings. I danced all the way home that Thursday evening after the announcement. "Mum, you'll never guess what!" I was breathless with running home. "I can learn ballroom dancing on Friday nights!"

My mother, being who she was, asked dubiously, "Where is this being held? And what grown-ups will be there?"

"Joan, our Lieutenant, and the Scoutmaster are teaching us. And only the patrol leaders in the Guides and Scouts can go. It's going to be held in the Scout Hut, just by the Parish Hall. Jean, my friend is going, and all the others. May I go, Mum?" I held my breath, and crossed my fingers behind my back.

"So long as you young people won't be by yourselves, you may go."

Now I would learn how to ballroom dance properly, and that meant being able to attend grown-up dances. Colin, Girl Guides and Friday night dancing, created an effervescent froth to life.

Once a week, at school, we learned swimming, though I could swim well already. But I enjoyed having the time out of school from regular lessons. That morning in June I burst into the classroom, ready to join those who had not been to the baths. The teacher, Miss Gertrude Shaw, commonly known amongst us as 'Dirty Gerty,' called out, "Joyce Bibby, you come and stand here immediately!"

Oh, dear. It must have been that arithmetic test I took last Friday. My light mood was evaporating fast.

"You've won the scholarship, Joyce," shouted a friend, Connie, seated at her desk.

I started for a moment, my heart beating faster.

Miss Shaw smiled, or at least what passed for a smile. "Yes," she interrupted primly, "There are five of you in our school who have passed, all in this class. I will give you each the paper, then you may go home and tell your parents, all of you."

My heart stopped. I had passed. I'd actually passed the scholarship! My mood soared. Along with the other four girls, I grabbed the precious paper, threw on my mac and ran home as fast as I could. I banged the knocker on the door hard. Mum opened the door, consternation across her face.

I tried my utmost to appear sick. "Mum. I've come home because I don't feel well."

"Whatever is the matter?" she asked. "You seemed fine this morning. Maybe you shouldn't have gone swimming."

I couldn't contain myself for one second longer. "I've passed the scholarship," I cried. "I've passed. I've passed!" I pranced around the hall in excitement.

She hugged me. "I'm so proud of you," she conceded with a broad smile.

That night I took out the familiar small red prayer book. I recited the evening prayer, already learned by heart, "Lord support us all the day long of this troublous life, until the shadows lengthen the evening comes, and the busy world is hushed and the fever of life over. Then Lord in Thy mercy, grant us safe lodging, a holy rest, and peace at the last." Then with a burst of thankfulness, I added, "Thank you God for helping me pass the scholarship." I paused, wanting to express how I really felt, "I truly thank you, God. Because now I can be a teacher." I suddenly realized, just before I closed my eyes, that on the form I had brought home it stated the name of the grammar school I would attend in August. It was indeed Calder High School, just as I had believed. I fell asleep, contented.

CHAPTER 16

TOUCH OF PRESENCE (1950-52)

Sometimes a light surprises; The Christian when he sings
William Cowper, 1731-1800

A smart new school uniform, navy and brown, complete with a brown and navy striped tie waiting to be neatly knotted at the neck of my white blouse, was laid out for me on the back of a chair. I waited impatiently to begin attending Calder High Grammar School. Only twenty-three students had passed the Thirteen-Plus Scholarship that year from many different schools, I learned later, all in our class.

Excitement buzzed as I took my seat in 3G. Four of my classmates I knew from Highfield School, whereas the rest had travelled from all over the city. One, I discovered, was a doctor's daughter, while another, who became a friend of mine, had a mother who cleaned homes, near to our new school, her dad having been killed in the war.

Mrs Goldberg introduced herself as our home room teacher, and informed us that she would also be teaching us maths. She warned us that we would have to work very hard because we had begun two years after those pupils who had passed the Eleven Plus Scholarship, and therefore would have to accomplish five years' work in three years, in order to be ready to take our General Certificate of Education at age sixteen.

With some slivers of trepidation intermingled with the thrill of a challenge, I listened to the curriculum presented. It was very different to that I'd experienced at the 'prison on the hill', in so far as, the stress was on academics. Quickly I relished being introduced to Robert Browning, Tennyson and Wordsworth, along with Shakespeare, Charlotte Bront and Dickens. Miss Ridiough, our English teacher, encouraged us to learn by heart and inwardly digest reams of poetry, which I did easily.

"Ah, but a man's reach should exceed his grasp,
Or what's a heaven for."

As soon as I read these words by Robert Browning, the image caught hold of my imagination. Yes, that was how I saw my life. I would reach always higher than where I was. Already a dream was unfolding, way beyond anything my family could even imagine. The quote rolled off my tongue, committed to memory. It had been written for me, I decided. Later that term, another poem by Browning was introduced to us. A portion from "Rabbi Ben Ezra" also resonated with me at deeper level.

"Grow old along with me,
The best is yet to be
The last of life for which the first was made
Our times are in his Hand
Who said, 'A whole, I've planned'
Youth shows but half, trust God, see all, nor be afraid."

I was but a youth. My life stretched before me with endless possibilities. I promised I would trust God to unfold the whole that He had planned for me. And if things didn't go my way, then that was all right too; because God knew what He was doing, all was well. Therefore as bumps and potholes impeded my life's journey, I mulled over Browning's sage words of wisdom time and time again.

I continued with my piano lessons, taking examinations and enjoying the sense of accomplishment as I mastered more difficult pieces. I was invited to play at school for a special concert, and was happy to show what I could do. Now that I could ballroom dance, and I was fifteen, Mum allowed me to attend the local dance hall where other teenagers gathered to dance. This became a highlight of my week. Sometimes I saw Colin, but now I preferred to go out with other boys too. After all, I reasoned, I was too young to be tied down.

Then I met Mike at a local dance club, and we began talking.

"I'm going to see a piano recital, with the Liverpool Philharmonic," he told me. "Would you be interested in coming with me? It's next Wednesday evening." His voice was earnest, his blue eyes clear and direct.

"That would be lovely," I replied, still holding back a little. I was always leery of any male I didn't know well, mostly due to

Mum's and Nana's remarks about the male sex in general. But I liked the way his blonde wave at the front of his head kept flopping into his eyes. I also mentally worked out how I'd get my homework done and still go out with Mike. By planning ahead and being able to learn the required poem of the week during recess time, I was able to get ready with a clear conscience, dressed in my long three-quarter length 'new look' skirt and a short jacket I'd borrowed from Mum.

One other major attraction nudged me along the way, and that was the fact that Mike had a car. My first boyfriend with a car! Very few people had cars, as petrol and cars were just too expensive.

He knocked at the front door, and I opened it, Mum behind me waiting to be introduced. I did what was necessary and rushed out, saying over my shoulder, "We won't be late," before Mum could say anything to me.

After the grand performance we slipped into a coffee shop for an expresso coffee, a big hit with teenagers. I found Mike was five years older than me and working. I told him I planned to be a teacher. I always made sure I mentioned that fact early on, so no boyfriend would get any ideas about becoming serious and turning me into a married wife and mother.

Afterwards he drove through the streets of Liverpool back to Thomas Lane, where we now lived, about a mile from our previous home. Then he took my hand. "I had a really good time with you this evening. May I see you again?"

As he squeezed my hand, I looked down at his fingers closed around mine and saw how pudgy they were. Inside, I felt like an icy shadow had slipped down my back. As gently as I could, and slightly shaken, I forced myself to smile.

"Why don't you give me a ring on the telephone next week?" I replied, as nicely as I could. "I have a lot of homework, and Girl Guides, and I also teach at Sunday school."

My voice trailed away with a tinge of guilt, but Mike didn't notice. He nodded, gave me a quick peck on the cheek, and slid his hand on to the gears of the car ready to take off, as I let myself out of the passenger side.

Mum was waiting. "How did it go? He seems like a very nice young man."

I sighed. "He is very nice, but Mum, but I can't go out with him again. He has pudgy fingers, and for some reason I just couldn't stand him even touching my hand."

Mum laughed. "Oh, you are too picky. You'll never get married. You're just too choosy!"

I shrugged. She was probably right, for once. I had been out with quite a few boys, just casually, and always kept my distance. I invariably found something wrong with them. Usually one, two, maybe three times out with a boy was sufficient, and then I made excuses that I was too busy. Mum's advice, along with Nana's stern words, had taken hold.

Music lessons and school work kept my mind steadily on course for college and a teaching career, along with continuing to teach Sunday school every Sunday afternoon. Now that we had moved further away, I always made my way to Nana and Poppa's house for tea on Sundays and then attended Evensong, which I found very meaningful. The familiar chant and the age-old words of the *Magnificat* and *Nunc Dimittis* spoke to me. Regardless of the worries of school and home, here I found encouragement and solace for my soul. As I said to a fellow schoolmate, who always was active in her church, " It feels like a warm shawl around me whenever I take part in that service."

At our Youth Group one evening, I commented on a newspaper article I'd read that day where it was reported that Hitler's remains had been verified in the bunker in Berlin, and he hadn't escaped, as rumour had it, to South America.

I proclaimed loudly, "Thank goodness he'd dead. That's the end of him!"

Our vicar responded to me gently. "Ah, Joyce, Hitler's body is dead, but the evil is still in the world. You see, you kill the body but not the evil."

I sat silent, taking in this profound thought. From that day on, I viewed evil in a totally different way.

About this time, I began to become even more involved in the church. Besides Guides, teaching Sunday school and Youth Group, I signed up to visit an elderly woman in a home for "indigent women" down town. We had been encouraged to become involved in service through our Youth Group. I had the address in my hand and wandered down the street passing old Victorian mansions, blackened with a couple of centuries of coal residue while more acrid smoke curled up from local chimney pots. "Home for Indigent Women", pronounced the sign. With some trepidation, I let the heavy brass knocker fall on the door. A uniformed nurse opened it, and I enquired if I could visit Miss Ivy Johnson. She stood aside so I could enter.

Dismay washed over me. About ten old iron beds lined up like tin soldiers against the wall, dressed with starched white sheets, and draped with washed-out green covers. A couple of worn armchairs graced the wall where the elongated windows looked out on to the grimy street. A bare wooden table and two straight-backed chairs completed the decor. A door opposite between the beds opened and I caught a glimpse of a dining room of sorts, with one long bare table set ready for a meal. A couple of women lay on their beds reading. Another approached me in a bath-chair and introduced herself as Ivy Johnson.

"Hello Ivy, I'm from St David's Church in Childwall, and I've come to visit you," I said.

Her face beamed with warmth. "How nice of you, child, to do that for me. Come and sit down, here." She motioned to one of the straight-backed chairs, while she wheeled her chair forward and positioned it beside mine. "Tell me about yourself," she said. "Where do you go to school, and what do you want to do?"

I told her that I wanted to be a teacher, and she beamed with pleasure, "Why my dear, that's what I was. I taught the little ones." Her grey hair was bobbed, held out of her eyes with a green slide. She wore a sensible woollen skirt with a slightly-shrunk jumper.

We chatted for a while. Then my curiosity overcame my politeness.

"Ivy, how come you are here?" I asked.

She gazed around reflectively. "Well, it isn't as bad as it seems," she explained. "They take very good care of us here. As I mentioned, I was a schoolteacher for many, many years." She hesitated. "I never married you see. In fact I took care of my mum and dad while I taught school. Then when they died my brother took over the house, and I moved into an old age pensioner flat, but after a while I couldn't stay there, as my arthritis got too bad."

She looked down at her heavy chair. "So here I am." Her voice brightened, "But they are good to us at the home," she repeated.

We talked some more, and for the first time, my heart reached out to someone in need, beyond my own family and friends, to someone I could see and touch who might like to have someone new to talk to, who might like a bar of chocolate and now and then, someone to care. As I rode the tram home, I thought about Ivy and her predicament and that night, asked God what I could do to help her. One thing I decided: I would continue to visit her regularly, which I did.

The following early summer, 1951, our vicar, Rev. Dunsby, announced to us Sunday school teachers an important event.

"If any of you are interested, there is a Sunday school teachers' school in the Lake District in July for two weeks. It is to be held at St Catherine's College on Derwent Water, near Keswick. If anyone would like to go, please see me."

There was no doubt. I had to go! After all, I now knew I was definitely going to be a teacher, so the more I could learn about it, the better. With great anticipation I waved goodbye to Mum and Dad and my sister Jean, who had come to see me off on the bus that had been hired to transport us there. About twenty-five of us, mostly young Sunday school teachers, male and female from various surrounding Anglican churches, crowded on to the bus. At the college we were assigned dormitories, with four to a room, and shared bathrooms, with girls on one floor, and boys safely on the floor above. Miss Smith, also affectionately called "Aunty", kept a close watch on her frisky teenage charges.

Almost immediately, I became homesick. It was the first time I'd spent any extended time away from home, except for the ill-fated Girl Guide camping trip and the brief stay with Dad's friends. However, this soon disappeared as I became immersed in the activities and explorations each day. Every morning we received instruction on teaching and some Bible study, and in the afternoons, we hiked over the surrounding Lake District. Evening concluded with Compline in the small chapel.

"Today, we are going to climb up to Ashness Bridge and on to Judith Paris's cottage," one of the residing ministers announced one morning (Judith Paris is a character in Walpole's *Herries Chronicles*). I loved walking and hiking, ever since Dad and I had climbed the hill to Pen-y-ball in North Wales so many years before, and after lunch, I eagerly donned my jacket and walking shoes. First, one of the leaders, a minister, rowed us across Derwent Water. Despite an awkward moment or two when someone almost fell overboard, we arrived safely and began our ascent.

Ashness Bridge, a well-known scenic location in Cumbria trodden by thousands through the years, brought us to a grassy area where we stopped. I turned around. Before me lay the sparkling expanse of Derwent Water, reflecting the green trees draped about the front edges of the shoreline and soaring mountains in the distance, beckoning to be climbed. I'd never seen such beauty. But more vistas opened up the higher we climbed, and the village of Keswick took on a miniature town appearance. I'd walked up hills and down into vales in Wales, but this vista suspended me in time.

After we'd enjoyed tea and scones at Judith Paris's cottage high in the hills, we climbed back down and across the lake in time for dinner. On successive days we explored Buttermere, the town of Keswick and Grasmere, reminiscent of William Wordsworth's poem on the daffodils, as well as venturing into Windermere. Between lectures in the morning and trips in the afternoon, I explored the bookstore set up with materials to excite Sunday school teachers and their pupils. Here I discovered flannel graph books containing drawings of Biblical figures and buildings, waiting to be coloured, cut out, have flannel glued to the back and then be used to illustrate the Bible story as told to the young children. I purchased two books, eager to begin the art of visuals to keep my young pupils' minds engaged, especially young Tony.

I smiled. During the last lesson I had taught I had spoken about how when we die we will see the wonder of heaven. My small pupil retorted: "Miss, we won't have to die to go to heaven. One day soon we'll have rockets that will go way, way up to there, so we'll be able to go any time we want!"

He sat back, content with the impact he'd had on the other children, as well as myself. I tried to explain otherwise, but knew he was convinced that rockets were the answer. I shook my head and paid for my purchases.

A couple of nights before we all left, I attended the usual service of Compline, entering into the beauty of words and cadences of phrases. We left the chapel in silence and I wandered into the stately English flower gardens stretching down to the lake, the evening hymn still echoing in my heart. A mystical sense permeated my being, as if I were floating ten feet above the ground. Fragrant lavender intensified into a musky sweetness. The warmth of summer roses gently brushed me, as I slowly trod the grass-matted path.

Then I simply stood, silent. The moon silvered the lake while the gaunt mountains stood guard on the far side. What was happening to me? What was this strange sensation of peace, of – other-worldliness?

Overcome, I sat down on a nearby stone bench, perplexed and a little afraid. It was beyond the comforting stillness I experienced in church. I absorbed all that this Presence offered, yet I was perplexed. The euphoric peace uplifted my soul even through the following day. That evening, as the beauty of Compline again infused my being, I stumbled into understanding; "It must be the presence of God," I half whispered to myself, yet I was still hesitant to identify such a holy experience.

The glow gradually subsided, but not entirely. The embedded ember continued to flicker, sometimes faintly, whereas other times it fanned into a shimmer of illumination, then again subsided into an inner assurance, like a soft mattress that would cushion the trials that lay before me for many years ahead.

Some months later I dreamed a dream. A vivid scene played into my senses, which I maintained after I'd awakened. I saw myself in a long white robe, walking in procession with others similarly clad toward a church. I passed my mother and father and a current boyfriend standing in a group watching, then processed into the building. Standing alongside my unknown companions in a long polished pew, we sang together. The words seared into my soul: *In simple trust like theirs who heard, beside the Syrian Sea, the gracious calling of the Lord, let us like them without a word rise up and follow Thee.* Excitement gripped me. It had to be that God was indeed calling me to be a missionary teacher. It was His message! I nurtured it warmly within, sharing it with no one – until a year or so later.

CHAPTER 17

CRUMPLED DREAMS (1953-54)

O Master from the mountainside, make haste to heal these hearts of pain
Frank Maison North, 1855-1936

At school our French teacher, Miss Sykes, announced that a trip to Belgium, including France and Holland, would be offered to all students studying French. Not wanting to lose an opportunity to travel, I cycled furiously back home and burst into the house.

"Mum, Mum! I have a chance to go to Belgium. Please will you let me go? You know how much I want to travel. I may never get another chance."

Her first question was naturally, "How many teachers are going?" The second one, "How much will it cost?"

I had anticipated both queries. I assured her. "Both Miss Sykes and Miss Bolton are going, and the cost is," I hesitated, "fifty pounds." I held my breath, then added, "I've got some money saved in my Post Office account, so I can pay some of it."

She looked at my face, flushed with excitement. "Very well. If you pay half of it out of your savings, I'll pay the rest."

I was overjoyed. Mum was right. By saving up for a 'rainy day' I had acquired enough money in my Post Office account to tip the balance in my favour. In order to be sure she wouldn't change her mind, I helped with the dishes, did some shopping for her, took library books back to the library when she was too busy, and even offered to change the beds every two weeks. It paid off.

The day arrived when we were to leave in the afternoon. The trip coincided with the school Easter holiday. My suitcase was tucked in a corner of the classroom, and I dizzed with anticipation. I hardly paid attention in Domestic Science later that morning. Miss Drake gave us end of term assignments. "Joyce," she said, "will you and Rita please polish the blackboards for me?"

I looked at Rita. "She said polish the blackboards. Do you think she really meant that?"

Rita shrugged. "I suppose so. Maybe they have to have polish on them to preserve them or something during the holidays."

Of course. So we both hunted around, and while Miss Drake fussed with other things, we finally found a tin of furniture polish. Next we rooted around and found a couple of clean rags, and then we were ready to commence our task. Thick globs of pine-scented polish were smeared across our cloths, and on to the blackboard. Then more polish, and more. After all we wanted to be sure that they were well preserved.

Finally we stood back. All three large blackboards were shiny with furniture polish. I told Miss Drake that we'd completed our task, and awaited her approval.

"Oh oh, no!" She exclaimed, her hands held up in horror. "You have polished the blackboards with furniture polish! Oh oh, dear, whatever will I do? You've ruined my blackboards!" She was almost in tears.

"But, but… you said for us to polish the blackboards," I explained, lamely.

"You silly girls! I meant for you to clean them, so they would be thoroughly washed, ready for next term. Now you've ruined them!" She sat down, head in hands, while we stood by awkwardly. She looked up. "Go, go away, you stupid girls. I've got to find Mr Chandler."

Mr Chandler was the caretaker, an old and rather cantankerous man with a yellowish-grey beard. We sneaked out as unobtrusively as we could.

After lunch, as I walked back to my Grade IV classroom, Mrs Goldberg, my home room teacher from the year before, sidled up to me. "Joyce, I heard about the blackboard incident. Don't let this Belgium trip go to your head."

I could have sworn she was trying not to laugh, but then a teacher would never do that!

Later in the day, we set off, first by train to Dover, then by boat over the English Channel to Calais, and again by bus to Bruges, where we stayed for four days. Our teachers encouraged us to explore around and practise our French. Hesitantly, Rita and I did a little window shopping.

I pulled up short. "Look at that!" I caught Rita's arm. "See - all those Easter eggs. Look - some are white even. I wonder what those are made of?"

Rita gazed in amazement. "I've never seen so many," she echoed. "Especially white ones."

This was my opportunity to practise my French. In I walked, trying to remember how to ask for chocolate Easter eggs. I was determined to buy a white one for Jean and surprise her on Easter Sunday morning, the following week.

"Comment les oeufs d'oiseaux?" I stumbled, pointing to the white egg encased in a chocolate cup.

"Ah, you want zee chocolate sweet," she replied, shaking her head at my attempt to speak her language.

"Oui, oui," I replied. At least I was sure of that word.

I could see now it was white chocolate and not just icing over brown chocolate. She wrapped it up carefully for me. I counted out the francs and carried my treasure back to the rooms where we stayed. I thought briefly back to the day when Margaret and I had lined up for just one regular iced chocolate egg so many years before.

After spending a day in France and another in Holland, we moved on to Brussels. Here we strolled in the main square, viewed the little Manikin statue (naked and spewing water) with snickers, then we noticed small square structures in the middle of the boulevard. The top and bottom were open, and at first we couldn't understand why men kept going in and out. We could see their legs and their heads, gazing at us gawking schoolgirls over the top. But what were they doing? Fortunately a couple of classmates had brothers and informed us loftily that they were having a 'wee'. Embarrassed by our lack of knowledge we quickly looked the other way, and hastened back to our guest house.

Later that week, another treat assailed my eyes – bananas. We had to queue to buy these back home, and then only one pound per customer. Here there were whole hands of bananas. My eyes grew larger. And they weren't even rationed! Before leaving

Belgium, I bought the largest hand of bananas I could find to take back home. At Boulogne, the French customs man laughed at me as I showed him my treasure, and waved me through.

On the boat back to Dover, I mulled over my experience. I was totally bewildered. Belgium had been occupied and bombed even worse than England during the war, yet there the shops overflowed with chocolate, bananas and other goods that were either still rationed or very scarce in England, which hadn't been occupied by the Nazis at all. But in the excitement of arriving home I forgot all about it and had no recollection of Dad's comment about the Marshall Plan so many years before. Jean was thrilled with her Easter egg, and Mum with the bananas, and life reverted back to normal.

However, one legacy the trip bequeathed upon me was the travel bug. I was hooked!

That summer I visited some other friends of my dad's, in the Peak District, some distance away by train. Greta, the wife, and I were out one day, having coffee and cakes in a café near where she lived. As adults do, she asked me, "Well Joyce, what do you want to do when you leave school?"

Without thinking, I replied honestly. "I want to be a teacher missionary in Burma or India."

Her faded fawn eyes sparked a glimmer of interest. "Oh, really? I've never met anyone who wanted to be a missionary."

A friend of hers stopped by. I was introduced, and Greta added, "And Joyce wants to be a missionary when she leaves school." The friend threw me a pitying glance, and the two passed a knowing look. I squirmed and looked down.

It wasn't long after I returned home that Mum announced. "Joyce, I have a bone to pick with you." My heart sank. What had

I done wrong this time? "Yes," she continued, "What is this nonsense I hear about you wanting to be a missionary?"

I tried to explain, but she cut me short. She continued, "You know other girls your age have left school by now, earning money to help out at home, and I'm still keeping you while you continue to go to school."

I kept quiet.

She took a breath, then continued, "You'll end up an old spinster and no one will want to ever marry you. You will be like one of these religious fanatics we see at the Pier Head wearing those religious billboards. You need to get that out of your head right now."

I nodded gloomily. I could see clearly the scruffy men in their long shiny overcoats and greasy workmen's caps on their heads, with a large board hanging each side of them, front and back, with messages like, "Repent: The End of the World is Near" weighing them down. I ignored her comments about leaving school, and no more was said right then.

But first I had to pass the General Certificate of Education at the end of Fifth Form. I studied hard night after night and was thrilled to pass in eight subjects. I needed a minimum of five, including Maths, English Language and English Literature, to be accepted to one of the teachers' training colleges. Now I had two more years ahead, in the lower and upper sixth forms, where I would take the Advanced Level examinations, then I'd be off, away from home, and on my way to being a teacher. I could almost taste it!

But now Mum's comments about wanting me to leave school began to become more repetitive. Other girls left school at fifteen, and those fortunate enough to attend a grammar school almost always went to work once they reached sixteen. Angela, Aunty Peggy's daughter, was now out working, and every time Mum arrived home from her house, I knew the litany that would follow. Not only was Angela working, she handed over her whole two pounds and ten shillings, her wage, each week to her mother, while her mum gave her ten shillings back for her tram fares and pocket money. Then followed, "And here I am keeping you in food and clothes when you should be out working."

I turned away, silent, continuing to harbour the dream, while doing my utmost not to rile her in any way.

At the end of my year in the Lower Sixth Form, the vicar at our church, in conjunction with other churches, arranged for some young Germans to come to Liverpool and stay with members of our Youth Group, in a reconciliation effort between the two countries. After Reverend Dunsby announced this to us, one of the boys burst out, "My Dad was killed by the Germans. I know my Mum won't want any Germans to stay with us."

A couple of my fellow youth friends agreed, but I wanted to have someone stay with us. I believed that doing something positive like this might prevent more wars in the future. So it came about that Helga stayed in our home.

Helga was the same age as me, and we enjoyed going on the various planned outings together, along with the other dozen or so Germans and their English hosts. One clear Saturday morning we all set off for North Wales, our vicar and some other church members leading all of us excited teenagers. Moel Famau (Movama) Mountain beckoned, with its distinguished oval hump on the top. Effortlessly we climbed up over rocks and scree, following, for the most part, a path worn down by enthusiastic climbers such as us. At the top, where the pile of rocks stood as a beacon, we gazed across the Rivers Dee and Mersey, where I again saw the finger of Liverpool Anglican Cathedral pointing heavenward, just as I had in Holywell. We munched on a picnic lunch that Mum had packed for Helga and me, cheese and tomato sandwiches, topped off with a Blue Riband chocolate wafer bar each. We sat together chatting.

"I am happy you have me in your home," Helga said, in her good English.

"I am glad that you could come," I responded and took her hand. We smiled at each other, two teenagers sitting on a mountaintop together, admiring the splendid view. I thought briefly of the German prisoners of war I'd seen as a young child on the picnic, but that seemed such a long time ago.

All too soon, our vicar gave the call and we all scrambled back down. As we scampered and chatted, moving a lot faster than we had on the way up, a young man, who I hadn't seen before, fell into conversation with us. On the bus and boat, he sat close to Helga and me, and then enquired if I might be going to the church dance that evening.

"Oh, yes, of course," I responded. "I love dancing. Helga and I are planning to go."

He smiled, his grey eyes warm. "That's good news. I love ballroom dancing too. I'll see you there, then."

"Sure." I also smiled in agreement. I found out his name was Roger. Colin had somehow faded far into the distance.

That evening, after our tea, Helga and I dressed carefully for the dance. I selected a sky-blue two piece which always seemed to bring me countless dance partners when I wore it. With my silver dance shoes in a bag and sensible shoes on my feet, I set off with Helga, with the usual warning from Mum for us not to be late.

Roger was already there. He glided over for the quickstep, and we turned and dipped, then bent in perfect harmony with the music. I followed his lead easily, and was glowing by the time he led me back to my seat next to Helga. I danced with him most of the evening, my Boy Scout friends forgotten in the presence of this man, who I found out was six years older than me. On the way home, he held my hand. Just as important was the fact that he was working. He had money to spend – on me, I hoped!

The following day Helga left for home. We promised to write and she invited me to stay with her in Germany the following summer. (Unfortunately this never happened.) I missed her company after she'd left.

So Roger and I began going out together. He introduced me to Chinese food. Being head chef in a large Liverpool hotel, he frequently showed off his prowess by creating delightful dinners at home, which endeared him to Mum. We danced as often as we could, usually on Saturday nights. I definitely liked him.

In the course of our conversations he mentioned a dance at the Village Institute. I remembered the pantomime I'd attended with Colin. "Do you happen to know someone called George Bradshaw?" I asked him.

"Of course, I do. He's a good friend of mine."

A flash of memory spun into place. "You didn't by any chance, take part in the Cinderella Pantomime?"

He laughed. "Yes, indeed I did. I was the older ugly sister. The one with the big wart." He stopped. "Were you there then?"

I nodded and laughed. "I looked in the programme to see who was playing that part. I remember your name now. You were really funny."

"What a strange coincidence." He smiled, pleased.

School began again – my final year. I had my required physical and an interview at an all-female college, and then applied to a couple of co-education teacher training colleges. I also stopped taking piano lessons, to the dismay of my music teacher, but I found there simply wasn't time to practise a couple of hours a day and get the required mountains of homework done. But when I had time, I relaxed, sitting on the worn, round stool, playing the now-tuned upright piano and losing myself in the beauty of a sonata or concerto.

Roger would sometimes meet me from school, if he were off, and I felt proud to have a boyfriend like him walking beside me to the bus stop. But then he began to talk about marriage.

"No, I can't think about that," I told him adamantly. "I want to be a teacher before I even consider marriage."

"I can wait," he said gently.

And so it was left.

Mum, in the meantime, still fretted about my plan to become a teacher, so she encouraged Roger, and conversations regarding me leaving school took on a new intensity.

"Angela, you know, had a promotion and got a wage increase." I waited for what was coming. "She's bringing home three pounds a week, working in a shipping office, and still gives all her wages to her mum." She waited a minute to see my reaction. I continued to bring my books out of my school satchel.

"I shouldn't be keeping you in school, not at seventeen years of age. You should be out earning your keep by now, like the other young people round here. I don't know that we can afford for you to go to college."

I stopped what I was doing and looked up. "But Mum," I protested, "It won't cost you anything. It's free, and it's only a two-year programme. Also the government will give me pocket money each term."

This appeared to offend her. "It still means I've got to feed and clothe you in the meantime. And you won't be bringing money in until you are at least twenty years of age."

"I want to be a teacher, you know that, Mum" I said quietly.

Now another caveat was added. "Besides, you and Roger seem to be serious and I am quite sure that Roger wants to marry you, he's made that pretty clear. If you marry him you have no need to go to college. It's a waste of time."

"Mum, I want to be a teacher," I implored. "You know I've wanted to since I first started school. Roger knows that too." Then I turned away, and continued getting my homework out ready to do. I liked Roger. He made me laugh and I luxuriated in being cossetted as he treated me to films, dances and expensive restaurants. Besides, he was a terrific dancer. I had to be honest, I thought more of him than anyone else, but teaching still came first.

Dad, in the meantime, didn't seem to be bothered one way or the other, though I heard him say timidly to her, "You know, Lil, you shouldn't get on to her like that." Mum then turned on him, and I could her hear terse voice as I closed my bedroom door. I already knew that he was afraid of her and found it difficult to disagree with her on anything.

Another turn of events complicated family life still further.

Mum had unexpectedly met up with her cousin, Hugh, who she had fallen in love with at fourteen years of age. Their reunion had all happened during the previous summer. A postcard arrived in the letterbox from Hugh saying that he and his wife were on holiday in New Brighton and would stop by to see her and Dad the following Wednesday. Mum was all of a dither. I knew she had been in love with him as a teenager. She'd told me that a number of times, but Hugh hadn't pursued it further, so she'd married my Dad. She hadn't seen him since she was twenty-one years of age, twenty-three years before.

On the day Hugh and Vicky were due to call I arrived back from school on my bike, excited to finally meet this old boyfriend of Mum's. Outside was parked a red two-seater Triumph convertible. As I wheeled my bike into the garage, my interest notched up several degrees. Mum was getting tea, and as I pulled off my raincoat a tall, tanned, rugged-faced man walked into the kitchen.

'Och, Joyce, it's nice to meet ye," said Hugh in a broad Scots accent. "I've heard a lot about you bairns from Uncle Jim and Aunty Peg's letters to my mother. Ye ken that my mother, your Great-Aunt Jessie, is your grandfather's sister?

"It's nice to meet you too," I offered inadequately, not knowing what else to say.

He then introduced me to Vicky, his wife, a full, rather blowsy-looking lady with faded blonde hair. They stayed for tea and we all made polite conversation. Then they roared off in the brilliant convertible.

A few weeks later, Mum informed us that she was going to Glasgow to see her Aunty Jessie, Hugh's mother, and Poppa's sister, for the weekend. "I haven't seen Aunty Jessie for such a long time," she told us. "You'll need to look after Jean and your father," she instructed me, which I did, without questioning or even thinking too much about it.

These trips began taking place on a regular basis and finally one day Mum confessed to me that Hugh had told her he was still in love with her, and apparently, she felt the same way about him. I suddenly realised that it hadn't been Aunty Jessie at all she'd gone to see, but I decided to keep this to myself. Now she began going north to Glasgow one weekend every month, returning on Monday morning. Dad, who, for some reason, claimed to love my Mum dearly, declared that he was willing to tolerate this, so long as she didn't leave him permanently. In the meantime, I took care of him and Jean while Mum was away. Sometimes Hugh returned with her, and slept some place, though I never asked where. Jean in the meantime was at Highfield Secondary Modern School, and kept out of Mum's way as much as she could.

Then the pressure intensified. "You should be out working. Here I am keeping you still in school…" the repetitious complaint I knew by heart. The atmosphere in the house hung heavy with apprehension as Mum became more agitated. I noticed that twin beds replaced the double bed in their room, and soon Mum had Dad sleeping in the small box room while I was instructed to sleep in the other twin bed with her. It wasn't what I wanted, but Jean had the other room, so felt I had no option.

Roger wanted us to get engaged before I left for college. I enjoyed his company, but marriage? A piece of me wasn't sure that I wanted to be tied down for that long.

The week before Christmas, after Dad had hung the

decorations and I'd made a fruit Christmas cake, complete with marzipan and icing, Mum arrived back from Scotland. I anticipated one more college interview, already scheduled for early January for a teachers' training college in Rugby, some eighty miles away.

Mum resurrected her usual tirade upon her return, "Here I am keeping you in food and clothes, and not a penny are you contributing. I have a hard time making ends meet and you are gallivanting off to interviews. You should be out working, like other normal girls. If you become a teacher, Roger won't want to marry you, neither will anyone else. You will be too bossy, and no man likes a bossy woman. You'll end up an old maid, with a bun at the back of her head." This was the dread of every young female in the nineteen-fifties. "Look at..."

An intolerable heat rose within me, red and blistering. I couldn't take it anymore and suddenly it broke open.

"If that's what you want," I exploded, "Then I'll leave school! I'll get a job! I'll give you my wage each week. Is that what you want? Will that make you happy? " I banged my school books down on the table as I fought to keep back my tears. Suddenly I realised what I'd done, and I couldn't take it back.

That was all she needed. The next morning I didn't want breakfast. I half attempted to say something, but Mum's face silenced me, and after I'd left for school she called the headmistress, Miss Baker. She informed her I was leaving school at the end of the week. The headmistress called me into her study and expressed concern that I should leave in the middle of the school year, but I shrugged my shoulders and made some kind of non-committal response, though I was in turmoil within. I knew beyond all doubt now that she had carried out her threat.

On the way back from school I stopped in at Nana's house and leaned my bike against her side wall. I knocked at the door and she opened it immediately. In I tumbled and made for the familiar well-worn kitchen chair. I leaned my arms on the table and cried, heaving from my deepest depths. I cried between sobs, telling her what had happened.

"I'll never forgive her for doing this to me. I'll never forgive her, as long as I live. I've wanted to be a teacher ever since I was little. She knows that. How can she do this to me?" I continued crying inconsolably.

Nana took me in her arms. "Now, now," she soothed. "Let's see what we can do." A flicker of hope caught my heart, but she continued, "I will pay for you to go to Machin and Harpers. That's a nice secretarial school in town where you can learn shorthand and typing, and get a respectable office job. There now, how will that be?"

I raised my red, tear-streaked face and after a while, conceding defeat, I nodded. "Thank you," I managed to whisper.

After I had calmed down a little, I left, slowly got back on my bike and let the oncoming brisk wind wipe the tears away from my face as I free-wheeled down the steep hill of Rocky Lane towards home.

I couldn't eat that night. Instead I quietly opened the door to the lounge in front of the house, closed the door, lifted the piano lid and sat down. I took a deep breath, my hands hovering over the keys, and played. Soothing notes of solace calmed my shattered dreams as Beethoven's *Moonlight Sonata* rose from my fingers. Tears ran down my cheeks.

As the final notes died away, I gently closed the piano lid and stole upstairs to bed. I pretended to be asleep when I heard Mum come to bed. The following week, I'd left Calder High School.

CHAPTER 18

BROKEN HEARTS
(1955-57)

Through all the changing scenes of life, in trouble and in joy
Nahum Tate, 1652-1715

I shelved my dreams and tried to deal with the reality of the moment. I buoyed myself up by thinking of the wage I'd soon be earning, and not having to slog away at school taking exams. Nevertheless typing and, shorthand, challenged me, for a while. *Ah, but a man's reach should exceed his grasp, or what's a heaven for* was catching me in its spell again. I felt compelled to exceed everyone else with my speed at such skills.

Our first task assignment, however, was more mundane. We were instructed to sew a cover for our typewriters, so we could learn, literally, touch typing. The old Royal typewriter clacked and clattered as I pushed the carriage over for each line, and rolled the knob to pull out the paper and begin again. Shorthand evolved into something a little trickier. Miss Mullins, our teacher, appeared decidedly elderly, with both a limp and a habit of nodding off during dictation.

She began, "Dear sirs, Thank you for your recent letter. We are pleased to inform you…" Her head dropped forward and a faint snore emitted. Titters circled around the class. With a jerk, she opened her eyes, "And that is why we are sending you this letter… " The words spilled out in a torrent, as she attempted to complete the letter in the allotted three minutes. Our giggles switched to frantic strokes and dots trying to capture the words.

Finally, after the required nine-month training, she declared, "Miss Bibby, you have reached 75 words per minute in your typing and 120 words per minute in your shorthand. You can now apply for a position as a shorthand typist."

Money, at last, sprung to mind. The days of dreaming of buying unlimited sweets had passed, but the thrill of buying my own clothes awaited me. The Eagle Star Insurance Company needed just such an applicant as myself, and I secured the position. With a dozen other, mostly young, women overseen by the white-haired, bespectacled, Miss Bamber, who took letters from the Manager, I settled into a boring routine. Each week I handed over my two pounds ten shillings to Mum towards my keep. Dutifully, I immediately placed half of what remained in the Post Office account, as Nana and Mum had taught me, the remainder disappearing mostly in tram fares. However as the holiday season approached, my priority became a particular dress I'd spied in the window of C&A. The fashionable longer length, sapphire blue fitted taffeta frock, sleeveless, with a pink lined stole, shimmered under the artificial light. That dress was for me, I decided; the first dance dress I had chosen by myself. I bought it and waited for the perfect opportunity to show it off.

Roger, the faithful boyfriend, escorted me on Friday night to the local cinema, as usual, and inevitably slid a quarter-pound box of Black Magic chocolates over on to my lap while his other arm slipped around my waist. I nibbled away during the film, then as the story ended with the usual romantic conclusion, he suggested, "How about some fish and chips?"

"Ooh, yes please." My reply had become predictable. We munched on fish and chips, wrapped in newspaper, after first generously sprinkling them with salt and vinegar. Eating greasy chips with our fingers, we strolled home from the Abbey Cinema, chatting and laughing.

"Where are we going dancing tomorrow?" I asked.

"How about the Rialto, or the Grafton, or do you want to go to the local dance at Christ the King? And before I forget, we are having a big do on Boxing Day at the Exchange Hotel. The Manager has invited all the staff and wives or girlfriends to come. It's free, and that includes drinks and food. Will you come as my girlfriend?" High expectancy hung in his voice, his slate-grey eyes questioning.

I assented eagerly. Images of the brand-new blue dress with the buckled cinched waist swirled in my head. A new nylon-flocked bouffant petticoat I'd bought from Marks and Spencer's hung expectantly on the hanger at home waiting to be worn and flounced underneath the dress's wide flared skirt.

But Roger also wanted to get engaged at Christmas. I balked, still not absolutely sure of my feelings. I enjoyed going out with him. He was fun to be with, but actually getting engaged! So it lay unanswered between us. Instead, much to my relief, I received a watch, for which I thanked him profusely.

Boxing Day, a public holiday in England, arrived. Very early that evening I took a leisurely bath, sprinkled on my Evening in Paris perfume, painstakingly applied my eye-liner, blue eyeshadow, to match my dress, and some black mascara. Yardley Pretty Pink lipstick completed the operation. I pulled out the clips from my newly-washed hair and carefully combed the curls into place. Another smooth to the skirt of my ballroom dress over my multi-layered petticoat followed, then I pulled the wide belt in another notch to show off my twenty-four-inch waist. I admired myself sideways in the mirror, and grinned, satisfied.

A knock echoed from the front door, and I pranced down the stairs, like Cinderella except that the silver dance shoes lay snug in my bag, while I wore the usual walking shoes to get there. My for-best three-inch black suede stiletto-heeled shoes I kept for short distances only.

Together we strode hand in hand to the tram stop and caught the number forty downtown. A brisk walk along Dale Street, then a turn right up to the Exchange Hotel, blackened with coal smoke from the adjoining train station. The ballroom inside glowed with Christmas lights, decorations and an open bar, with *Moon River* just calling to be danced to. I felt light-headed at the prospect of a festive, joyous night ahead.

After a glass of port, I slid into his arms, and we danced the night away, interrupted only by a sumptuous buffet with unlimited ice cream. Eleven o'clock rolled around too fast.

"We have to run to get the last tram," I said, suddenly realising.

"We'll get a taxi if we miss it," he assured me.

Part of me considered lingering a little longer, tempted, but we caught the tram after a quick scurry as it drew to the nearest stop. Neither of us wanted to face Mum's displeasure.

Valentine's Day celebration came next, and on the tram ride home from a romantic walk along the promenade on the other side of the Mersey, Roger handed me a package from his large winter coat pocket.

"I have a shirt here" he said. "I wondered if you could sew a couple of buttons on for me?" He smiled, somewhat smugly, obviously certain I would say, "Of course."

"No way." My response was swift. "You have a mother to do that for you. Remember, I'm not your wife."

His crestfallen face created a small wave of guilt. "Open it anyway," he pleaded.

Reluctantly I tore open the package. Enclosed in a cellophane heart lay a fresh red rose nestled on a bed of cotton wool .

Shamefaced, I stammered, "Thank you. That's very nice." The words appeared trite. Some devilish quirk within me wanted to giggle at his seriousness. I pressed my lips together. "Oh, God," I prayed silently, staring down at the rose, "What am I to do?"

I sensed that marriage would arise sphinx-like yet again. I guessed right.

"You've got to give me an answer. You have left me hanging long enough," Roger insisted, not long after Valentine's Day. "We've been courting almost two years. Will you marry me or not?" We had our arms around each other saying goodnight, in the hall at home, at the end of another evening of enjoying Chinese curry at the Chanticleer restaurant.

I hummed and hawed. I fast forwarded to the future. If I

married him, did I love him enough for a life together? I sighed within. I didn't know. Then suppose I turn him down?

I gazed over his shoulder. I imagined Miss Bamber, ready to retire, a spinster with no family, living by herself in a little flat in the Wirral on the other side of the River Mersey, having worked for years and years, taking dictation and pushing a clanking typewriter. I shuddered. A lovely white wedding, and then of course the honeymoon, shimmered tantalizingly on the horizon. As good girls waited until marriage for sex, that appealed to me and set my pulse racing. Also it would prove to Mum I wouldn't be left on the shelf after all.

I pulled back to face him. "Very well, I'll marry you," I said. He gave me an extra hug, and the following Saturday we purposefully made our way toward Samuel's, downtown, to choose an engagement ring. Of course, I had been surveying the ring windows of the local jeweller's for a few weeks, just in case I said yes. I settled on one with five diamonds on a slant, and wore it proudly.

I showed off my five-diamond cross engagement ring to office colleagues, church friends and anyone else who was around. We decided we wouldn't get married for about two years, when I was twenty-one. That, I felt, would give me some breathing room to get used to the idea.

Sunday school teaching was still an inviolable commitment for me on Sunday afternoons, followed by tea at Nana and Poppa's, then on to church for Evensong. If Roger wasn't working, he joined me there, usually saving a space beside him in our usual pew. This particular afternoon, after our tea, Nana, Poppa and I sat in the living room idly watching an interview on the small box-like black and white television, beside the winter fire. David Sheppard, the famous England cricketer, who had just become an ordained curate of the Church of England, was the person being interviewed.

Suddenly I burst out, "That's the kind of man I would really like to marry".

Nana and Poppa stared at me.

"But you're engaged to Roger!" said Nana, horrified.

Poppa gave me a long look. "Och, lass," he said gently, "I'm thinking ye have got some sortin' out to do."

Embarrassed, I stood up. "Oh, look at the time. I must hurry, I don't want to be late for church." Red-faced, I rushed into the hall, Nana after me, and pushed my arms into my swagger coat, then grabbed my handbag. "Ta ra, see you!" I called out as I hastened through the open front door, Nana watching me.

Once out of sight of their house I slowed down, allowing the damp breeze to cool my face to normality. Why had I said such a thing? I wasn't sure.

One evening, in the middle of the week, a short time after my engagement, there was a rat-a-tat on the front door. Mum answered it, and in walked Colin, who I hadn't seen for over a year. As he had been my first sweetheart, although we had grown apart over the last few years, I perked up at seeing him.

Almost immediately, there was another knock at the door. Mum, again, opened it, and Tommy sauntered in. "Oh, dear," I whispered to myself, "this isn't so good!" Tommy was an erstwhile boyfriend, the son of one of Dad's friends. He loved classical music, as I did, and was a super dancer. I welcomed him in, and invited him to sit down too. Dad was working nights that week, and Jean was visiting one of her friends overnight, so it was up to Mum and me. Conversation stumbled.

Then came another knock. I couldn't imagine who this might be, but I opened it this time, leaving Mum to entertain the other two boys.

Roger stood there smiling. "I got out of work early, so thought I'd surprise you and drop by."

My heart sank, but I had to ask him in too. His smile dropped to a stony stare as he entered the living room. He glared at the two males already seated in armchairs while a silence you could cut with a knife hung in the air.

Mum hissed, "Joyce, get in the hall. I have a bone to pick with you."

Oh, dear, Mum always said that if she'd thought I'd committed some offense. I really needed her help to come up with a plan to get rid of all three young men. She shut the living room door firmly behind her.

"That's it!" she hissed. "I've had it with you and your boys. How many times have I made excuses for you when a boy has called on the phone for you, and you haven't wanted to speak to him? I can't count the times I've said you were out, when you were standing right there. No more. You got yourself into this mess. You get yourself out of it." She pulled on her coat. "I'm off to Mrs Butterworth's across the road. She invited me over earlier today."

"Mum," I pleaded, "You can't go. You've got to help me get out of this. I don't know what to do. Please don't leave me with them all. "

"Oh, yes, I can, and I will. You make sure they are all gone by the time I get back, or you'll be in big trouble!" She clamped her hat on her head, marched to the front door, opened it, went out and slammed it behind her. She was gone.

"Oh, God, help me!" I cried. Nothing happened, so I thought God probably agreed with Mum. With a deep breath I turned the handle of the living room door, "Well now," I declared in a bright voice, "who would like a cup of tea?" It barely chinked the icy atmosphere.

"No thank you," came a unified voice.

"What do you think about Sudan declaring independence?" I asked next, referring to the latest news.

"Very interesting." responded Tommy politely.

Sporadic stilted conversation followed, then more deadness. Eventually, Tommy stood up to leave. I escorted him to the door, thanked him for coming, and wished him well on his next tour of duty in the Army. He was leaving for six months in Germany.

Colin came next. But at the front door, he lingered. "Joyce," he hesitated, "The reason I came tonight was to see if we might get back together. I still care for you very much."

Oh, dear God. Where are You in all this? I sent up the arrow prayer. But silence ensued. I vacillated, flummoxed as to what I should say. I managed to ease him out of the door. Now only Roger was left. His grim face told me everything. "I don't want you having anything to do with those two boys again," he informed me.

"But they are friends of the family," I attempted to explain.

"I don't care. I will not have you seeing anyone else. You are engaged to me." His eyes gazed grey stone.

My stomach turned. What had I done? He stormed off, but at least he didn't ask for his ring to be returned. He banged the front gate and strode off up Thomas Lane back to his house.

I closed the front door, made my way to the living room, and sank into a chair exhausted, relishing the comfort of the coal fire. Shortly after, Mum's key turned in the lock. The front door opened and after a pause, it closed. After an unusually long time, she appeared at the doorway.

"Good, they are gone. Gone, gone!" Her voice sounded strange, disjointed almost.

"Yes," I agreed, hesitant. "They've all left." I stared. "Mum, are you okay?"

She smiled in a sloppy way.

I cried, amazed. "You're tiddly, Mum. You're tiddly!"

"I only had a couple of sherries," she explained, carefully pronouncing her words. "And the glasses were small, you know."

I'd never seen Mum like this before in my life. Suddenly I burst out laughing. After a moment or two she joined in, giggling like a schoolgirl. Together we laughed uproariously, tears rolling down our cheeks, washing away the tension of the evening. Still laughing, and with me holding her steady, we trundled off to bed. Mum lost some of her edgy control that evening, as I realized she wasn't next to God after all.

The remnants of that evening cast a pall over my relationship with Roger. Yet I did my utmost to cast it from my mind, and focused on wedding plans. Another topic had to be discussed, as I needed to be sure that religion was as important to Roger as it was to me. Normally we simply didn't discuss it. However, one Sunday evening after a moving sermon during Evensong, I tentatively enquired, "Have you ever felt the presence of God?"

"No, I can't say I have. Have you?" He turned to me, his face grave. I nodded, then paused, unsure of what to say. "Perhaps you will one day too." I tried to be understanding.

The silence between us hung with discomfort, so the subject was changed, but we continued to attend church together. However, knife-points of discord now crept in to our relationship. "Why do you have to teach Sunday school every Sunday?" he demanded yet again.

I tried to explain that I didn't want to disappoint the children, and I felt I would be letting God down too.

Mum took his side. "When I think of all the times you have been there, week after week, surely you can take off a Sunday now and then and let someone else do it? I'm sure they all take time off. Besides, you still visit Ivy in the old people's home. Can't another person from the church at least do that?"

Roger chimed in, "Aren't I more important to you than Sunday school and other church stuff?"

But I stood my ground. To me it was important. God had called me to do this. If I couldn't be a real teacher, at least I could be a Sunday school teacher. Besides I loved teaching the children about Jesus.

The subject continued to create tension between us, but I pushed it away. After all I was engaged and once we were married it would be different. He would change, I was sure. Any shadows that crept in I dismissed, and instead filled my mind with the kind of wedding dress I wanted, where we might spend our honeymoon, and all the excitement that accompanied such thoughts.

The subject of summer holidays arose. Roger suggested to me one day, "How about us going to the Isle of Man for a week? We could stay with Mrs Williams. That's where my mum goes each summer to help her out, so she would be there." The fact that we would have separate rooms went without saying.

I asked Mum. She drew herself up to her full height and threw us both a scornful look. "Of course not!" she retorted. "Don't you think I know what happens when two engaged people go off on holiday together?"

"But, Mrs Bibby," explained Roger. "My mum will be there, and I promise nothing will happen." His earnestness impressed me.

I watched with fingers crossed. She threw him a glance loaded with disbelief. "No, and that's final. If you want to go over, you can go on the midnight ferry, spend the day there and come back on the next midnight ferry."

Which is what we did. I took the week off from work, and along with the Isle of Man we took day trips to Southport, to New Brighton, and enjoyed days of swimming, picnicking, and taking train rides to places we'd never been to before. Any misgivings were squelched into a no-man's land.

On Monday morning, reluctantly, I climbed the stairs to the fourth floor of the insurance office, only to be called into the Manager's office. Mr Turnbull told me to sit down. I sat on the edge of the upright chair, perplexed as to what was taking place.

"I'm sorry to inform you, Miss Bibby, but we are consolidating our offices, and our main office will be in Manchester. Therefore, we are letting our married typists go. Because you are engaged to be married and won't need a job once you are married, we have to tell you, that you will be losing your job also."

I couldn't believe it. The men downstairs were all keeping their positions, though some were moving to Manchester, I discovered. But I needed a job. I wanted money for my trousseau!

Roger didn't seem too concerned about it. Neither did Mum. But I was devastated to have actually lost my job. Each evening I read through the *Echo*, circling jobs available for shorthand typists, and eventually found one with the Dunlop Rubber Factory office in Speke. The man who was my new boss swore and cursed all day. The office appeared as large as a football field, crammed with men and young girls. *Is this where you want me to be, Lord?* I asked. Then immediately came my own response, *But you will be married soon, and you won't need to work.* Then I forced myself to take a hard look into the future. Housework, which never thrilled me, a couple of children, and then what?

Dancing somehow lost its gilt, and the Black Magic chocolates tasted tedious. A restlessness pervaded my spirit, manifesting itself in petty arguments with Roger. Even the glamorous wedding plans and the thought of the honeymoon lost their allure. I struggled with the bleakness of the roiling thunder clouds that gathered before me. The sun had gone down on our engagement.

Roger kept asking me, 'What's the matter?"

I shrugged it off. "Nothing."

What would happen if I broke off the engagement? I thought of our vicar, my friends and people at church. Girls didn't jilt their fiancés, at least not church-going girls. I prayed harder. "Oh God. You know how I feel. I think I've been in love with the whole wedding and honeymoon idea. I feel desperate about the future, yet how can I hurt Roger and his family in this way? Please God, give me a sign."

But God has his own ways. No thunder rolled down from the skies, no words streaked the air from lightning bolts. I opened my Bible at random, desperate for some enlightening verse. Instead, an innocuous verse from Leviticus lay dormant on the page in front of me. I didn't discuss it with anyone. I wanted God to tell me, and no one else.

Tommy returned from Germany and, still in uniform, came to visit. It was good to see him again and the family warmly welcomed him. He held out a small box to me. "I've brought a little gift for you. I thought you'd like it," his honest ocean-blue eyes were anxious.

Carefully I peeled back the fancy paper, and opened the box. I gasped, "Oh, Tommy, it's beautiful!" Carefully I lifted out a small gold cross and chain from the cotton batting. The gold glinted in the firelight as I held it aloft. Immediately I fastened it around my neck, and fingered it reverently. I hugged him, which obviously pleased him, and he stayed to have some tea. Only Mum, Jean and Dad were around that evening, for which I gave thanks.

As I knelt before my bed that night, I held the small cross, still around my neck, gently with my fingers. "Lord, Jesus," I prayed. "Is this the sign I wanted? Are you telling me, I should break my engagement to Roger? Is it your will?"

A little later as I lay back on my pillow, I saw the gift as the sign I'd sought. It was sufficient. Tomorrow I would tell Roger, and return my engagement ring. Instantly relief flooded my being. I slept soundly for the first time in several weeks.

The following morning, rained poured down as I avoided puddles on my way to the tram stop. The drops on my face washed any remnants of doubt away, and I felt as if chains around my heart had fallen away too. The decision had been made. Now I must do the deed.

CHAPTER 19

ENDINGS AND BEGINNINGS

Heaven's morning breaks, and earth's vain shadows flee
in life, in death O Lord, abide with me

Henry Francis Lyte 1793-1847

Guilt plagued me after breaking off the engagement. Hurt feelings, misunderstood comments, shock, surprise, and, above all, Roger's mother's comment to me, "My poor son. How could you do this to him?" Her words haunted me. Perhaps one lesson I'd learned was not to make a serious commitment for the wrong reasons.

However, such remorse did not deter me from jumping on the back of Tommy's motor bike and roaring off into North Wales and the Lake District, or from dancing with him with gusto on Saturday nights. Nevertheless, I began to seek other avenues to fulfil the inner desire to serve my Lord in a more purposeful way. Teaching as a career was no longer viable, so I turned to nursing, the only other female profession available. I told God that I could help others in this way far more effectively than I could pounding a typewriter. Also the dream of becoming a missionary gravitated from the back burner to the front once more.

I dreaded telling Mum. After all, she had accepted the broken engagement with equanimity, giving her usual refrain: "You know you will never find the kind of man you are looking for. They don't exist. You need to set your sights a little lower, like the rest of us." However, most weekends, she had liaisons with her cousin in Scotland, and when home she lived for his telephone calls, or raced downstairs first thing in the morning to get the post, just in case he'd sent her a letter.

"Mum, I am thinking of going into nursing," I finally announced one Saturday morning. "Actually I'm thinking of St Bartholomew's in London."

Silence followed my statement. Then she spoke. "Why on earth do you have to go there? Why can't you go to a local hospital and do your training nearer home?"

"Well," I reasoned, "It is one of the best hospitals in the country, and I'll be twenty-one soon. I think it is time for me to make that move."

She cast me her stony stare. I sighed, knowing that there would be more obstacles ahead. I pointed out, "I'll have my keep provided for, and my uniforms and I will receive eight pounds a month pocket money." I thought some more. "Also I have fifty pounds saved in my Post Office account, so it won't cost you anything."

She was getting ready for another trip north, so her mind was wavering between my news and her desire to be off to catch the bus, buses having finally replaced the trams.

I threw myself into filling in forms, lining up my General Certificate of Education passes, and references, then attended the all-important interview. My letter of acceptance arrived early one morning a couple of weeks later, with my starting date, Monday the first of September, quite some months away.

A couple of weeks later Jean arrived home in tears. She'd started her first job several weeks previously at a local factory. All students attending Highfield Secondary Modern left school at fifteen years of age, and were expected to find a job in a shop, factory, or as office girls, getting coffee, running errands, a general gopher.

"Whatever is the matter?" I tried to console her.

Mum stepped in, "Jean, tell us what's happened? Are you ill?"

Jean shook her head, crying harder. "Miss Jackson, you know my supervisor, she told me," She blew her nose. "She told me I was repugnant!"

Mum and I gasped simultaneously. "You're not repugnant," I cried, considering her dark curling shoulder-length hair and flashing brown eyes. "You are very pretty." I thought too of Mum's comment a couple of years ago to a neighbour, in front of me, "Oh, yes, Jean is the beauty of the family".

"How can anyone call you repugnant?" Mum's voice rose in amazement.

"Well, she did." Jean sniffed hard. "And she told a couple of the other girls they were repugnant too."

Mum and I passed a knowing look. Somehow it just didn't add up.

"Tell us some more, Jean," I asked, teasing out more information.

She wiped her face with a hanky. "It happened this afternoon, before we left work. She came over to me and said I was repugnant, and I wouldn't be going back there to work on Monday."

A few moments passed as the full extent of what she really meant dawned on us both. I tried to stifle a grin. Mum actually gave a short laugh. Then we both chortled out loud. Jean, highly indignant, exclaimed. "It isn't funny! How would you like to lose your job?"

"You're not repugnant, by any means," I tried to say, still shaking. "What you mean is, she told you you were redundant."

"That's what I said," she retorted back. "Now I'll never find another job."

"Of course you will," I reassured her. "In fact we'll look in the *Echo* this evening and I'll help you write a letter of application."

We worked on the letter, and a couple of weeks later the office in Hunter's Handy Hams factory, within walking distance of our house, hired her. Within a couple more weeks she started raving about a young lad of eighteen years of age, in her office, who, she thought, 'liked her'. On Saturday nights they would take off for the Cavern Club, in downtown Liverpool, where they rock'n rolled and listened to a young foursome.

Brian, who we had now met a couple of times, brought her back one evening after visiting the Cavern.

"You'll never guess what," said Jean, spilling over with excitement, "Brian knows one of the boys in the group. He went to school with him."

Brian chimed in. "Oh, him. We got into a fight when we were at Quarry Bank together."

"Oh, you went to Quarry Bank?" My interest notched up. "I attended Calder High."

Brian grinned. "Some of the lads in my class used to climb over the wall and meet a couple of the girls in your school."

I was shocked. Boys and girls were clearly segregated and any student at our school found fraternizing with a boy from Quarry Bank found themselves in severe trouble. "How did they get away with it?"

His grin widened. "They used to meet in the middle air-raid shelter."

I chuckled. The air-raid shelters, still standing from the war, hugged the high brick wall separating the schools. I vaguely remembered seeing a fellow student slip out the door, but never saw any boys. I couldn't figure out why anyone would want to go into one of those sleazy air-raid shelters. That explained it. And they never got caught!

Then I asked, "Oh, what is the name of the boy in the band, you know?" just in case I knew him.

"John Lennon," he replied. "He's not much of a fighter, I can tell you. I beat him easily."

Jean joined in. "You should come and hear them. They call themselves The Beatles, and their music is smashing. It's like a real different beat."

I declined to go, though I wished in later years that I'd accepted their invitation.

Winter still hung around, and summer holiday plans clamoured to be made. A couple of friends invited me to go with them to visit Lake Lucerne, but Mum would have none of it. In the end I settled on the Isle of Wight, off the coast of southern England. I'd never been there before, and it had to be sunnier than Liverpool. Also it was a Christian Endeavour Holiday Home. I'd visited a couple of others for holidays and always had fun with a group of young people who attended these resorts, although they were well chaperoned. That made it 'safe' as far as Mum was concerned.

"Why don't you take Jean with you?" she suggested, possibly having premonitions that Brian might come up with his own ideas.

"Sure," I agreed readily. "Would you like to come?" Jean thought it was a super idea, and I filled in the forms.

After sending in the form that cold January night I had a vivid dream. I found myself dawdling along a narrow road with some of my work friends until we arrived at a small footpath on the right, winding uphill with hedgerows each side. I left my friends, and with curiosity climbed up the dirt path to the top. There on the right stood a small church. I passed through the swing gate, pushed open the oak church door and entered the coolness of the sanctuary. A small altar with a plain gold cross brought my focus to the centre. About eight pews filled the church, with a side aisle leading to the front. I knelt down for a few minutes in a front pew then arose, trod softly back down the aisle, and out through the church door again, which I closed behind me. I crunched up the path, stopped at the gate and drew in my breath. Unfolding before me, stretched a wonderful vista of trees, fields and in the distance a sparkling blue band of water, almost blending in with the clear, guileless vaulted sky.

Still absorbed in the beauty, I woke up.

I was always happy to babysit for the vicar and his wife. This particular Friday evening they both returned early and as I put on my coat the phone rang. Reverend Dunsby called out, "Wait, Joyce. Don't go yet." He came out of his study and placed his hand on my arm. "That was your mum who just called. You need to go straight to your grandmother's house." He stopped.

I took a quick breath. Something was wrong.

"I'm so sorry to tell you that your grandfather has just died."

I flew out, half stumbling, half running to get to Nana's and Poppa's house, only a few hundred yards down from the vicarage, my heart beating fast. Mum opened the door even as I pushed open the front gate.

"What were you doing there, babysitting?" she said. "You should have been at home where you belong." She spoke harshly. Although she knew where I had been, for some reason she didn't like me to do this service for them. But her staring face was worn with grief, and I understood her hard-sounding words.

Nana was crying into her handkerchief, seated at the kitchen table. The comforting teapot sat on the table, with two half-drunk cups of tea in the familiar blue and white china.

"May I see him?" I asked.

Mum nodded. "He's in the front bedroom. We're waiting for the undertakers to pick him up." She turned back to fill the kettle, to replenish the almost empty teapot.

I crept up the creaky stairs and into the front bedroom. A white sheet covered Poppa, and slowly I folded back the top. He lay in bed, his shock of silvered hair still combed back, mostly in place. He looked so peaceful with his eyes closed. It didn't seem possible he wasn't merely sleeping. Tenderly I bent down and kissed his cheek. He was cold, lifeless. Feeling numb, I sat on a nearby chair watching him, and remembering.

The image of Poppa with his legs twisted behind his neck suddenly sprang to mind, and tears flowed. I remembered his dry humour and the outings on Saturday mornings when he'd take me to his favourite pub where I'd enjoy a glass of lemonade. Then I heard his voice, "Now be careful, lass, I dinna want ye to fall off the bench", as he held on to my coat as a little girl, balancing on the back of the seat to see the trains. Or the times we'd inspect the green tomatoes, in the heavy, rich fragrance of the greenhouse. I closed my eyes and could see his toasty-warm kind eyes searching mine when I asked him a question, and how he'd commented about the Reverend David Sheppard. I smiled as I pondered the times he'd sneak me a drink of his tea in his saucer when I was too small to properly hold a cup, and Nana proclaimed, "Jim, that child is too young to drink tea!" And he would respond, "Och, get awa' with ye woman. It'll noo hurt the bairn". Sometimes I wondered how they ever managed to get along, but they did.

Now he was gone. Never again would I hear that rich Scots burr and the deep-throated chuckle when he was exasperated with Nana. Somehow it didn't seem real. It was more like a bad dream.

A car drew up, the headlights catching the bedroom window; the bang of a car door and then the rat-a-tat. That would be the funeral people to take his body. "Bye, bye, Poppa," I tried to whisper. Slowly I turned the sheet up again over his beloved face.

I offered to stay with Nana, at least until after the funeral, to help her with arrangements, for which she was grateful. It was decided that she would sleep in the spare room. "I can't face sleeping in the same bed," she anguished. "I will miss his cold feet on my legs." She blew her nose hard. I ran home to get my nightclothes, my sponge bag and a change of clothing along with my Bible. I rode my bike back up Rocky Lane to Nana's house.

After drinking several cups of tea, Mum turned to leave. Wanting to be by myself I excused myself, climbed the stairs, closed the door to the front bedroom behind me and pulled back the clean top sheet to get into the four poster double-bed with the hollow in the middle. I had no problem sleeping in the bed where Poppa had died. In fact it brought me comfort in some strange way.

In the street-light dimness of the bedroom, I pondered sadly. I wish I'd been there. Mum and Nana told me how he'd stared up at the ceiling as if he'd recognized someone. They told me they looked up too but saw nothing, and couldn't understand it. I glanced at the corner chair where Poppa always placed his clothes, and started. I could see him, pipe in mouth, wearing his familiar ginger-coloured tweedy jacket standing beside his chair. I wasn't frightened, but a little unnerved, then he was gone. *What is death? I* asked myself. *Is there really life after you die? How do we know? What actually happens to us? Is our life on earth all there is?* What I had learned in Sunday school and church, and even what I taught the five-year-olds, had vaporised now that I faced death in someone I loved so very much. I lay on my pillow struggling with my tears and my faith, wondering at what I had seen.

After several minutes and hardly daring to breath, I switched on the bedside lamp. My Bible lay on the stand and with a shaky hand I opened it at random. My eyes fell upon John's Gospel. "*You have believed because you have seen, Thomas, but how much more blessed are those who believe but have not seen.*" My head fell back on the pillow. I lifted up the book and read the whole story of Thomas. That had been written for me. Jesus had said those words just for me. I marvelled at their message. Peace stole over me. *Thank you,*

Lord Jesus. I thought for a moment or too, then added, *Thank you Poppa.* Then I fell into a dreamless sleep.

The harried life of work kept me busy during the day, and in the evening, I enjoyed the company of Tommy, or girlfriends. Sometimes we danced at the Floral Hall in Southport, if I stayed with my friend Jean, who now lived in Waterloo, a seaside resort some distance away. Other times she visited me, and we danced at a local hop. I longed for my summer holiday, and especially September when my new life in London would begin.

The fifth of July finally arrived. Jean and I, amidst excited hustle and bustle, caught the train to London, then another one to the southern coast, where we boarded the boat to Ryde on the Isle of Wight. Another bus ride took us to Ventnor and to St Rad's, as the Christian Endeavour holiday home was called. Early that evening, we sized up the other young people, including the two leaders, Gilbert and Des. I wrote in my diary that night regards these two males, "Not much!"

However, before dinner, we took an evening stroll, down along the cliffs, up a pathway, then wended our way along the narrow road back to St. Rad's. As I strolled with the others, a cold wave washed over me. "I've been here before," I whispered to Jean.

Her large brown eyes were sceptical. "No way," she retorted. "You've never been here before!"

"I'm going to come back after," I told her, all the while glancing to the right, waiting for the upward footpath to appear. There it was, with a sign attached to the stone wall and an arrow, "To the Church of St. Lawrence." With reluctance I followed the others back for dinner but immediately after, I rushed back along the road, my heart beating fast. As I climbed up the hill, there were hedgerows on each side exactly as before.

At the top, I halted. A lime-washed stone church stood sentinel, just like in my dream, except it lay on the left of the road, rather than the right. Trembling a little, I opened the latched gate, walked down the gravel path and pushed open the heavy wooden door. A sanctified coolness helped to ground me. Slowly I walked down the single aisle on the right towards the small central altar, again as in my dream. I knelt in wonderment and asked, "Lord, what does this mean? Is this significant?"

Eventually I reverently rose up and slowly moved to the door. Closing it quietly behind me, I gazed out to the anticipated glorious expanse spread out before me. Green trees, patchwork fields, and beyond, scintillating like diamonds in the evening sun, the stalwart English Channel which curled its edge out to the azure sky. At that moment I experienced a strong sense that what we call reality and time are not what they appear to be.

During the fortnight there Jean and I swam, swapped stories, eyed the males and thoroughly enjoyed ourselves. However, after the first few days, one of the leaders, Des, started conversations with me. I learned he was in theological college in Richmond, just outside London, studying to be a minister. My interest ratcheted upward slightly. Before long he held my hand on the evening walks. By the following week, he had proposed and arrangements were made for him to come to Liverpool to meet and Mum and Dad, before I set off for London. However, I wrote in my diary, *We must wait and see.* I made it clear, I wasn't ready for any commitment as images of

Roger and a broken engagement still rubbed raw in my memory.

The weeks passed and the romance progressed. He not only loved the Lord, he had even dedicated his life to become a minister. I was convinced that the winter dream had endorsed the relationship. Now I had an additional reason to anticipate my future in London.

CHAPTER 20

LESSONS TO BE LEARNED

As even, ere the sun was set, the sick, O Lord around Thee lay
Henry Twells, 1823-1900

The day arrived to leave home. "Bye Mum, bye Dad, bye Jean."
With some tears and sudden fears, I set off, suitcase in hand, for
London, specifically Letchmore Heath, where the Nurses'Training
Centre for St. Bartholomew's was located. Twenty-five or so of us
prospective nurses settled into our starchy uniforms, carefully-folded
caps and a rigorous curriculum. Again the challenge of learning
and succeeding stimulated my intellectual appetite. The navy capes,
lined with red wool, wrapped about us as we walked from
classrooms to sleeping areas. Once Desmond had returned to his
seminary in Richmond, just south of London, we met at Euston
Station and relished exploring London. In the middle of our
training, Desmond called me.

"You'll never guess where I'm assigned to preach in two weeks' time."

I had no idea. "I don't know. Tell me."

"I'm going to Aldenham."

"Really?" The Aldenham Methodist Chapel was close to our training centre and a number of us had gone there to worship a couple of times.

"I will be sure to go to the service," I assured him. In fact, a couple of the people there invited us trainee nurses to dinner on several occasions, which we all greatly enjoyed, so much so that they became highlights in the midst of our heavy studies. So to actually see Desmond in the pulpit preaching thrilled me. In addition, one of the families invited us both for dinner following the service.

Sunday arrived. I dressed carefully in my charcoal grey wool suit, with the pencil slim skirt, relieved with a rose coloured blouse. I slipped my feet into stiletto black leather shoes. I had to look my best! The worship service began. Desmond stood tall in the pulpit, distinguished in his clerical collar, and preached on 'Friendship'. Pride filled my being. People congratulated him on a fine sermon, and I swelled even more.

Soon we sat around the Simmonds' dinner table to a mouth-watering meal of roast beef, roast potatoes, peas, gravy, and the traditional Yorkshire pudding. Just as the apple pie and ice cream were served, the youngest boy of the family spoke up.

"Mummy, how come we only eat like this when the minister comes?" I stifled my laughter, and placed a reassuring hand on the arm of his embarrassed mother as she attempted to smooth over his too-honest comment.

"Please, don't tell him off. We all go to extra trouble when a visitor has dinner with us. We understand perfectly."

She smiled gratefully. After dinner, she ushered Desmond and me into the cosy front room by ourselves, whilst she took care of the dishes, "so you can have some time alone together." Her thoughtfulness impressed me warmly.

I continued to see Desmond on my days off, and we combed London on foot and by tube, climbing the steps up to the tower in St. Paul's, enjoying a quick lunch at the local Lyons, surveying the Thames from Westminster Bridge, and exploring the park at Richmond. The subject of marriage soon found its way in our conversation.

"I mentioned to Mam and Dad that we were probably going to get engaged at Christmas," he said, after returning from a weekend at home.

I didn't answer for a minute or so. Once again, I vacillated, trying to sort out my feelings. I reasoned Desmond was exactly the kind of man I'd always dreamed of marrying; moreover, he was Christian and had given his life to serve God. As a minister's wife, I'd be a helpmate; one who could serve alongside him. I thought of the dream I'd had, surely a sign that this was meant to be. He even shared the fact that he hoped to be a missionary. The corner piece of the puzzle appeared to fit perfectly.

I gazed at him fondly. "Yes, of course I'll marry you." The decision was made. Happiness cascaded through us as we walked the streets of London hand in hand.

My training concluded and I felt pleased with attaining high marks in my exams. Now actual nursing commenced. My assignment was to the Ear, Nose and Throat Ward at the St Albans branch of Barts. Sister Smith, who was a favourite instructor at Letchmore Heath, had transferred to be Sister of our ward. Apprehension and trepidation, mingled with excitement, was spun into the daily duties of those first few days.

Taking temperatures was a task assigned probationer nurses. Tentatively I tucked the thermometer under the patient's arm, in the first bed in the Men's Ward. I felt the pulse – normal.

The patient in the next bed beckoned me. "Nurse, can you fix my pillow?"

I hastened over, to be as helpful as possible. The pillow was plumped, then I turned back to take the thermometer, anticipating the usual 98.4. I gazed in horror at the reading; 112 degrees.

"I've got to show Sister" I exclaimed, convinced the man was about to die. The patient grabbed my apron.

"Nurse, come on back," he laughed. "Don't get your knickers in a twist. We do this to all the new probationers." The man who'd wanted his pillow fluffed lay back, holding his belly in laughter. I stared at him, bewildered. "What's going on?" I demanded, looking from one to the other.

The patient brought out a dead match beside the bed. "We always light a match and put the thermometer over it," he explained between guffaws. "We get them every time!"

I wrote down a 98.4 on the chart and hustled away, embarrassed.

The following day, I noticed that one of the patients, a Mr Moore, had a 'bed bath' assigned on his chart. I took a deep breath as I pulled the screens around the bed. A bowl of warm water was placed on the stand and I set out the required two facecloths alongside the towel on the bed, one for the face, the other for the genitals. I washed the upper body, legs and feet, then hesitated.

"Don't forget the rest of me," he ordered.

Taking a deep breath, I pulled back the blanket further down and hesitantly moved his hospital gown further up. I'd never viewed a naked man before. The nearest had been clinical diagrams on a chart. I tried to look elsewhere as I rinsed out the flannel. Carefully, I moved his manly parts around to wash underneath, feeling sweat running down my neck.

"You've missed a place," he said pointing downwards.

I didn't think I had, but who was I to argue? My face burned. "There, that's it," I said briskly, as I pulled the gown down and the blanket up.

"Will you give me another bed bath tomorrow, nurse?" He grinned wickedly, a front tooth missing.

"Someone else will probably be assigned," I informed him primly, and took off for the sluice room as fast as my legs could go without running. There I took a couple of deep breaths and splashed some cold water on my face. Then, despite myself, I grinned, remembering my Nana's refrain yet again, *those damn men!*

The male patients were all good sports, and as Christmas came, they clubbed together and bought each of us nurses on the ward a small gift. Christmas Eve held excitement as Sister helped us drape the ward with decorations, and put up a Christmas tree that stood watch in the corner resplendent with multi-coloured paper chains. A star on top completed the picture.

Jackie, my fellow probationer and I, scurried around to complete our chores. Bandages boiled on the stove, as we washed dishes left by the kitchen staff, who disappeared early after imbibing too much sherry. At half-past eight that evening, with our chores done, we searched for Sister Smith to be dismissed, knowing that at half-past seven the next morning, we'd have a long day ahead of us, as all the nurses were expected to work Christmas Day, a thirteen-hour shift, to keep the patients company and the children, especially those without family.

"Have you seen Sister?" I asked Jackie.

"No" she replied. "I'm so tired, I don't think I even have the energy to go to the party tonight."

"I know what you mean," I agreed, dragging one black laced-up shoed foot in front of the other.

"Where can she be?" Irritation welled up. "She must be here somewhere."

We searched all the side wards and the sluice rooms. "Well, that's it. I'm going," declared Jackie.

"Me too. She must have left and not realized we were still here."

Slowly we made our way through the ward, passing the attached Children's Wing, where half a dozen children lay quietly sleeping, dreaming possibly of Father Christmas, then into the hallway leading into the main corridor. The kitchen lay on our left now clean and dark, and the nurses' room, where one could have a cig or sandwich during one's break lay on the right, the door closed.

"We should have cleaned the nurses' room," I reminded Jackie with a grimace.

"I'm just too tired," came her response

"Me too. I'll take a quick look."

I opened the door. There on her hands and knees knelt Sister Smith, scrubbing brush in hand, soap suds skimming the sad, worn linoleum. Embarrassed, we fidgeted and looked down at her, not knowing what to say.

She sat back on her heels and smiled warmly. "That's all right nurses. It's Christmas Eve. You've had a long day, and you'll have an even longer day tomorrow. You go and have some fun at the party. I'll take care of the floor here. Off you go."

I hesitated, still unsure.

"Go on, go ahead." Sister waved her scrubbing brush, then bent back down again to the soapy foam.

I closed the door silently. There wasn't anything to say.

"Well, I'm off." Jackie turned right in the hallway and trod down the nearby stairs.

For a few moments more, I stood, unsure what to do. Should I go back and apologise, or offer to help? Then faintly from down the hallway between the wards drifted the sound of carols. Flickering torch lights lit the way in the darkened corridor as white figures wrapped in red cloaks processed solemnly towards our ward. Their voices rang clearer, "*Once in Royal David's City, in a lowly cattle shed, where a mother laid her baby, In a manger for his bed...*"

Tears sprang to my eyes and rolled down my cheeks. Jesus had lain in a cattle trough, He had come down to earth for me, and I couldn't even check the nurses' room. Sister, the most important person in the ward, had stooped to clean the messy floor.

That Christmas Eve, God showed me the gift called humility. As I wrapped my navy woollen cape, lined with brilliant red, closer to myself when facing the biting air, on my way to our dormitory, the warmth of that lesson caught hold in my heart.

CHAPTER 21

WEDDING BELLS (1960)

Unless you build it, Father, the house is built in vain
John Ellerton 1826–1893

The damp from the river and the wintry mix caused us to huddle as we meandered along the walkway flanking the River Trent in Nottingham. New Year's Eve 1958 promised to be an evening to remember. Desmond slipped an engagement ring on my finger and I gave him a gold signet ring. Once the ring exchange had taken place, we pulled our gloves back over our chilled hands, then scuttled back into the city to catch the bus to his parents' home and a warm fire.

His mother and father had greeted me warmly as we met for the first time that afternoon. When we arrived back shivering, excited and engaged, they congratulated us, and told us both that they had planned a celebratory outing on New Year's Day at The Grange, a rather posh restaurant. Asparagus was served, the first time I'd ever tasted it, and roasted duckling. His parents raised their sherry glasses. "Congratulations to you both."

We gazed deeply at each other, basking in our unfolding love for each other. Then the next day I returned to London.

Unfortunately, a déjà vu situation circled back on me. St Bartholomew's, along with other prestigious hospitals in London, had a ruling. Only single women were employed as nurses. Once a nurse married, she lost her job in that hospital. Anyone who became engaged brought forth an ultimatum: "Either you make a commitment to stay four years, or you leave now!"

The dilemma caused some sleepless nights. I talked it out.

OK, Lord. You brought Desmond and me together. We plan to be married next year, and that means I will have to leave nursing. If I stay and complete my four years, Desmond will be off some place, possibly overseas in missionary work, and I'll be still here. Is that what I am meant to do?

God didn't say anything particular. So I played out the situation a little more, to help Him along.

You know I want to go to Selly Oak for the missionary training with him, after we are married, which means we will go overseas the year after next.

I stayed quiet for a few moments. I had to be honest with myself.

I know, I know, Lord. Of course I'm going to go with him, and I'll leave nursing. In my heart, I realised, I'd already made up my mind. Besides, nursing wasn't the passion I thought it might be. It was only second best.

"Of course, it's the right decision," Desmond assured me. "You'll easily find a job in London as a shorthand typist and I know Miss Porter at Methodist International House, who will help you find a place to live."

He was proved right. I began almost immediately as a shorthand typist at the Royal Exchange Insurance Company, in the well-known London landmark by the same name. I eventually found a bed-sitter, hidden in a basement in Queensborough Terrace in London's West End. New friends were made, and with Desmond as my fiancé, life shone with a golden glow.

My bed-sitter consisted of a small room, about sixteen feet in either direction, with a single bed, a chest of drawers and a small washbasin, along with a card-size table, two upright chairs, and one faded and scratched semi-armchair. A gas ring sat on a small asbestos mat to provide fuel for cooking, whilst a gas fire popped its heat for warmth. An important meter-slot for shilling coins lay embedded into the wall close to the fire. Shillings became a precious commodity, for these fed the gas into the ring for hot soup as well as the fireplace to counteract the dull cold that seeped in through the window high in the wall. A toilet was next door, also used by the family that owned the establishment, and two bathrooms were situated at the top of the stairs on the first floor, offering weekly baths for all the tenants.

I met Bronja Nissenbaum, who lived on the third floor, while volunteering at the Methodist International House. She introduced me to creative cooking, war stories about the German underground and spiritual reading. As the months passed, her friendship grew to be a warm and compassionate mainstay of my life in London, and beyond.

"Joyce, you must read *A Private House of Prayer* by Leslie Weatherhead," she announced one day in her brusque, slightly accented English. "It is just what you need." She sported short wiry curly hair and had a slightly stocky figure, but her eyes caught my attention. They were brown, wide and penetrating, and I knew she was someone I had to be honest with as well as a friend I could trust.

I glanced over the book she handed me, then read it some more that evening in my small domain. The devotional led me through readings for each day covering a whole month. Weatherhead's prayers, and above all his poetry, caught the attention of my soul:

Said the robin to the sparrow
I should really like to know
Why these human beings
Rush about and hurry so.
Said the sparrow to the robin,
I think that it must be,
That they have no Heavenly Father
Such as cares for you and me.
("Overheard in an Orchard" by Elizabeth Cheney)

Bronja introduced me to another close friend of hers called Frances Petch, or 'Petch' for short. Bronja brimmed over with energy and mischief, whereas tall, willowy Francis exuded refinement, right down to the grey-streaked russet bun she wound neatly into the nape of her neck. Francis also volunteered at Methodist International House and had been a good friend from childhood of Miss Porter, also fondly called 'Aunty Hilda', the founder and manager of the hostel, and a former missionary to China. Of course I introduced Desmond and Bronja to each other, and a couple of times when I smuggled Desmond into my room the night before we were to spend a day out together, or he had missed the last tube train to college, Bronja made room for me. I would have lost my bed-sitter if the landlady had caught any man in my room after eleven o'clock at night.

Desmond and I continued to delight in the hidden gems of London, savouring the history, the sights, sounds, and even smells of the city. On Sunday mornings, when he wasn't preaching, we attended City Temple, to listen to Rev. Leslie Weatherhead or Martin Lloyd Jones at Westminster Chapel. On occasions we visited All Souls to hear Rev. John Stott. A regular stopping place became Hyde Park Corner to enjoy observing Rev. Donald Soper deflect the hecklers. He made impassioned pleas for the impoverished, later taking his cause before important Members of Parliament.

One Sunday afternoon, while basking in the late autumn sunshine in Kensington Gardens, Desmond said to me, "We had Len Tudor come and speak to us from Home Missions." He squeezed my hand. "He spoke about the Shetland Islands and how they need ministers to go there." He waited.

"Who would ever want to go there!" I exclaimed. "It's miles from anywhere. Isn't that where the Shetland ponies come from?"

He gave a quick laugh. "Yes, and not only that, but any minister who goes there has to be married. No single men are allowed, and they have to stay at least three years."

"Good luck to them. The powers that be probably don't trust them with the local lassies up there!" I gave a short laugh.

"Oh, no. It isn't like that," he assured me, his face serious. "You see it can be pretty lonely, so being married helps the minister to have a helpmate for company."

I muttered half to myself, "Same thing!" but covered my tracks by adding, "Anyway, we are going to Selly Oak next year, and then to the mission field, overseas. So our future is settled."

I thought no more about it until a few months later when Desmond, with obvious disappointment, told me, "I was told today, that because of my age, I'm to complete my three years' probationary period in the UK. The overseas mission people feel I need to be older than twenty-three before going for training and overseas."

This was a bitter blow. "You mean we have to wait three years, until you are fully ordained, before we can even go for training?" I wanted to be sure I heard aright.

He nodded. "I'm afraid so."

We walked on in silence, each with our own thoughts as we attempted to grapple with this disappointment. I had been so certain that God had it all arranged, and now this. I shook my head. Even though I thought I knew God's will, it appeared I didn't. A niggling suspicion slid into my consciousness. Could it be that even 'good' plans we dreamed of to serve God weren't always fulfilled? But why not? We didn't say too much more about it.

A day or two later, I read in the book Bronja had loaned me, "Streams in the Desert" by Mrs Chas. Cowman, and the following verse:

> *I'll stay where You've put me; I will, dear Lord,*
> *Though I wanted so badly to go;*
> *I was eager to march with the 'rank and file,'*
> *Yes, I wanted to lead them, You know.*
> *I planned to keep step to the music loud,*
> *To cheer when the banner unfurled,*
> *To stand in the midst of the fight straight and proud,*
> *But I'll stay where You've put me.*

In the meantime our wedding plans unfolded. The eighteenth of June 1960, coinciding with the commemoration of the Battle of Waterloo, became the chosen date for our wedding, and the flurry of excitement overcame somewhat the disappointment of being turned down for missionary work.

In the meantime I continued pounding my typewriter at the Royal Exchange, and often visited Bronja upstairs. One evening over a creative meal of mince, potatoes and green beans, all cooked over her gas ring, I plucked up courage to ask, "Bronja, I know you were in the German Resistance. Can you tell me anything about it?"

She laid her fork down and threw her head back and laughed. "That Hitler!" she declared. "I'd have done anything to get rid of him." She pondered for a moment, then began her incredible story. "I'm a fully-qualified nurse, so I met a number of high-ranking officers both in the hospital and outside." Her accent grew more pronounced. "I was pretty attractive then, with a good figure, so I used my assets to get secrets out of them."

My eyebrows raised, wondering, had she really...?

She chuckled at my expression. *"Nein, nein."* She shook her head. "I would never give any Nazi officer the satisfaction of having my body." She gave me a quick glance and continued, "I'd play them up. We'd go out, and have a good time, then back to their flat. Of course, they expected one thing. We'd have a few drinks, though I always made one last all evening, but I'd make sure my beau, so called, was plied with plenty. Then he'd start talking. I'd flatter him, pretend ignorance, then he'd pull me towards the bed. We'd get undressed. Then I'd slip a mickey into his drink beside the bed, making sure he finished it before actually getting under the sheets. I'd get more secrets out of him, and prolong the lovemaking until he fell under the drug." She laughed a deep belly laugh. "Then I'd slip out of bed, leave him a note thanking him for being a wonderful lover, knowing he'd never remember otherwise, get dressed, and get in contact with my British counterpart, passing on whatever I'd learned."

"Gosh!" I responded, awestruck with her audacity and courage. "You never got caught?"

"No no. I got out before that happened." She took a deep breath. "Now how about those custard tarts you brought up for our sweet?" The subject was closed.

Sometime much later, in fact several years later, Frances shared with me the fact that the Gestapo had wanted Bronja, and she had been smuggled out of Germany with a high price on her head. I was thankful that God had spared her and brought the richness of her friendship into my life.

Mum promised to sew my wedding dress for me, so on a trip home to Liverpool one weekend we made our way to Blacklers, in downtown Liverpool. The store displayed its merchandise in the same old warehouse it had taken over after being bombed out during the war. I found an off-white flocked satin material, keeping in mind my mother's admonishment that I should never wear pure white, and found a simple princess-style pattern with a sweetheart neck. A coronet of imitation orange blossom and a waist-length veil completed the outfit, except for a pair of white stiletto shoes.

On the way back we bumped into a neighbour getting off the number forty bus.

"Oh, I see you've been busy shopping at Blacklers," nosed the neighbour.

"Yes, Joyce is getting married in a few months," Mum informed her.

"Oh, really!" The neighbour's interest perked up her plain features. "And who is the lucky young man, and what does he do?"

Mum immediately answered, "He's a parson."

There was a brief silence. "Oh dear. I'm so sorry to hear that," then seeing my face, she hastily added, "but I am sure there are some very nice ones around."

"Yes, there are, and he is one," I righted her decidedly. She bustled away, head down, whilst Mum popped into the corner newsagent's to buy a block of Lyons Cornish ice cream, now our favourite, then we turned to hurry down Thomas Lane back home for a cup of tea, to indulge in ice cream and to delight in my wedding purchases.

A week or so before the Christmas prior to our marriage, Desmond knocked on my bedsit door.

"What are you doing here?" I asked, surprised.

He came in and closed the door. "Guess what?" He smiled delightedly. "We're going to the Shetland Islands."

"We're WHAT?"

"Yes, I thought seeing we couldn't go overseas, I'd volunteer for us to go there instead. They only take volunteers you know."

I sank into the armchair, flabbergasted. "But, why didn't you ask me first?"

"I just thought that because I wanted to go, you would too."

A fast somersault spun within me. This was what he wanted, but did I have any choice? Is this how it works when you're married to a minister? It wasn't quite what I had envisaged.

I glanced at his crestfallen face.

"I could go back and tell them you don't want to go." He stopped, waiting.

I thought further. That might be quite an adventure. It would certainly be different. After a few moments I nonchalantly replied, "No, no, don't do that. Let's talk some more more about it."

The more we discussed it, the more interested I became. Soon we were told we'd been assigned to live in Scalloway, a village of eight hundred inhabitants on the west coast of the main island of Zetland. His appointment to three churches would begin on September first, two a half months after our wedding.

Desmond's parents were meeting my mum and dad for the first time that Christmas, and on Christmas Day we made the announcement.

"Guess what. We have something to tell you," said Desmond. I glanced at Mum and guessed immediately what had sprung into her mind. I patted my flat tummy with a clear conscience. He continued, "We've been assigned to the Shetland Islands, and that is where we'll be going on 1st September." I sat beside him, beaming.

Dead silence ensued, then his dad spoke up, "Well, it'll be a good chance to visit Shetland, won't it?" The ice was broken, though I sensed Mum was not happy. In her dismay, and wanting Christmas dinner to be perfect, she stumbled as she brought the custard out of the oven where it had been placed to keep warm, ready to accompany the rich plum pudding. Right over the matted rug it streamed.

"Oh, no," she cried. "What can we do now?"

"Never fear Mum," I said, as I gathered a nearby spoon and began scooping up the custard off the floor.

"That's the pea spoon," she whispered hoarsely.

"They won't know the difference," I assured her. "It will mix in with the plum pudding and they'll think it's a raisin, if they find a pea!"

And it worked. Everyone complimented her on the wonderful Christmas pud and the creamy custard, whilst we didn't enlighten anyone.

The wedding day arrived. Sunlight streamed in between the heavy drapes, sending shafts of dusty motes on to the faded carpet. My wedding dress, complete and beautiful, hung on the curtain rail. Mum had even sewn in the silver threepenny piece Poppa had given me that he'd found in the Christmas pudding when I was little.

Suddenly I panicked. What on earth was I doing? A sense of urgency to run and run and run seized me. *Breathe deep Joyce,* I told myself. *You can't run away now. It's only wedding nerves.*

A couple of deep breaths steadied me slightly. I tumbled out of bed and knelt beside it. A book of prayers by William Barclay lay on my bedside table and I turned to the reading for the day. Immediately the soothing words calmed my trembling nerves, and a semblance of peace enabled me to rise from my knees and meet the day.

That afternoon, resplendent in my wedding attire, I walked down the aisle of my home church of St David's, holding tight to Dad's arm. Desmond, tall and slim in his new charcoal grey suit and sporting a crisp new clerical collar with a peace rose boutonnière, stood waiting until I reached his side.

The service began, "Dearly beloved..." Prayers and promises followed the ancient ritual and then the final hymn rang out.

We sang, *O Father all creating, Whose wisdom love and power....*
Then the organ led us heavenward with the last verse:

> *Unless you build it, Father,*
> *The house is built in vain;*
> *Unless you, Saviour, bless it,*
> *The joy will turn to pain.*
> *But nothing breaks a marriage*
> *Of hearts in you made one;*
> *The love your Spirit hallows*
> *Is endless love begun.*
> (John Ellerton 1826 – 1893)

The words winged through my being: *Unless you build it, Father, the house is built in vain: Unless you, Saviour, bless it the joy will turn to pain.* The melody died away, but the words lingered.

The wedding breakfast proceeded beautifully at the Mansion House at Calderstones Park. As I proudly showed off my gold wedding band, any lurking doubts melted away in the brilliant sunshine. Then Dad's car, with the tin cans tied on the back fender, stood ready for us.

One last task lay before me. On our way to Lime Street railway station to begin our honeymoon in Somerset, with the tins rattling and bumping behind us, I asked Dad, who was driving us, to stop the car outside the Home for Indigent Women. In my powder blue going-away suit with matching hat and white stiletto heels, I knocked at the main door. A nurse in the traditional deep blue and white starched uniform motioned me in, and on a wooden table in the now empty room, I left my fragrant wedding bouquet of pink-tinged yellow peace roses with a note, "For Ivy, with love, Joyce." Then I walked back to the car, smiled happily at my new husband, and we were on our way to married bliss.

Almost fifty years later, in Maine, while attending an Episcopal church called St. David's, I met one of the former students who had stayed at Methodist International House in London during the two years that I volunteered there. Although we had never formally met, we shared happenings and tales of Miss Porter and Francis Petch that brought back many fond memories and much laughter. And a new friendship was formed.

CHAPTER 22

WELCOME TO SHETLAND

Eternal Father strong to save; whose arm doth bind the restless wave
William Whiting, 1825-1878

The St Ninian rose and fell as the slapping waves of the North Sea hit the bow. Except for a brief stop-over in Kirkwall, in the Orkney Isles, we'd suffered twenty-eight hours of constant rocking. I walked lopsidedly from the bunks downstairs to the outer deck, only to hold my stomach and then watch my new spouse throwing up over the side of the rails, whilst white-caps coated the heaving waves. Pewter wind whipped skies swept over the sullen sea.

At last we sighted the main island of Zetland in the distance. Seagulls cried their screeching welcome overhead as rain splattered the deck. Slowly, murky hills merged into the grey washed sea. Bare land, bereft of trees, passed us on the left, and small fishing boats, securely moored in Lerwick Harbour, rode the wake from the ship. The slightly calmer waters soothed my churning stomach.

I watched in silence. Then I spied something. "Look," I cried. "The houses, by the water. Why is that opening like a garage built right into the water?"

"Aye, tis so, lass," gurgled a hearty Shetlander at my side, leaning nonchalantly on the rail. "They be logberries built there, so the fishing boat can be brought up to yon house and placed underneath in a muckle storm. Just like some folks have garages for their cars."

"Oh, I see," I responded, but didn't really. Desmond, still pasty-faced, said nothing. As we drew into the quayside, the houses, grey granite, sturdy and stern, blended into the hills, sea and sky. Then I noticed people scurrying about on the landing. With a couple of bumps, we arrived in the Shetland Islands.

"Ahoy there!" Someone shouted and waved their arms from terra firma as the gangway was lowered. We waved back, in case it was meant for us. Desmond disappeared to drag our suitcase up the stairs, and together we trod carefully down the slatted gangway, holding tightly to the rope at the side, our legs still shaky.

Desmond, in his clerical collar, stood out. The man who'd waved came over to us, a broad grin creasing his face. "Hullo there. I'm Johnny Mac, and this be Lowery, and here is John T. Just so everyone kens the difference between him and me. And then, here be Jim Duncan. He'll be bringing ye fresh fish."

Desmond managed to smile, somewhat weakly, "How do you do. So nice to meet you." We shook hands all round.

Darkness began lowering its cloak as we were hustled into a car, whilst the rest bundled into a small truck. As we drove the outer road, leading around and between the darkening hills, the vehicle braked occasionally for a wandering sheep, anxious to gather with the flock before night fell completely. "Look ye now, there." Johnny Mac pointed down the hill to a small broken-down castle, perched near a harbour. "That there be where yon Earl Fitzpatrick lived. Ah, that was one mean body. And, it's said, it's haunted." His voice dropped. Then he coughed. "We'll share the tale another time, ye ken. That there island," he pointed toward the blowing waves. "That be Trondra. That keeps Scalloway safe from the worst of the storms."

We dropped down the hill, passed small squat stone cottages blinking warm lights from windows, then along Houl Road and up Manse Lane to the manse, our home for the next three years in the small town of Scalloway, its eight hundred souls in solid homes huddled about the harbour. With still unsteady legs, we trod two steps down into the pathway and through the back door. This led into a narrow hallway, encompassing a kitchen, with an indentation for an ancient electric stove, a wash boiler, sink, and a small narrow table. We walked past a bedroom on the left and into the living room.

As we entered, seven or eight women rose in unison. My heart sank. All I wanted to do was have a cup of tea and go to bed. But I smiled.

"Welcome, lass. Welcome Reverend. Come ye yourselves and get warm." Meg, wife of Jack Moore, one of the many men who'd met us, spoke. "Ye must be besides yourselves after that journey. Come along and sit yeself down. We have some hot tatties and neeps and reested mutton, all ready for ye." I learned quickly that this meant potatoes, turnips and dried sheep meat, soaked and cooked.

"Aye, come and sit down." Someone called Jessie invited me to sit beside her, and gave me a sympathetic smile. "Yon minister doesna look too good," she whispered to me with a wink.

Feeling more at ease, I explained. "Yes, I'm afraid he was seasick."

"Och, he'll soon get used to it," she reassured me, "Especially once he gets his sea legs riding the *Tirick* to and fro to Burra Isle."

Somehow we made it through the small talk, until the women and men began to disperse. I longed for bed and sleep. On her way out, Meg stopped. "I'll call on ye at half-past eight in the morning," she said, "And be sure ye mind yon milk pail." She pointed to a metal can with lid on the small table in the kitchen.

I nodded. The back door closed.

"Bed!" exclaimed Desmond with a loud yawn as the coal fire burned low in the grate.

We entered the main bedroom, off the living room, and found the double bed already made up for us. Someone had loaned us sheets and blankets until ours were unpacked. One square, wooden tea chest stood in the corner containing all our worldly goods. Fortunately all Methodist manses in the United Kingdom were furnished, so that was a help.

Stumbling around we found our nightwear, and rolled into bed, immediately falling into a deep sleep.

Suddenly jolted, I grabbed Desmond's arm and whispered, "Who's that on our roof?"

"Shush," came his reply.

Silent, shaking with fear, we heard the clumping of heavy boots on the black tarred roof of our house. "Who can it be?" My voice quaked.

Faint moonlight cracked through the curtains at the top, the wind having pushed the rain back out to sea.

"Maybe you should go outside and see," I suggested with a gulp.

"No chance! I'm not going out there. Who knows what might be going on?"

No street lights shone reassuringly into our bedroom window, only silvered darkness.

"What if he comes through the roof?"

"Shush, be quiet," was his reply.

After a while, the clumping around ceased, without any boot appearing through our ceiling, and with pounding hearts we lay back down in silence, sleep having been banished. What place had we come to? I knew that there was no television, and electricity was found only in the few main villages on Zetland. The islands were 180 miles north of Aberdeen, and I'd read somewhere that people still believed in trolls in the rural areas and remote islands. But someone clumping around in boots on one's roof in the middle of the night… it was beyond my imagination.

Eventually, we both fell back to sleep, instinctively holding on to each other, until daylight streamed in. I looked at the time – eight o'clock!

"Wake up, wake up!" I urged Desmond. "They are coming for me in half an hour so I can find out where to get the milk." I jumped out of bed, as Desmond sleepily rubbed his eyes. I scampered into the bathroom, splashed cold water on my face and threw on the clothes I'd worn the previous day.

Just before eight-thirty, there was a rap at the back door. I groaned at the sink full of dirty dishes from the night before, but caught hold of the wire handle of my milk pail, and managed a sincere smile as I opened the door.

Meg and her sister Nell stood there, their pails swinging slightly.

"Och, I see ye're up and aboot," said Nell brightly. "We'll show ye the milk shop, and also the bread shop. Maggie runs that and she's a good chapel-goer."

"Thank you. That will really help me a lot," I replied, making sure I'd remembered to put my purse in my pocket. I had. That was a relief!

We walked briskly down Houl Road as my companions stopped to greet other shoppers along the way and introduced me as 'yon new minister's wife', then past the small grey weather-beaten chapel into the main street, where a few shops straggled the winding road that led down to the quayside. "Here, now is where Jamie sells the milk," said Meg, turning into a small shop. In front of us stood a broad man with a ruddy face and wide smile, sporting a large white apron.

"Well noo," he said, "Ye must be yon new minister's wife."

I smiled and nodded my head.

"Welcome to Shetland, lass," he said. "And noo, you'll be wanting yer milk."

"Yes, please," I handed up my pail.

Taking a large ladle he dipped it into an outsize silver metal churn and poured a couple of ladlefuls of insipid-looking milk into my pail. "That'll be fivepence," he said.

I handed him sixpence and he gave me a penny change.

By happenstance my hand brushed the outside of the pail. "Oh my goodness, this milk is warm!" I exclaimed. "It isn't even cold," as I placed my hand around the curved surface.

Jamie Jamieson smiled again and leaned forward. "Och, of course it's warm, lass. This milk is straight from the coos. We don't go for modern new-fangled machinery here!"

"You mean it isn't pasteurized?" I was horrorstruck.

"Nah, nah," interrupted Nell, "We dinna go for such things here in Shetland."

I said no more, but my perturbation diluted my new enthusiasm. I waited for Meg and Nell to get their milk and we crossed the road to the bread shop.

"This here is Maggie." Meg introduced me to a tall silver-haired woman, dressed completely in black, including her pinny and headscarf.

"Ah, ye must be Mistress Parker, yon minister's wife," she said with a smile.

"Yes. It is so nice to meet you," I replied shaking her hand.

After a quick visit to the local grocer's we made our way back, with Meg instructing me to wash my pail thoroughly before I took it back down to the milk shop. They left me at the gate as I walked into the house to recount my morning happenings to Desmond. I found him at the small wooden table against the wall in the kitchen, drinking a cup of tea. One of the neighbours had left us a cup of milk from the night before, and he'd found some tea in the walk-in cupboard alongside the table.

"Well, I bought some cornflakes and some other groceries," I said, spilling out the contents from the cloth bag Meg had loaned me. "And wait until you hear about the milk!"

"Wait until I tell you about the toilet," he rejoined quickly. "However, I'm hungry, believe it or not," he said with a grin. "Never thought I'd want to eat again after that voyage." He poured some cornflakes into a dish and then topped them with fresh milk from the warm pail." He pushed a generous spoonful into his mouth, then gagged.

"Whatever is the matter?" I asked. "Are you all right?"

"This milk," he spluttered. "It's awful!"

I bent my head to smell the white contents. "It does smell a little funny," I agreed. "But it is fresh from the cows, according to Jamie."

"I don't care" he said, taking a swallow of tea to mask the taste.

I tried just a little. It was almost fishy in flavour. "Maybe if I boil it, it will be better," I offered. Quickly I found a pan and placed it on the Calor gas burner on top of the large zinc boiler in the corner of the kitchen (a large tub for boiling clothes). That would be quicker than trying to boil it on the rusted antiquated electric stove. I boiled the milk, thinking to make a custard sauce, then place the rest in a clean milk jug, covered over with a cloth, ready to leave on a shelf in the same cupboard, that served as a larder and hideaway for every other utensil, food items and cleaning supplies. However, the milk, to my horror, separated.

"It's useless," I cried. "Look at it!"

"Desmond leaned over my shoulder. "This is a rum deal, isn't it?"

"I know. I'll go down to the corner grocery shop and buy a couple of tins of evaporated milk." I threw on my coat and ran down Manse Lane to the corner, where I purchased two large tins of evaporated milk.

"How will I tell Meg I'm not buying the local milk?" I asked Desmond later.

"Oh, just make some excuse. You'll think of something."

We both laughed. That helped.

"Now," he said, after we'd made another pot of tea, "read this note." He handed me a piece of paper from an envelope on which was written, 'Rev. Parker' then sat back to watch my expression.

I read it out loud. "Dear New Minister and Wife, Please be

careful with the toilet in the bathroom [a lean-to leading off from the narrow entrance]. One of the previous ministers added the bathroom before I came. However, when you pull the chain, stand back, as the tank tumbled down once when I pulled too hard. We thought you would want to know. Good luck." It was signed 'Rev. Bowes.'

"I can't believe it!" I exclaimed. "What else are we going to find out?" However, I always made sure to stand well back whenever the chain was pulled after that. Fortunately the tank stayed in place, but we likewise forewarned the minister who eventually followed us.

That afternoon Jessie called us on the telephone. "How would ye both like to come out on my boat and see Scalloway from the harbour?" she offered.

"We'd love to," I responded immediately.

Arrangements were made and she planned to pick us up the following afternoon. The day was chilly, so I dug out a pair of warm tartan trews, a jumper and windcheater, along with my usual war paint - lipstick, eyeliner and eye shadow. With sturdy walking shoes on my feet, and a husband bundled up likewise beside me, we walked down Manse Lane toward the dock to meet Jessie. She stood on the dockside holding a rope to a small row boat.

"Come," she said, "I'll help ye get into the boat. Careful ye dinna fall overboard." We all laughed, me somewhat nervously. That water gleamed cold and choppy.

Desmond and I sat side by side on a narrow board while Jessie pulled the oars, her dark curly hair blowing in the wind. Her bright cornflower-blue eyes sparkled full of laughter as she pointed out various landmarks.

"Now, see over yon. Trondra used have folks there, but now it's just sheep. See up on yon bank? That's where I live. There are a couple of old wartime army huts left there that's been made into homes. Ye must a come and visit me."

Our heads twisted this way and that taking in the snippets of information and the austere yet timeless scene of a village, hugging the heathered hills, standing up bravely to storms and gales over the centuries. She pointed out small brown animals moving around the hills, along with sheep. These were Shetland ponies, allowed to run wild, then rounded up once a year. Those likely to fetch a good price were shipped to the mainland, and many over to America. Apparently their small size is an adaptation of nature to withstand the fierce gales, so they wouldn't get blown over, likewise the sheep with their shorter legs and thick fine wool.

"Aye, Scalloway used to be the capital of Shetland," Jessie continued, pulling hard on the oars. "Then Lerwick took it over. Only about twelve islands have people on them now. A peerie [little] bit of advice for ye. Never let a Shetlander hear that these islands are part of Scotland. Most trace their ancestors to Norway, for until the 1700s that is where they belonged. Then a king gave the islands as a dowry for his daughter when she married the king of Scotland."

I made a mental note to remember her advice.

She continued: "Now yon castle. It's no so very old, but Earl Fitzpatrick in the seventeen hundreds decided to build himself a big hoose. So he built yon castle. In order to build it he told every crofter to bring the whites of the eggs of their hens to bind the sand together to hold the bricks in place. One feisty ole wife refused, it is said, and the earl took her and hung her by a hook in the castle wall, and left her there to die." She paused, "And her ghost still walks, ye ken. Talking about ghosts, see yon hill, up there?" She pointed to a high hill above the manse. "That there is Witches Hill, where they used to burn those said to practise the art of magic. It's a bonnie view from the top, and there's nothing between that hill and America except the Atlantic Ocean."

I decided to climb it as soon as I had the opportunity.

She invited us back for a cup of hot tea and told us about her four children, two being in the navy, a daughter in grammar school, hoping to go to St Andrew's University, and Rob, a ten-year-old. "Ye'll get to meet him in Sunday school," she informed me. Her home was small, basic but warm from the peat-fired stove to the side of the room.

Somewhat hesitantly, I asked her about the fishy-flavoured milk.

She laughed. "Och, that farmer up country. He'll feed his coos fishmeal if there be no fresh grass or hay available." That explained it.

Thinking over the conversation on the way back home, I thought about what Jessie had said.

"Does that mean I've got to teach Sunday school? " I asked Desmond, as I slipped my hand into his. His lanky frame strode large steps and I walked quickly to keep up.

"It seems like it." He squeezed my hand reassuringly. "But you've had lots of practice already." He smiled.

"I know," I agreed, secretly pleased that I would soon have the chance to teach a group of children once again.

A day or two later, Sunday morning dawned clear with a stiff breeze off the sea. We walked down the road to the chapel. My heart was beating hard, hoping that Desmond would do a good job. He'd been running to the toilet ever since he tumbled out of bed. I hoped he wouldn't have to go in the middle of the service, as there was no bathroom on hand.

He preached on 'friendship,' which I'd heard at least three times before, but he knew it well. It was a good sermon, and I was proud as people congratulated him. The chapel itself seemed plain to me though and I missed the warmth of the candles, the cross on an altar and the comfort of the liturgy. The people were friendly enough, I thought, and then I overheard a conversation between a couple of older women.

"Humph, yon minister's wife comes here with her city ways," said one.

"I dinna think that she should wear breeches, neither should she paint her face, being married to yon minister and all." The second woman caught a glance from me and quickly turned away. I raised my head up a notch higher. *I'll show them,* I said to myself. *From now on, the first thing I'll do in the morning, after washing my face, is to put lipstick on.* And I did!

Another expectation was thrust upon me. "Ah, there ye be, Mistress Parker. I want to be sure ye ken that you'll be speakin' on Thursday night to the Methodist Women," another pleasant older woman, dressed in the ubiquitous black, informed me.

"Er, yes, or course," I answered, determined to please, yet quaking within.

At the manse over Sunday dinner, I shared my conversations, conducted and overheard after chapel that morning. Desmond chuckled at the paint and breeches piece.

"But what about speaking at the Women's Group?" I pleaded. "I've never done anything like that before."

"You'll do just fine, love," came the response. "I'll help you. Why don't you speak on John Newton? That's easy to do, and I'll show you how to set up a talk like that." Which he did.

The following Thursday, with a trembling heart, I entered the small vestry attached to the chapel. The heat from the peat fire almost suffocated me, but the women smiled and nodded their welcome. I sat tentatively on the chair facing the small semi-circle, the burning smoky fire facing me. A constant clicking of needles provided the background noise, apart from a peats falling into the fire.

Someone opened with a brief prayer, and silence reigned briefly. As soon as the 'Amen' was said, the needles were raised up and each knitter took her right needle and jabbed it into her side. I winced.

"Och, dinna mind us and our knitting," laughed Jessie. "See. We all wear knitting belts." She pointed to an oval shaped piece of stuffed leather belted to her side with a needle sticking out from it. "Did you bring your sock?"

"Yes, I brought my knitting." Hesitantly I took it out of my bag and laid it to one side. I cleared my throat. "I thought I would speak on John Newton." I stopped, waiting for an expected cessation from the clicking and clacking of steel knitting pins. But no respectful quietness descended.

"Dinna be concerned about us," Jessie continued. "We always take our sock wherever we go in Shetland, be they meetings like this. Aboot the only time we dinna knit is when we go to chapel."

I took a deep breath, and as the women knitted away at a fast and furious pace, I tried to look away and focus on my notes. Somehow I got through my three points, and the group were gracious enough to thank me.

"Now, then, get busy on ye sock," said one of the women nodding toward my knitting.

I'd been knitting since I was seven years of age and considered myself pretty accomplished, but as I watched these women passing stitches over their needles at an incredible rate and using two different coloured wools at the same time, one on each hand, creating intricate Fair Isle patterns, I very reluctantly picked up my knitting.

Noting my consternation, Jessie took pity on me. "Och, lass," she said, "I'll get yet a knitting belt and teach ye the Shetland way."

"Thank you. I'd like that very much." As soon as I could I pushed my knitting into my cloth bag, and accepted the welcome cup of tea in my hand. As I took a hard gulp, one of the women showed me the Fair Isle mitten she'd just knitted, mostly in the past hour or two. I was amazed and decided at that moment, I'd do my best to learn.

On my way home, I looked over the houses to a fishing vessel pulling into the small pier. As the fishermen cut off the heads of the fish, they tossed them over the sides of the boat high into the air before they fell into the choppy water. Then they dropped the body of the fish into the wooden barrels. Overhead a cloud of anxious, squawking seagulls caught herring heads in mid-air, while others dived into the chilled water to secure a tasty meal, all the while creating a raucous uproar as they competed for the food. Some successful birds flew higher, gripping in their beaks their large, protruding, grisly prizes.

"You greedy things!" I called to them, not too loudly, in case someone heard me.

As I pushed open the gate leading to the two steps down into the path to the back door, I stopped suddenly. There on the roof of the manse waddled two seagulls, their mouths barely holding on to their coveted fish heads. One banged the fish head on the roof, then the other smashed his on it. I watched, mesmerized, as they continued to do this until the fish-heads were broken into manageable beak-size pieces, whereupon they gobbled them down. Then one flew off, straight back to the treasure trove of glorious fish food, followed by its mate. Soon another gull appeared, heading directly towards our slightly pitched roof, and dropped the fish head from above. *Thud.* It fell hard and broke apart, then with a scream befitting only a seagull, it dived and swallowed up both pieces before a rival could spy them. Now I laughed out loud, and turned the door knob to go inside. "Wait until Desmond returns from his visiting", I thought, still chuckling, imagining now the look on his face.

The mystery was solved. Indeed no boots were clumping on our roof, merely local seagulls, breaking up their food into edible chunks. When Desmond arrived back at the manse, I shared the seagull story, and merriment filled the house.

True to her word, the following week, Jessie invited me down for tea, and she produced a knitting belt, some Shetland wool, and a pair of very fine steel knitting needles or pins, as the local women called them, having two points on each needle. She showed me how to fasten the belt around my waist, how to push the right needle into the belt to keep it taut, and then to loop the wool over the fingers of my right hand. I practised diligently.

"Next time ye come, I'll teach ye how to do Fair Isle using both hands," she promised.

"I'd really like that." Already I could feel the familiar challenge rising within me. The saying from my school days, echoed yet again, *Ah, but a man's reach should exceed his grasp, or what's a heaven for.* I determined that I would indeed learn to knit Fair Isle as a Shetlander and thereby increase my knitting skills. From then on, I always knitted the 'Shetland way'.

Many years later when living in Florida, we were told to evacuate as Hurricane Ivan barrelled up the Tampa coastline. The first item I packed was my knitting belt, which I still use!

CHAPTER 23

OUTPOSTS AND OUTHOUSES

'As o'er each continent and island, the dawn leads on another day.'
John Ellerton, 1826-1893

Although I'd planned to work for a couple of years, I was informed, in no uncertain terms, that "ministers' wives don't work!" So I accepted my lot and immersed myself in the Methodist Women's group, teaching ten-year olds, visiting parishioners with my husband, dabbling in some writing, beginning the process of becoming a local preacher, attempting to master Fair Isle and trying to manage the finances.

But on this morning, the clanging of a bell outside caught my attention.

"That's Jim!" I shouted to Desmond.

I grabbed my plate and ran up the two steps into the lane where Jim Duncan held on to his barrow. He saw me, placed it down, and rang again the attached old school bell for good measure.

"Tis a braw day," he offered nonchalantly.

"It is indeed," I agreed shivering without my coat. "What do you have today?"

"We have some bonnie skate, some whiting and fine haddock." He pointed to the fresh fish laid out on his hand-pulled barrow.

"I'll take some haddock." I handed him my plate.

He placed two good-size fish on the scale, filleted them there on the cart, and slid them on my plate. "That will be fourpence, Mistress Parker," he said with a smile.

I gave him my money, and we had fish again that night, as we seemed to most evenings. Meat was expensive and I had to travel the seven miles by bus to the butcher's in Lerwick usually to purchase it. We were on a tight budget, so fish it was.

Desmond had pastoral responsibility for three churches, one in Scalloway, another in Nesting, about fifteen miles north, and the third on Burra Isle, about forty minutes away by boat, namely the *Tirrick*. A welcoming soiree concert had been arranged on the Saturday evening at the chapel on Burra, we were told, and all the islanders would be there to see what we looked like! Then on Sunday morning and evening there would be regular worship services.

"They will be expecting you to come with me," Desmond said.

"But where will we stay? The boat leaves Saturday and doesn't run again until Monday."

"Everything will be fine. They'll have a place for us." He gave me a hug. "You shouldn't worry over such things."

Reassured, I packed our overnight wear and a change of clothing to get us through the couple of days. On our way down to the landing stage to catch the boat, we met Nell Duncan and the organist, Ellie. "It's a bonnie day," announced Nell. "I suppose ye be on ye way to yon boat to get to Burra?"

I nodded.

She continued, "But ha' ye no heard, that young Willie Sandersun is awa'?"

"Really," I replied, "And where has he gone?"

Silence.

Desmond looked quizzically at the two.

"He's gone awa' means he's dead!" came Ellie's flat answer.

"I, er, I'm so sorry. I didn't realize that 'away' meant he'd died." I stammered in my ignorance.

"Aye, twas sudden like. He was enjoying his salted herring and tatties, and just fell into his dinner," Nell added.

I could feel a telltale giggle tickling inside. I struggled to compose myself and present a suitable expression of concern.

"I'll be sure to see the family as soon as I return from Burra," Desmond assured them.

"Aye, then. We'll tell 'em."

We scuttled as fast as we could, fearful we'd miss the boat over to the island.

"Come awa' on board," cried the owner. "I saw ye running down yon hill."

We jumped on the motor launch and it chuntered out past Trondra towards what seemed to me like the open sea. Immediately the waves slapped the boat, and the tossing began. Some of the passengers huddled inside the small cabin, but I preferred to sit outside, holding on to a rail. "It's a little choppy," I yelled to Desmond above the ever-present wind, and the noise of the engine.

"I can't hear you!" he yelled back.

"Never mind." But I watched him closely. He seemed to be handling it better this time than the trip up on the *St Ninian*.

The forty-minute ride passed uneventfully and the packed vessel drew into the small dockside. People jostled about waiting for the boat and the various supplies that were piled up at the back, mostly bags of groceries and the all-important post. I noticed another small motor launch moored close by, apart from the fishing vessels that were scattered about the sheltered harbour.

A passenger noted where I looked. "That there be Dr Durham's boat," she said. "He's the doctor, ye ken, in Scalloway, and he comes out here to see the local folk."

Just then a tall, good-looking man with a traditional black doctor's bag in hand came towards Desmond and myself. "I'm Dr Durham," he announced with a faint Scots burr. "I'm very glad to meet ye both."

We shook hands.

"Ye'll have to come over and meet my wife. She's from the mainland, so you can enjoy a good cup of tea together." With a warm smile and a wave of his hand, he jumped into his small boat and sped off back to Scalloway. I would get to know him well.

I gazed around. Houses, mostly sparse and modest and made of solid stone blocks, stood haphazardly against the sloping hillside dipping down to the water. It seemed as though someone had had a pinafore full of homes, thrown it up, and the houses had jumped out, falling haphazardly and settling there. A few dry stone walls and straggly potato plots formed a patchwork among the homes.

"It looks as if everyone went and built wherever," I whispered to Desmond.

"Shush," he admonished, "Someone will hear you." He nudged me for extra measure.

"Where's the chapel?"

"It's got to be around here somewhere."

He asked a fisherman hauling out some lobster traps.

"Och, yon chapel is about two mile from here. Just follow yon road there." He pointed toward a narrow strip of road winding between a few of the houses and over the hill. He eyed us both. "Ye both have sturdy legs. It will no take ye long to get there."

We looked at each other, and off we went.

Neither of us had ever had a car for transport. In Scalloway, Desmond had been supplied with a motor scooter for travelling the main island and the northern isles, but it only allowed for the driver. Cars were expensive to buy and expensive to run, though I vaguely remembered my dad having one before the war. Despite the fifteen years that had passed since the end of the war, and six years since rationing ended, people still lived fairly spartan lives. (My Dad did buy a small Ford Poplar just before I was married.) So, at a good pace, we set off, with our rucksacks on our back. Once out of sight of the houses, we held hands, taking comfort from each other in the bare treeless landscape. We had been told that because of the winds, no trees could grow, unless shrubs and bushes were protected by stone walls. Out here wandered sheep, grazing on whatever blades of grass they could find amidst the gorse, craggy hollows and heather in this barren landscape.

"Just look at the crofts," I said, pointing to one set back from the road. "It's a wonder anything grows here."

"Hmm, it does appear desolate. But it is an adventure. You don't regret coming here, do you?" He stopped and gave me an earnest look.

"Of course not." I glanced around. Yes, it was an adventure, and I wondered at what other adventures lay ahead.

"There, there it is, I think." I pointed up the hill to a windswept grey squat stone building, barely discernible against the outcropping of rocks jutting out of the scrabbling hillside. We drew closer. No other cottages stood near, except for one we could barely see, down the stark ribbon of road.

We pushed open the chapel door. Inside stood the sentry-like pews, with the central obligatory pulpit keeping watch up front. Tentatively we walked down the centre aisle, noting the austerity and the damp chill. Desmond pushed open a door at the back to the left of the pulpit, where we found a small, square room that hugged the back of the chapel. This must be the vestry. In the centre spreading out warm fingers into the damp blanket of air surrounding us, was a peat stove, with a scuttle full of peats at the side.

A note was nailed to the wall. I placed our bag on an upright wooden chair and pulled it note down.

"Welcome Reverend and Mrs Parker," I read out loud, shivering in the clinging dampness. "We set a fire for ye both, so be sure ye keep it stoked with peats, especially at night. It is hard to set in the morning. In the tin on the table there are sandwiches for your dinner and breakfast. We'll bring some more at chapel tomorrow. The couch pulls out into a bed and sheets are in the trunk in the corner."

My heart sank as I placed the note on the table.

"Come on," said Desmond, falsely cheerful. "It's all part of the adventure. Now give me a hand to pull the bed out."

We pushed and pulled and eventually an old double bed sprang out. I found a couple of blankets, along with two sheets, two pillows and two pillow cases in the trunk, as instructed. "They're damp!" I cried. "We can't sleep with these."

Desmond's face was set. "We'll have to. There isn't anywhere else."

"Bring that other chair over," I commanded. "See, we'll spread out the sheets over the chairs in front of the stove, so at least they'll dry out. And we'll drape the blankets over the table. And let's throw more peats on the fire."

He pulled open the small iron door and threw three or four more peats on to the dull red glow that peats produce. A blast of wind shook the smoke out of the door into the room.

"Close it, close it!" I shouted.

"I'm doing it as fast as I can," he yelled back, frustrated and trying to hook the latch into place.

"I need to go to the toilet," I announced. "Where's the bathroom?"

I searched around, but all that was there was the cupboard, tightly fitted with shelves. An old stone sink with one tap hung to the corner on the wall.

"Oh, no!" I moaned. "Don't tell me."

Desmond moved to a door at the back end of the small vestry room. "Maybe it's in here." He opened the door and a blast of North Sea air blew its whistling chill into the room. I grabbed my windcheater and yanked the door shut behind me as I stepped into the buffeting wind. Immediately in front stood a cockeyed wooden hut. With trepidation I pulled the lathed door open, the wind almost pulling it off its hinges. Set squarely before me was a wide wooden plank complete with hole. The slight odour informed me immediately what it was, despite the automatic air freshener that blew constantly. A long-handled shovel rested against the inner wall and some sheets of paper hung from a nail in the door, wafting in the breeze.

Desmond joined me and laughed. "Well this is just like when I grew up in Ashwell Street," he said.

"What do you mean? You had running water and a bathroom when I visited you."

"Yes, but I'm talking about the house where I grew up. It was a small terrace house, with a backyard toilet, similar to this."

"Well, I've got to go," I said, "Otherwise I'll wet my knickers."

I closed the door and held my breath. Chinks of daylight wrinkled through the top of the uneven door along with wafts from the brisk breeze. Afterwards, I dug a shovelful of dirt from the hillock alongside and threw it into the hole. I vowed that if I needed to come in the night, Desmond would have to come with me. I recollected seeing a torch on the table. Now I knew what that was for. At least we had electricity, so I should be thankful for small mercies.

"Come and look at this view," called Desmond. Pulling my gloves on, I climbed up to the crest of the hill to gaze down upon a deep velvet-blue voe, with the water cutting in deeply into the hillside. As I followed the fathomless water toward the horizon, it stretched out its limbs around spits of land until it disappeared into the open sea. Absolute silence wrapped itself around me. I sat down on a rock to allow the beauty to bathe me. A couple of scories (cormorants) dived into the breeze-rippled water, but that was all. The air, crisp, fresh and tanged with salt, whipped across my face, while an azure sky spanned overhead, bringing water, hills, rocks and even sheep into one unified sense of being. I'd never seen such stark wonder, or experienced such utter silence.

Desmond broke into my reverie. "We'd better get going. There are a couple of parishioners somewhere here I've been asked to see. Will you come with me?"

"Of course," I agreed, and turned my back on the serenity of the moment.

He'd been given a rough sketch as to where some of the crofters lived, close to the Methodist Chapel. We made our way down the road about half a mile, then turned into a small dirt path. A stolid croft squared itself at the end of the pathway, windows barely discernible. Desmond rapped on the door.

"Och, come awa' in." The woman, bent over towards us, was wearing the conforming black clothing that almost all women over the age of forty years wore. Her rosy face contrasted with her outfit as she beckoned us in. I blinked, trying to see in the peat-smoked room.

"Come, come now, and sit ye down." She motioned to a couple of sagging chairs.

"This here is ma man," She poked a gently snoring form next to the open stove.

"Jackie, wake yeself up. Yon new minister and his wife are here to visit us."

With a splutter, he stirred himself. "Oh, aye, glad to meet ye. Are we no going to ha' a cup of tea?"

"I'm jus' getting it." Rosie bustled, lifting a blackened pot from the top of the stove. She reached for some cracked cups from an open shelf, then set them down on an oil-cloth covered table, and asked, "Ye take some milk?"

"Yes, please," I answered, hoping the local cows hadn't been fed fish meal.

I glanced at the grime-encrusted furnishings and the questionable cups. "Lord, please look after us," I prayed silently as I took a drink of the dark, stiffly-brewed tea. I watched Rosie pour some more hot water from a boiling kettle next to the teapot into the blackened pot, give it a stir, then fix the lid back on ready for the next cup.

Jackie supped his tea noisily and said not a word, but Rosie proceeded to bring us up to date with the gossip of the island, in particular how nearby 'ole Jamie' had advertised in the *Shetland Times* for an 'ole wife' to cook his food, clean his house, and keep him warm in bed. Rosie laughed.

"Did he get any replies?" I asked amused.

"Och, no!" she threw her head back with a laugh. "Everyone in Shetland knows ole Jamie, and noo ole wife would ever have him."

After an appropriate stay, we made our excuses and breathed deeply the clean air outside.

"I think we'd better get back to our sandwiches." I said. I pointed up the hill to the sombre chapel. "Otherwise we'll be late for the big shindig tonight."

"Maybe they'll be good sandwiches," suggested Desmond.

I didn't get my hopes up too much. But as we let ourselves in, a wind-blown woman dressed in blackbird-like attire came running down the road from the other direction with a saucepan in hand, her pinny blowing like wings each side of her in the wind. "Och, och, I'm glad I caught ye" she said, gasping for air. "I've brought ye some hot tatties for ye dinner, to eat alongside yon sandwiches." She emptied the boiled potatoes on a plate, then took off, calling, "I've got to run, ye ken. Can't be late for the soiree tonight."

She left. "Well now," said Desmond slowly, "that was nice of her to bring those."

"Boiled potatoes and cheese sandwiches," I answered. "That's different."

We were hungry and soon cleared the makeshift meal. After we'd washed our plates in the cold water, and made sure the second packet of sandwiches was still in the tin for breakfast, we made our way into the chapel to be greeted by the faithful.

We listened to the local talent warble ancient shanties, folk songs and sentimental hymns. A young Scottish dancer performed an intricate dance with swords and an elderly fisherman brought toe-tapping music from his fiddle. Everyone agreed it has been a grand evening. However, neither of us slept too well that night with the wind whistling around and having to drag ourselves up out of the now warm and dry bed to pile more peats on the fire. The sandwiches were welcome the next morning and once we'd splashed cold water on our faces from the stone sink tap, we were ready for the morning worship. The pump organ wheezed its way through old familiar hymns, dragging and squeaking with reedy voices following the melody. As usual almost no men attended, claiming it was 'women's work' to do that.

Sunday night followed the same pattern, with more sandwiches supplied for our tea before the evening service. Then Monday morning we hiked the two miles down to the quayside and caught the boat back over the water to Scalloway.

Later, as I got to know Jessie better, I mentioned the sandwiches incident in the Burra Chapel vestry. She laughed loudly. "Och, dinna be put off by yon. All the island folk dinna have anyone stay in their homes unless they be family. You should hear what happened when the Queen herself visited Foula."

"What happened?" I asked, edging towards the edge of my chair.

Jessie put her knitting down in her lap. "Seems like when yon Queen docked in her fancy boat, all the island folk disappeared inside their crofts. No one was there to greet her, being a stranger like. Only when yon boat of hers took off did they all come out." she laughed again. "But that's how island folk are."

I wondered what the Queen might have thought about her island subjects.

The following weekend, Desmond took off for the island of Yell. Not only did the Methodist ministers preach in their own churches, often twice on Sundays, they also preached in all the other Methodist churches in the circuit. This meant visits to the northern islands of Yell and Unst. To serve these remote chapels Desmond left Saturday morning, puttering his scooter down Manse Lane, along Houl Road and off north to Tofts Voe to catch the ferry over to Yell. I knew he wouldn't be back until Monday, or if the weather was bad, Tuesday. Sometimes, I was warned, it could be even Wednesday, especially coming from the most northerly of islands, Unst.

I was anxious for his return, but busied myself in cleaning the house and rising to the task of using my knitting belt to knit my first pair of Fair Isle mittens, using both hands for the two different-coloured yarns. On Sunday morning I gathered my six or seven ten-year olds for Sunday school. The children complained that there was nothing to do during the weekdays after school. I had a brilliant idea. "Why don't you come to the manse on Wednesday nights, after school? We can have a Bible story, then do some fun things, and I'll have biscuits and milk."

"Hey, I'd like to come!" cried Morgan.

"Me too!" chimed in Robbie, youngest son of Jessie.

"And me!" added Billy from the house down at the back of the Manse.

"Right. I'll see you all at four o'clock."

I felt excitement ripple through me. We could do some interesting things, and I hoped that something of God's love would wend itself into the hearts of these great young children. I also saw it as another opportunity to teach! (Several months later I submitted an article about our 'Wednesday Night Sunday School' and had it published in 'Christian Life' (USA). I received my first cheque for five shillings and was thrilled.)

Desmond arrived back from Yell and I couldn't wait to tell him about our 'midweek Sunday school' but he couldn't wait to tell me about his adventures either. I made the usual pot of tea, and we sat in front of the coal fire to chat.

He began. "I was made very welcome by a Mr and Mrs Johanson on Yell, close to the chapel. I had no problems getting over, and was able to transport my scooter on the boat. But before long I had to go to the toilet."

"Oh, another toilet problem," I teased.

He laughed. "Well, Mr Johanson assured me that he had running water and everything and he'd show me to where it was." He took a breath. "He took me out across a couple of fields, and I had a feeling that it wasn't what I expected a toilet to be. Then there was this wooden hut right in the middle of a field. We trudged over to it, and Mr Johanson opened the door for me, pointed to the hole in the plank, balanced on two posts of wood, and underneath was a running stream."

I began shaking with laughter.

"There,'" my host said, "'This here is our toilet with running water.'"

Desmond sat back. My hand shook so hard I had to place my cup on the hearth.

"That's the best one yet." I pulled myself together. "My news is a bit more serious, but I am really excited about it." I shared with him my plans and Desmond shared my enthusiasm. We talked back and forth and finished our cups of tea.

I stood up. "Now then, how about some nourishment to keep us going? I have fried fish for our tea."

"What, again?" he cried.

"Yes, again," I said and turned to go into the kitchen, trying to figure a different way to cook fish rather than frying. As I stepped into the narrow hallway I called over my shoulder, "By the way, you're going to have your first wedding in a couple of months." I knew that would take his mind off the fish!

Desmond bounced up from the chair, the one that had a loose spring in the seat, and cried, "What do you mean? I didn't know there was a wedding coming up."

I moved into the kitchen, with Desmond following. "Jim and Alma are getting married on New Year's Eve," I crowed. Taking pity on him, I explained. "Alma and I were having a cup of tea this afternoon, and she told me that Jim will be calling you to see if you can marry them on New Year's Eve. But don't let on I told you!"

He nodded, "Okay. I'll act surprised." The happy grin stayed on his face even after eating his fish, and continued as he left the table to go in to his study to resume writing his next sermon.

CHAPTER 24

CELEBRATIONS ALL ROUND

Sages leave your contemplation; Brighter visions beam afar
James Montgomery, 1771-1854

Alma and Jim had been going out since before we had arrived and had recently got engaged. Alma worked at the *Shetland News*, taking the bus into Lerwick each morning, and was about my age. The village throbbed with the thrill of the news. It had been a while since a wedding had taken place in the chapel and after all, everyone knew Jim, our fish man and a Methodist local preacher too, as well as Alma and her family, who were also staunch Methodists, especially her Dad, who was also a local preacher.

But Christmas was coming first. I had mixed feelings every time I thought about it. It would be the first Christmas without family, but we had been invited to the Methodist Superintendent's manse in Lerwick, along with a couple of other Methodist ministers, all of us young, and married of course. I planned on purchasing holly to decorate the house, and maybe a small evergreen tree, to be brought in from the mainland of Scotland.

However, just as 'Jingle Bells' crowded the airwaves on our wireless, foot-and-mouth disease was announced on the mainland. The word circulated. No greens for Christmas this year. The islanders could not afford to have any possibility of contamination getting to the islands and decimating their sheep and cows, mainstays of many people's livelihoods. Though the ponies would not be affected, mice, rats and horses could pass it on to other animals.

Shetland, being bereft of trees and most greenery except for gorse and some heather, offered no local substitute. "What can we do for Christmas?" I wailed to Desmond.

He shrugged. "We'd better a get a small artificial tree from the chandlers in Lerwick, and put up with it."

Despondent, I half-heartedly began some preparations. A small scant apology for a tree was purchased, along with a dozen or so miniature ornaments. I placed the tree on the sideboard, pulled down the dry wired branches and arranged the shiny ornaments the best I could. I succeeded in posting the Christmas parcels to Mum, Dad and Nana as well as Jean and Brian, who were now engaged, along with one to Desmond's mum and dad in Nottingham.

Mum had rung me and said she'd just mailed our parcel, and we should get it in time. She'd been sick so she was later than usual getting it to the Post Office. I waited anxiously for these gifts from home.

However, another happening now caught my attention.

"Have ye noo heard," shared Jessie, after chapel on the Sunday morning. I perked up. She lowered her voice. "It seems that Jackie Ollason from Burra brought in some holly from the mainland on his fishing boat." She paused. "And his neighbour saw him. Of course she rang some others and told her man." She grinned wickedly. "Seems they all came a runnin' and surrounded the boat, yanking out yon greens, and burned every last leaf right there on the dock. My cousin Bessie rang and told me this morn."

"Gosh, I bet he was sorry he'd tried to sneak them in," I said.

"Aye, but tis a good thing they found them. It could have caused muckle havoc on the island."

Others joined us, all talking about Jackie Ollason and the holly. No one else dared to smuggle any more greens on to the islands that Christmas season.

A couple of days before Christmas Eve, the wind, which blew constantly, picked up in velocity. Whatever might be loose was caught up, given wings and flew hundreds of yards to be caught in the gorse bushes on Witches Hill. Sheep hovered close together in the leeward side of hills and stone walls, built for ever, with a few stragglers even seeking shelter in our back garden against the stone wall separating the Manse from our neighbour.

Word sped around the village. "Tis a braw day. No boats or planes, you ken, will come today. And, aye, how aboot poor Robbie Magnuson? He's a'going to Aberdeen. Did you noo ken, he had a heart attack last night, and is in yon Lerwick hospital, waiting to be flown down. And, it doesna look like the weather will turn any time soon."

I pulled my coat closer, trying to stand against the wind, as I heard the news outside the bread shop. "But what will happen to Robbie if he can't be flown down to Aberdeen?" I asked, all thoughts about the non-arrival of Christmas pressies forgotten.

"Och, he'll be in the hands of God," came the solemn reply.

Murmurs of agreement rose and fell, then each turned away, doubled over into the relentless gale, still whipping up its ferociousness.

Bent into the howling yet invisible force, I pushed my way up the hill back to the manse and slammed the door shut. Relieved from the incessant buffeting, I felt ten pounds lighter and walked into Desmond's study. "I heard that someone called Robbie Magnuson has had a heart attack and is waiting to be flown south," I told him. I removed my hat and coat and pulled off my mittens.

Desmond looked up from his typewriter. "Oh, dear. That is bad. Where's he from?"

"Whiteness, I think," I replied, trying to remember the details of the conversation. "I hope he's going to be all right."

Desmond changed the subject. "On a happier note, take a look at what I've written for the wedding."

"I hope I can enjoy the wedding breakfast," I said hopefully, taking his paper.

He turned back to his desk. After all, this was a female problem. Dr Durham had confirmed I was pregnant, so what could one expect!

The gales continued right through Christmas morning, then the wind dropped to its usual blustery pattern. But no planes flew, and no boats sailed until the following day.

It was too late for Robbie Magnuson, and a funeral was planned for him instead. Some of the glamour and sense of adventure dissipated that day, as the realisation hit me that living on these islands literally meant the difference between life and death at times. Robbie was buried up country, and life resumed its island pattern.

After chapel on Christmas Day we got a taxi ride over to Lerwick and good cheer filled the air the moment we stepped into the manse there. Laura, Mrs Searle, as we respectfully called her, demonstrated her skills as a good minister's wife. Her warm hospitality embraced us, as did her steaming kitchen, cascading over with roasting turkey and Christmas pudding smells as they greeted us through the open door. "Merry Christmas, Merry Christmas!" rang out from us all.

Pam and Graham, the Methodist minister and his wife from Whiteness, further north, were already there. Despite some loitering morning sickness, I managed to consume a healthy dinner with two helpings of Christmas pudding. I thought of Poppa all the years before and the silver threepenny piece hidden beneath his pudding dish, which I still had tucked away in a small purse in the chest of drawers Desmond and I shared. I had been sure to rescue it from the hem of my wedding dress.

After the meal, all of us women helped with the washing up. Then we sat down to play some games around the spitting coal fire in the sitting room. 'Password' appeared the favourite, accompanied by Christmas carols from around the world on the nearby record player. Following a traditional Christmas tea of cold turkey, bread and butter, trifle and Christmas cake, we played 'Murder'. The old three-storey stone manse lent itself to mysterious happenings. Thick stone walls muffled screams. Empty bedrooms, with dustsheets covered old furniture and secrets, with steep, back, servant staircases that no one used any more, all contributed to our dastardly setting for our game of Murder! We drew cards, keeping impassive faces. Who knew who the murderer was, and the detective, not to mention the victim?

We scattered through the house. I hid in the bath tub, only to have Rev. Searle, portly, still in clerical collar, in his mid-sixties find me, and murder me! The screams and yells would have been enough to make an unsuspecting visitor's blood chill to ice. Then it was over. Breathless, with faces red from exertion and our adrenalin high, we hurried one by one our way back to the warm arms of the living room.

"This is one Christmas I'll never forget," I declared to everyone, stretching out my feet towards the now blazing fire.

"Me too," echoed Pam, her face still flushed as she held on to her rounded tummy. Her baby was due a couple of months hence.

"Imagine if the chapel-goers could have seen us half an hour ago," chuckled Mrs Searle. We all joined in the laughter.

She then hurried about and brought in hot cocoa with biscuits. After a while the conversation lagged, and with a well-satisfied weariness from rich food and good company we all trooped up the dank stairs to the cold rooms upstairs. Mrs Searle, bless her heart with her thoughtfulness, had slipped a hot water bottle between the smooth icy sheets, warming the bed for us. Then Desmond and I fought over who would get to hug the hot water bottle. We all stayed overnight, and soon sleep spun its soothing web through the manse as we soundly slept. Only the old watching grandfather clock broke the silence.

"That turned out to be a really good Christmas after all," I told Desmond on our way home on the bus the day after Boxing Day.

"Yes, that was really kind of the Searles to have us all over. But do you realise that this time next year there will be three of us celebrating Christmas?"

I smiled at the warm thought and patted my tummy. Mum's Christmas parcel awaited us on the step at the back door, which completed the holiday celebration.

New Year's Eve dawned bright, sunny and bitterly cold, but not so windy as usual. The wedding was planned for late afternoon, and I was almost as anxious as the bride.

The Methodist Chapel in Scalloway was crammed with well-wishers and guests. Alma walked down the aisle on the arm of her Dad looking beautiful in her satin wedding dress, while Eunice, her older sister, and another sister, who lived on the mainland, accompanied her as bridesmaids. Soon the service was over, and we trooped back to her house for the celebration meal.

"I wonder what we'll have for the wedding breakfast," I whispered to Desmond as we walked part way up Houl Road to the Williamson's family home.

"I'm hungry, so I hope it's something good."

"I'm still a bit off my food, so I trust I can keep it down." I felt doubtful. I was never sure when the sickness would raise its spectre, though I'd been lucky over Christmas.

Stamping our feet to get warm, we entered the peat-heated home. The rack hovering over the fireplace had a couple of legs of reested mutton hanging from it, waiting to have chunks cut off for future dinners. Our coats were taken and we sat down in the other room, all cleared and set up with a long table laid out for the festive meal. The food smelled tantalizing as heaping dishes of the traditional tatties, neaps and mutton were laden on to the table.

Despite Lowrie, Alma's father, claiming to be a teetotaller, we noticed a telltale bottle being passed between the men under the table. Jim, however, resolutely passed it on, as, of course, did Desmond.

"You know," I leaned toward my husband, "This is good, really good! I'm enjoying every mouthful." And it did taste delicious. Also I wasn't in the least nauseous from that day on. Toasts in non-alcoholic beverages were raised, and the home-made wedding cake cut, whereupon the bride and groom, and most of the cake, disappeared. In keeping with the Shetland tradition, Jim and Alma, still in bridal finery but with a warm coat now over her shoulders, stepped outside to visit the local infirmed to offer them a piece of wedding cake, so they too could have the opportunity to wish them a happy life.

Eventually they returned. Alma changed into her smart going-away outfit and matching hat, and a taxi took the happy couple with beaming faces off on their honeymoon to the southern part of the island. It was midnight and guests began to disperse.

Desmond and I started up the hill of Houl Road, then stopped. I caught my breath.

"Wait, just look at those fairy dancers, as Jim calls them." I whispered. Awestruck, we gazed, hand in hand, our faces heavenward, absorbing the dancing lights of the Aurora Borealis jumping and almost laughing across the northern sky. Pinks, aquas, metallic blues, deep greens, burnt orange, violet and sunshine yellows performed an unending dance, in perfect harmony. I felt drawn up, wrapped around with their beauty, wanting to leap up and swing with them across the starry sky.

Eventually the cold night air worked its frosty fingers into our hands and feet and we slowly walked back up to the manse.

In bed that night, I thanked my God for letting me experience such wonder. He touched me profoundly through His omniscient show streaming the heavens. I was uplifted into His Presence way beyond the experience of sitting through any Sunday morning or evening service. After the comfort and richness of a liturgy-based worship I found the rambling prayers and extemporaneous sermons sincere, but for me, usually without meaning and jarring. That night though, I fell asleep, with a grateful heart.

At the end of January, we visited the manse in Lerwick again, this time to view the ancient festival of Up-Helly-Aa. Some said it meant the end of the holidays, whereas others claimed it stood for the return of the sun as winter days were desperately dark with only about four hours of daylight, even on a bright day. We caught the last bus into Lerwick and were reminded by the driver that there were no buses out of Lerwick until the next morning, the day following the celebration being a most necessary holiday, particularly for the night-owl revellers.

That evening, bundled up against the North Sea's penetrating wind, we stood on a strategic street corner to wait, along with other islanders anxious for the festivities to begin.

"I hear them!" a child shouted.

A cheer arose as evil, dancing flames sprang from burning torches when the guizers turned the corner to our street and moved in procession towards us. Leading the marchers strode the Guizer Jarl, the chief Viking, resplendent in his leather outfit, complete with the Viking horned helmet upon his head. His fellow warriors followed, dragging a life-size Viking galley with study ropes attached to the proud ship.

Then the singing began. Strong fishermen's voices, now Viking marauders, sang the Up-Helly-Aa song. Their resonance echoed through Lerwick, right down to the harbour, filling every nook and cranny with their vibrating sound. It thrilled me to the bone. There was indeed something primordial as the men moved by, shadows from the burning torches accompanying the stirring music. Behind the Vikings and their ship came the squads, groups of men in costume, ready to provide entertainment in the various halls through the small town.

We ran through a side street to catch the procession yet again, then doubled back to the park, where eventually the marching men convened. Silence now fell as the Vikings surrounded their galley, torches held aloft. Suddenly a loud cry came from the Guizer Jarl through the crowd, and the men began throwing their lit torches into the stately ship. Soon the wooden vessel ate up the flames and, like an ancient dragon, spewed up into the air the yellow and orange flares from the burning ship. In time the fuel burned away and the women hustled their children home, while others swarmed to the halls for dancing and entertainment. Each squad was now ready to move into the first hall assigned to it to perform the skit, long prepared.

We wandered back to the Seales' manse while the merrymaking continued through the night. While we sat by their fire, the various squads meandered between the numerous halls, entertaining the enthusiastic merrymakers. The ever-present dram was shared and celebrated at the end of each skit until the halls closed and the crowds dispersed.

The next morning we allowed the first bus to Scalloway to take the local inebriated performers back to their respective abodes, where their wives waited to get them into bed, along with a couple of aspirin, to sleep off the after-effects of too much revelry. We wisely caught the almost empty afternoon bus instead.

The winter raged and retreated. Gales sprung up, then died down to allow thick fog to roll in, and I grew more pregnant. One bright spot was when Rev. and Mrs Searle came to visit us. Of course we allowed Rev. Searle and his wife to sit in the easy chairs by the cheerful fire.

Suddenly he jumped up out of the chair. "Something nipped me!" he yelled, holding his bottom. We smothered a chuckle. He'd sat in the chair with the broken spring. "Its companion isn't much better either," I told him. Mrs Searle agreed wholeheartedly.

A few days later, two new armchairs arrived from Lerwick. The Superintendent Minister was able to work the miracle that we had tried to bring about with our local stewards, unsuccessfully. Life around the fireplace became decidedly more comfortable.

Slowly, the weather notched up a few degrees. June arrived at last, and a visit back home was scheduled. This time we flew down. It felt so good to be back in civilization with reliable plumbing, hot water, trees and family. Jean and Brian were engaged, and a wedding was planned for the following year.

"How about if we all go up to the Lake District for a day or two?" Mum suggested to us all.

"Yes, oh yes!" I clapped my hands. My beloved mountains, the green valleys and serene lakes once again beckoned like heaven.

Arrangements were made. Dad was working so Jean, Brian, Mum, Desmond and I set off, getting the bus to Windermere. We climbed up Orrest Head, wandered around part of Lake

Windermere, enjoyed fish and chips, then decided to find a bed and breakfast for overnight. First we tried one, then another, but no accommodation could be found. Finally Mum knocked on the door of yet another B & B.

"We just have two double rooms," the woman said. "But I do have a foldaway bed I could put up in one of the rooms." She looked at the five of us.

"We'll take them," answered Mum immediately.

We breathed a sigh of relief. After our walking and climbing, at least we were now assured of beds for the night.

As we drank a cup of tea in a local café, Mum announced. "Well, that is taken care of, thank goodness. Brian, you and Desmond can share one room, and Jean, Joyce and I will share the other."

"Oh no," said Desmond. "Joyce and I will have one of the rooms. After all, she is my wife, and we aren't going to be separated."

I stared at him in dismay, but knew better than to get into an argument with him in front of the others.

One of Mum's if-looks-could-kill stares was thrown Desmond's way, and I sighed. She was not happy, to put it mildly. Mum drew herself up. "I think you're being very selfish," she said.

Desmond was adamant. I, like a coward, slunk further into my chair and looked elsewhere, churning within. My time-rooted fear of Mum resurfaced, alongside a new spectre – that of displeasing my husband.

Without saying another word, the five of us made our way to the B & B and up the steps to the front door. Mum immediately asked the landlady, "Do you have a large screen that we might borrow?"

The owner looked quizzical. "Yes," she said hesitantly, "I believe I do have one in the cellar. I'll go and see, but you'll need to help me carry it up." She nodded at Brian and Desmond.

As Mum, Jean and I climbed the stairs to the two rooms, and took note of where the bathroom was further down the landing, the two men, huffing and puffing, lugged the heavy screen up two flights of stairs and into the second bedroom.

That night Desmond and I slept in one room, saying very little, while Mum, Jean and Brian settled down in the other. The next day I asked Jean, when we were by ourselves, how the sleeping arrangement had worked out.

"Well," she said, "You know Mum. She had Brian set the screen down the middle of the bedroom between the double bed and the foldaway bed, to be sure he wouldn't see anything he shouldn't."

We laughed together. Without saying anything we knew too well where Mum stood on any hanky-panky before marriage. Brian and Desmond were sufficiently afraid of her that both knew better than to try and go too far before the wedding bells pealed.

"So," I urged, "What happened?"

She turned to me. "Nothing, of course. Mum and I got undressed, and presumably Brian did the same. We put on our coats to go to the bathroom down the hall, and so did he. This morning we got dressed well within our side of the screen, and so did Brian on his side. Then we came down to breakfast."

I grinned. "Poor Brian. He must have been tormented to have you so close, all undressed and not be able to do a thing."

Jean chortled. "I bet he had a hard time getting to sleep. After all, he'd never dare do anything that would get Mum mad with him. If she ever thought he'd got up to something, the wedding would be off."

I sometimes wondered how Mum ever managed to conceive Jean and me!

However, Brian had the last laugh. Several years later, now safely married to Jean, he confessed to us that he had seen everything that night, and the next morning. Despite Mum's elaborate plans, he'd seen their complete nakedness through a mirror right opposite his bed!

CHAPTER 25

PENNIES AND POUNDS

Through days of toil when heart doth fail; God will take care of you
Civilla Martin, 1866–1948

I was delighted when I first felt the baby within me stir, and sought advice and assurance from Jessie.

"Och, 'tis something like that of a bad toothache," she said. She waved her knitting needle in dismissal. So my days of pregnancy passed uneventfully and August arrived quickly. Mum came up to be with me when I had the baby, and the dispute in the Lake District was never mentioned.

A Sunday school teachers' meeting had been held that evening in the manse, rather than the vestry. I'd provided biscuits and tea and at eleven o'clock they left. At one o'clock, I shrieked. Labour had started. Toothache be damned, I thought as I yelped with the contractions. Unexpectedly I suddenly thought of the cats squealing and meowing the night Jean was born, but now I was too taken up with the latest waves that assailed me to even laugh.

Half an hour or so later the ambulance arrived from Lerwick, and I was bundled into the vehicle while Desmond and my mother stayed in the manse to wait. At 3.15 am, the call was made to Desmond.

"Reverend Parker, you have a fine baby girl," they told him. And so Kathryn Joyce became the third member of our family.

My knitting needles worked overtime. Knitting almost as fast as the local Shetland women, I pushed my right knitting pin into my knitting belt and stocking stitched and cabled furiously, turning out baby jackets, bonnets and leggings for my adorable baby daughter. I delighted in pushing the pram about the village and even across the voe to Castle Head, relishing the fresh air and the miracle of our child.

Christmas rollicked its way toward us. This time I'd covertly brought a miniature bottle of sherry back with me from home, after our visit there, specifically for the trifle on Boxing Day. We spent Christmas Day with the Searles, as was our custom, but on Boxing Day we invited a fellow minister and wife to our home for tea.

Wesley and Doris had taken the place of Pam and Graham in Whiteness and Doris was due to have her baby any time now. Wesley, a large, good-humoured minister, seemed to fill our small house with his presence. We sat down to tea.

"This looks good," he said. Then he added, "You know how much of a problem drink is here in these communities. It's a good thing Scalloway is dry." He and Desmond commiserated on the evils of drink, as I eyed the sherry trifle sitting in the middle of the table.

"Yes, indeed," boasted Wesley, "Alcohol has never passed my lips. I wouldn't even know what it tasted like."

I gave a slightly nervous laugh and nudged Desmond's knee

under the table. We had our bread and butter and cold ham, then I served the tell-tale trifle. I held my breath.

"This is very good trifle," said Doris, eating her sweet with relish.

"Mmm. I like this," said Wesley. "In fact I'll have another helping." He pushed his dish toward me. I didn't dare look at Desmond. "In fact," he continued, "This is the best tasting trifle I've ever had in my life. What's in it?" He licked his lips, while coveting the last portion in the bowl.

I shrugged indifferently. "Oh, just the usual; home-made sponge cake in the bottom, soaked in the juice from the peaches. I added the peaches on top of the sponge cake with jelly, and custard, then topped it off with some tinned cream." I prayed silently, *Please God, forgive me for my sin of omission!*

He smacked his lips. "It must be the peach juice." He turned to Doris. "You'll have to make us trifle like this."

She smiled. "Maybe you could write out the recipe for me. I'm still not a very good cook."

I smiled back. "I'd be glad to!"

The rest of the afternoon and early evening passed uneventfully, and they left for Whiteness in a car Wesley had brought with him to the island.

"Whew, that was a close call," I remarked, kicking my shoes off and lifting my toes to the warming fire. "Throw some more coal on. It's a cold night."

Desmond threw some coal from the scuttle by the hearth and sat back in the comfortable easy chair. I nursed Kathryn, then leaned her on my shoulder.

We laughed about the sherry in the trifle. "But you'd better not do that again," he warned.

"It turned out fine in the end," I pointed out.

"Yes, but another time, it might be different."

"You're probably right. I'd better not risk it."

Christmas was over, the presents put away, and now the wrappings and boxes from England and family had to be disposed of. The bin men came on Thursdays. I surveyed the small empty sherry bottle. Knowing myself, I could just see the bin men emptying our bin and the bottle rolling out, right down Manse Lane, whereupon some chapel-goer would be sure to see it, and trouble would brew! I then had the brilliant idea of wrapping the bottle up in the torn Christmas wrapping papers, then placing all these in a cardboard box, tying it up with string and positioning it next to the bin ready to be picked up the following morning.

"That's it," I told Kathryn. She gurgled and gave me a watery smile.

As she sat in her pram in the living room watching me, I thoroughly and securely wrapped the bottle in as much discarded Christmas paper as I could squeeze into the box. With the glass bottle safely ensconced in the very middle, I tied a couple of strands of strong string around it, knotted it well then placed it beside the bin ready for collection the following day.

"I'm off to deliver some Methodist magazines," I told Desmond that afternoon. "I'll probably be gone an hour or two."

"I'll see you later," he called from his study.

Kathryn was bundled warmly into her home-knitted pink coat, bonnet and mittens, with a soft blanket wrapped about her and laid into her pram. I pulled the pram up the two steps into the street and off we set. Opposite, Geordie Nicholson was busy on his small piece of land raking up old grass and other debris. He and his wife lived just a couple of doors up from us. Mary was a staunch and active chapel-goer, whilst Geordie, now a retired fisherman who still did some crofting and fishing for trout now and then, seldom visited the chapel, except for funerals.

After delivering the magazines and enjoying cups of tea with several of our Methodist members, I pushed the pram back up Manse Lane to our home. I undid the latch on the gate, then stopped, horrified. The box, neatly and securely tied up with string twice over, had gone! I stood, frozen to the spot, unable to move. My heart hammered. *Where had it gone?*

Geordie strolled over. "Och, lass," he said. "I saw yon box waiting for the bin men, and thought I'd get rid of your rubbish for you."

My heart almost stopped.

"And I found this!" His hand whipped out from his pocket, the miniature empty sherry bottle. I stared at the tell-tale bottle, unable to say anything. He laughed at my obvious discomfort.

He patted my shoulder. "Och, dinna worry lass. I'll noo say anything to anyone aboot it." He put it back in his pocket. "Anyway, you'd noo get drunk on that." Still chuckling, he sauntered away, back to his bonfire on the lot opposite the manse. Slowly I let the pram wheels fall down the two steps, then wheeled Kathryn back to the door, and pulled her into the shelter and safety of the manse. I tickled her chin. "You'll never remember what you heard today, will you? One day I'll tell you about it." I decided not to tell Desmond about what had happened to my well-packed box, at least not for now. And Geordie kept his word.

One evening as Kathryn lay asleep, we had a couple of parishioners around for tea and biscuits. Mary and Charlie McKinney were faithful members of the local chapel, but Mary was special. She had an additional small toe, which ran in the family, and that meant she had 'the gift'. After finishing our cups of tea, she brought out her small crystal ball and I held it in my hand for a minute or two. Feeling a little nervous, I handed it back to her. Mary never accepted any fee for her readings, as she consider this ability as a gift from God. I waited as she peered into her crystal ball.

"Ah, I see all kinds of adventures for ye both." She turned it slightly. "My, I see yon a great body of water, like an ocean." She stopped again. "Aye, I see yon a laddie in the family too. And he will give you much worry, but it will be all right." She glanced at me. "Ya, ya, you will travel a great distance, across this body of water to another continent. I see yon lassie all grown-up, and walking down the aisle in white. Ye will be proud of her. And ye'll do well. I see ye later in life quite comfortable." She turned it again. "Tis fading awa' noo." She laid it down and slipped it back into the velvet cover, and we sat back to have another cup of tea.

That evening in bed I wondered at what Mary had told us, but dismissed it as fanciful, at least at that time.

Spring was almost upon us again. The round of washing nappies by hand and hanging them out to dry, along with our clothes, was an almost daily occurrence.

Next door Mary O'Pappa lifted her heavy bosom on to the stone wall separating our houses. Her real name was Slater, but she came from the island of Pappa, now uninhabited, so she was called O'Pappa.

"Mistress Parker," she called. "I see yon minister's breeches up there on the line." She heaved herself a little more on to the fence. "I tell ye, yon minister is as thin as to slip down the plug hole." She pointed to his underwear. "I've told ye before. Ye should be feeding him more porridge, then he'll be a peerie more fatter."

"That's just the way he is," I told her, taking a clothes peg out of my mouth.

"Did I tell ye about knitting a Fair Isle waistcoat for Winston Churchill?"

I smiled. I'd heard it before, but didn't want to be impolite.

"Aye, that I did. I knitted him a bonnie waistcoat and sent it to him, and he sent me a note back, just to me, he did." She paused to see my reaction, then continued, "Can you believe the grand ole man himself did just that?"

"That's very nice. Very special" I said, still pegging the white terry squares on the line and trying not to get slapped in the face by the others, as the mischievous wind blew the droplets out of the nappies. No washing machine, or even a wringer, was provided in the manse, just the electric boiler, which cost too much to heat.

Eventually, Mary left me to finish my task. I stood back, surveying my billowing squares, like sails in the blowing wind. Over in front lay the harbour, with Trondra Island dividing up the Atlantic's grey, whipped waves into two sections, thereby sheltering the quayside. The mainland stretched to the left and I could almost see St. Ninian's Isle this brilliant March day. A peace settled on me. The washing, done for the day, stretched out, flapping, straining to fly away, was somehow satisfying to me. I thought of the poem I'd learned in my London days, from Leslie Weatherhead's book, *A Private House of Prayer.*

I could not find Him where the ventured priests
Intoned the ancient ritual of prayer.
My neighbour bowed the knee,
And yet to me
He was not there.
I could not find Him where the bugles called,
And men cried, "Hallelujah" to the sky
My neighbour sobbed His name -
To her He came
But passed me by.
Yet on a busy day when spring winds blew
My billowing linen to the bleaching sun,
That Man Who served with wood
So clearly stood,
Smiling: "Well done!"
(Doris M. Holden, *To Each His Vision*)

Yes, Jesus was here, He knew, He understood, and it was sufficient.

Another problem however, caught my attention. We had struggled with managing our money ever since we came to Shetland. We'd stopped switching on the hot water heater because of the astronomical electricity bill we'd received that first quarter. Coal took a major chunk of Desmond's meagre stipend. What made matters worse, his £36 per quarter pay cheque didn't always stretch to cover the bills due during the last couple of weeks. This brought out my most creative streak, especially concerning fish. It was the cheapest commodity on the island and I cooked it every way I could imagine, despite Desmond's weariness of monotonous meals.

However, we also tithed. It began during our first year on the island when Desmond received a small booklet in the mail.

"You know," he said, "I think you should read this. It's about tithing."

I wasn't sure exactly what that meant, but I read it.

"Maybe we should start tithing too, and trust God to supply whatever we need," I suggested.

We both felt that this is what we were called to do, and began putting ten per cent of our money away each quarter to go into the plate on Sunday mornings. This particular morning I emptied my purse. "Desmond, I don't know what to do. We only have two shillings left until the end of the week. I've got baby food in for Kathryn, and evaporated milk. I also have some porridge oats, tea and sugar, but that's about it."

He patted my arm. "Don't worry about it," he reassured me, as he usually did. "Something will turn up."

"Maybe, but you're not the one who does the grocery shopping or pays the bills."

He patted my arm again and disappeared into his study.

After he'd gone, I prayed softly. "Lord, you know our problem. You know we don't have enough food. Can you please help us in some way? Thank you, Father, Amen."

Methodist magazines were delivered monthly, and once again it was my task to take them to the homes of the members and collect their money. This was set aside and given to the treasurer whenever I'd finished the job. Six magazines were waiting on the table that afternoon after my impromptu prayer. Kathryn, in her pram and I, layered against the brisk wind, set off. First house of call was Mary Nicholson, wife of Geordie, just up the road.

"Och, come along in," Mary greeted me warmly. I gave her the magazine and she gave me her one shilling and sixpence, which I placed in a special envelope marked "Magazines." We chatted for a while, then she turned to me.

"Would ye like a couple of eggs for ye tea?" she asked. "Yon hens are laying good right noo."

I nodded eagerly. "A couple of eggs would be lovely. We'd really enjoy those for tea."

She took three eggs from her cupboard and put them in a bag. Just then Geordie came through the door.

"Och, there you are lass. I've got a bonnie catch of fresh trout. Would ye like some?"

"Oh, we'd really enjoy that too. We can have that for our dinner tomorrow."

He wrapped two good-sized trout in newspaper. I tucked them into the bottom of the pram along with the eggs, and continued on my way.

The next house of call was Lyddie Sanderson. Her fifteen-year-old daughter shyly handed me a tissue-wrapped gift. I opened it and inside was a beautifully-knitted shell-pink coloured cardigan for Kathryn.

"Oh, Mary, how lovely. Did you knit this?" She smiled and nodded.

"Kathryn will like to wear this, I know. It is so kind of you to knit this for her."

We had tea and a biscuit, and I made to go on my way.

"I have some new rhubarb growing here, in a sheltered spot by yon wall" said her mother. "Could ye like some?"

"I love rhubarb," I enthused, thinking of the sugar I had on hand. It would be a perfect sweet for our tea, after the boiled eggs.

"And, I have here a cabbage. I had a few left from overwintering and just brought them in. Ye may as well have one, if ye can use it."

I assented gladly, and after thanking her profusely, made my other calls, then went back to the manse. As I went to pull the pram up the step into the house I saw beside the door a large bag of potatoes. I almost cried, my heart spilling over with thanks.

After settling Kathryn, I placed the food into the cupboard, and fell to my knees by the fire, after I'd poked it back to life. "Thank you, Lord. I will never doubt You again." Tears rolled down my cheeks. "Help me to always put You first, because, I know You will look out for us, even down to a sack of potatoes."

Of course when Desmond came in, I shared with him the good news.

Kathryn crawled her way into everything that wasn't tied together. String tied the two sideboard cupboards together, and after finding her in the kitchen walk-in cupboard with two precious eggs being rolled on the floor, I had to purchase a gate to go across the narrow passage into the kitchen alcove.

The weeks passed, and Jean's wedding plans were falling into place. The twenty-first of June was the set date, and I was to be Matron of Honour.

CHAPTER 26

FAREWELL TO THE ISLES OF THE SIMMER DIM

Farewell in hope and love; in faith and peace and prayer
George Watson, 1816-1896

We flew down to Jean and Brian's wedding, thanks to contributions from parents. And the night before the wedding Jean and Brian spent the evening with Desmond and me.

"Well, you never guess what your sister said the other evening," said Brian as we sat around the fire.

Jean rolled her eyes. "Here we go again," she said. "He'll never let me forget this."

I leaned forward. "What did she get up to this time?"

Brian leaned back and grinned. "We were coming home from the cinema in town after seeing some film that had all kinds of monsters in it, including a very big octopus." He looked at us. "We got the last bus back, and as usual we went upstairs. Once we got into our seat, Jean began telling me, and everyone else on the upper deck, about this great big octopus, with the big huge testicles." He began shaking.

"Oh, no!" I cried, laughing at the thought.

"But that's not the worst of it," broke in Jean. "He kept asking me questions."

Brian interrupted. "I asked her, 'tell me again, what made that octopus so scary' and she would give another description of the unusually large testicles. Of course everyone else on the bus upstairs was in stitches, and it was packed!"

By now gales of laughter filled the room, and Jean laughed as heartily as anyone.

Finally she said, "It's a good thing our wedding is tomorrow, or I might be tempted to call the whole thing off."

"But you know you'd never find anyone as handsome as me," teased Brian.

And on that note, Mum brought some tea and biscuits into the room for us. She looked at the clock meaningfully, and reminded Brian, "Remember you need to leave soon. You have your wedding day tomorrow and you can't sleep in."

She was determined to make sure her second daughter got to the altar untainted and worthy of her white wedding.

The day dawned fair and bright as only an English summer's day can. We set off for the local church of St John's. Mum and Desmond took care of Kathryn, pretty and dainty in a lemon-flocked dress, while I relished my role as Matron of Honour. Brian's niece, Dianne, was bridesmaid, and together in our bouffant blue dresses we walked down the aisle, as Jean, beautiful in her gown and veil, walked with Dad towards Brian, her long-patient boyfriend. The ceremony was over and we drove to the Calderstones Park Reception House, where two years before Desmond and I had enjoyed our wedding breakfast.

Toasts were proposed. As Dad lifted his glass of wine, I glanced at Mum. Her face beamed triumph. I'd never seen her quite so content before. She smiled like a cat that had finished a saucer of cream and was licking its whiskers.

Suddenly I realised why. She now had both daughters safely married off. Not only that, but they had both been married in white, with all that it symbolized, and no pregnancies on the way. Now she could relax. However, I began to suffer morning sickness once more and suspected that a brother or sister for Kathryn might be starting its prenatal journey!

Jean and Brian set off for the Isle of Man to enjoy their long-anticipated honeymoon, while Desmond, Kathryn and I travelled up to Glasgow to catch the plane back to Shetland.

As Halloween crept up on us that last year, our friendly family doctor confirmed that I was indeed pregnant, with a due date of February 22nd. The Youth Group that Desmond had started had grown and it was decided to celebrate with a Halloween party in the village hall, complete with costumes. The young people insisted that Desmond must wear one too, so I had to think hard.

"You must have something different," I insisted.

"But you don't have a sewing machine to be able to make a costume." Desmond was right, but he hadn't counted on my creativity.

"Let me think about it," I told him, and think I did. I

considered what we had on hand, what oddments were pushed into corners of my tea-chest, and how I might utilize the clothes we owned. A brilliant idea came to me.

"I know what you can be," I proclaimed delightedly. "You can be a devil!"

"I'm a Methodist minister," protested my spouse. "I can't go as a devil!"

"Why not?" I stood with hands on hips surveying his thin frame. "You have a black shirt already. Leave your clerical collar off, of course. I have some black tights that I wear to keep me warm in winter. You have black socks, black shoes, and a black pullover." I clapped my hands. "Voila, you can be a devil!"

I brought out my sewing basket and began cutting up an old black curtain I'd found in a cupboard. A black nylon stocking, with a couple of runs in it, was rescued from the rubbish. I bought a yard of wire from the chandler's shop, and found an old woolly hat in the bottom on my tea-chest. I clipped away, sewed, and fashioned a great-looking tail, complete with fork at the end. I back-stitched it securely on to the back of an old pair of black trousers I'd found, on which he'd spilled a little white paint when decorating the small box room we had for Kathryn. The stocking became a mask, with a couple of eyes cut out, so he could see where he was going. Then I stitched on two horns, one on each side of the pull-on hat.

Halloween arrived. "Now, first put these trousers on," I commanded. "Now the shirt. Tuck it in good. Take the socks and pull them up over the bottom of your trousers." The tail swished to and fro as he bent and stood. Very effective, I thought. Then came the stocking mask, tucked into the black shirt, covered with a V-necked jumper. Finally I pulled the woolly black hat on to his head.

One horn seemed a little too bent, so I straightened the wire, and stood back.

"No one will recognize you in that outfit," I declared, chuckling away.

Desmond was dubious. "I'm not sure this is a good idea." He shook his head. "What will people say if they see me?"

I giggled. "They will never guess it's you, so they won't know. You can take the stocking mask off once you get into the hall and after the youth guess it's you – if they do! Go on. Off you go, or you'll be late!"

He left the house to walk down the road to the village hall. I wished I could have been a fly on the wall when he walked into the youth group, but I had to wait until he returned.

At ten o'clock the back door banged and he stormed in, the stocking mask stuffed in his pocket. He yanked off the horned hat throwing it on a chair. As he did so his tail swung wildly.

I glanced up. "Well, what happened?"

Desmond sat down, holding his tail to one side. His sigh came big and loud. "I got to the hall without seeing anyone on the way, thank goodness, but when I got to the hall…" He hesitated, then groaned slightly.

"Go on, go on," I urged.

"Well, except for the main hall, the place was in darkness, so I let myself in by the side entrance into the kitchen where I saw Old Willy, the caretaker, bent over doing something by the sink. The door was open to the main hall, so I could see where I was going and I approached ask Old Willy to ask why the other lights weren't on, but he didn't hear me." Desmond was silent. He grimaced. "I tapped Willy on the shoulder." He shook his head.

"Well, what did he say?"

Desmond gave me a hard look. "He yelled bloody murder and almost collapsed on the spot. I thought he was going to have a heart attack. I yanked off my hat and mask, as I could see he was scared stiff. He grabbed the sink and kind of stuttered. "O God, it's you. I thought Old Nick had finally come for me. I've got to sit down." I guided him to a chair just inside the hall and he took a swig from the small bottle he had inside his jacket pocket. I think it must have been whisky. That took care of the shock, I think, but his voice was still shaky."

"Oh, that's so funny!" I doubled over in laughter. Everyone knew that Old Willy was a reprobate with a reputation known throughout the island. "Maybe he will mend his ways after that," I said, tears streaming down my cheeks.

"It isn't that funny," Desmond said. "What if he had died? I could have killed him by being a devil."

That set me off again. In response Desmond scowled, "That's the last time you ever get me to dress up for Halloween. I should never have listened to you." He strode off to the bedroom to rid himself of the tell-tail trousers with the still-swishing forked tail, taking with him the hat, with now two rather crumpled horns. He was not happy!

It was the following week that Jessie reported to me. "I heard that yon minister gave Old Willy a fair fright," she said with a mischievous grin.

"Oh, you heard."

"Aye, I did that, and all yon village heard too. Old Willy is telling any that will listen that yon minister was dressed as the devil, and he'd thought Old Nick had come for him. He said that he almost fell on the floor." I laughed. "But that's no all. At yon prayer meeting on Saturday night, after hearing about Willy's tale, Jimmy Henderson prayed for the minister. To use his exact words, he said, 'we pray for our young misguided minister, that he might be shown the error of his ways'." She stopped for a minute.

I groaned and pulled a face. "Oh dear. It was all my fault. I put him up to it. I feel a bit like Eve and the apple, complete with serpent. This sounds like I've really created a problem for him. Is there anything I can do to put it right?"

"Och, dinna worry aboot it," Jessie reassured me. "They'll only talk aboot it until something else comes along."

But I did worry about it. Fortunately we were leaving the following August. Nevertheless I was concerned that someone might tell the District Superintendent and he'd believe that Desmond wasn't worthy of another church. But as the months passed no one said anything and I began to relax, leaving only twinges of guilt.

Christmas that year passed uneventfully that year and on 23rd February 1963, Kathryn had a baby brother. It was late evening when I began labour, and once again, the ambulance whisked me into the hospital in Lerwick. The old wartime Nissen huts that served as the islands' hospital where Kathryn had been born, had been replaced with a spanking new building, now called the Gilbert Bain Hospital.

An hour or so after our arrival, Christopher Russell slithered into this world. As I lay in bed recuperating, an older woman climbed into the bed beside me. Minutes later she was wheeled down to the labour room, and thirty minutes later she emerged with a baby cradled in her arms.

"My, that was a quick labour," I observed casually.

"Och, aye," she replied cheerfully. "I always have the bairns quickly."

"Oh, have many do you have," I asked politely.

"This is my thirteenth, but I had two baby bairns not make it, and a miscarriage too.

"Golly, how on earth do you manage?"

"One just does what one has to. The bigger bairns take care of the peerie ones and so it goes." She sighed. "I really think this has to be the last, though."

"But why did you have so many?"

"I tell my Harold that this is the last, but he just ses, *'we'll see aboot that,'* and then I find myself in the family way again next year."

"But thirteen, that is so many."

"Aye, tis a muckle job to feed so many mouths." She shifted the baby to the other breast. "At fifty-four, I think I've had enough."

I almost fell out of the bed. I couldn't imagine being fifty-four years of age and having your sixteenth baby. Dr Durham had already told me that they didn't believe in birth control, and if I wanted to have any kind of contraception, we'd have to send away to the mainland. "However," he reassured me, "They come in a brown paper wrapper so Tootsie the postman would never know what was in it!" That explained the exceptional number of large families on the islands.

At six weeks old, Christopher began throwing up and crying incessantly. Dr Durham was away on holiday, so a locum had taken his place. She came around to the manse and examined him thoroughly.

"He has a severe ear and bronchial infection," she pronounced. "I'll give you a prescription for tetracycline."

I dutifully gave him the drops, but he didn't improve. That evening, his screams shattered my self-control. I was in tears on the phone again. "Please, please, you've got to do something. He is crying, and can't breathe because he is wheezing so much." I was beside myself.

"Continue with the drops," she said, "and call me in the morning."

I sat up in bed, holding Christopher in my arms while Desmond lay beside me. My baby's cries wrung my heart. "Please God," I prayed fervently, "Please, please, don't let him die. Don't let him die!"

Part-way through the night, his breathing eased slightly and the crying died to a whimper. Tentatively I laid him in the cot, but I couldn't go back to sleep, afraid that he might slip away. Eventually morning light crept through the opening of the curtains that didn't quite meet together, and Chris stayed with us. However, it was some time before he finally recuperated, and then he had difficulty in catching up.

Springtime arrived and with it, the spreading of daylight hours. A watery sun emerged from time to time amidst the splattering rain against the windows. Local people called the Shetland Isles the 'Isles of the Simmer Dim' because of the long summer days, with only a twilight settling briefly between each day. August approached in its own time and the day of leaving drew near. Now the children were dressed, everything was packed and Desmond and I stood by the living room window of the manse taking in the familiar scene of stone cottages leading down to the quayside, with the hills of Castle Voe stretching up and beyond into the horizon.

"This was our first home" Desmond said fondly, putting his arm about me. "We will always remember this place in the years ahead as being special."

I agreed with a nod of my head as I took one last look out towards the harbour with a fishing boating chugging in and seagulls flocking above the catch to be squabbled over. So much had cascaded into my life these past three years. Laughter gurgled up briefly as memory replayed some of the more humorous incidents like the bottle of sherry and the Halloween party. I thought of Jessie and her wisdom and friendship, along with the hospitality of the Searles in Lerwick, Jim and Alma, my knitting belt, and the glimpses of ethereal beauty as one turned a corner to view an ice-blue voe against the backdrop of stark peat-embedded hills.

Plans for overseas work were on hold, as we heard about missionary families who we knew were fleeing the field because of local uprisings and violence, such as the Mau Mau in Kenya. I glanced at our two little ones and realised that I could never subject them to such tumultuous danger. Now I was impatient to take the next step, back to civilization, friends and family.

A horn blasted outside. Quickly I took Kathryn's small hand whilst Desmond carried Chris. I closed the door behind us and our family began the journey back to England and, for me, home. I wondered what new adventures lay ahead.

EPILOGUE

A few years later Mary McKinney's crystal reading came true. A deep ocean was crossed by our family of four, but it was westward across the Atlantic to America. Our earlier missionary dreams had dissipated when more violence spread its bloodshed across the colonies as they sought their independence from England, and missionary families hastened home.

Upon our arrival in Boston and after being met by another ex-patriot ministerial couple, we were driven north to Maine. Along the way we made our first stop, at a Howard Johnson's ice cream parlour. Inside the shop we were confronted with twenty-nine flavours of ice cream. Overwhelmed with blueberry (what were blueberries?), banana, rum-raisin and other exotic tantalising tastes, all four of us settled for familiar, old-fashioned vanilla. For a moment I thought back to the paucity of such treats when I had been a child and shook my head in disbelief.

Twenty years after my mum had called Miss Baker to inform her I would be leaving school, I finally received my Bachelor's Degree in Education, with highest honours, from the University of Maine at Orono. Another thirteen years passed and I received my Master's Degree in Administration. After a total of twenty-five wonderful, fulfilling years in public education, I finally retired.

I brought the square cardboard box back to Maine. Now once again I gently replace the remains of the once-malevolent gasmask, along with the memories. As I pull down the lid towards the box I notice it is officially called a 'respirator' and there are specific instructions on how to correctly pull it up over the face and adjust the taped straps at the back.

I shake my head with a smile as I fold the lid down and tie it up with the original string. "Well, Mum," I say out loud. "You never did get rid of my gasmask after all, did you?" I take the box to the bedroom and carefully lay it on the top shelf of my closet and close the door.

So the journey continues. God has brought me to this place up steps and stairs as well as down slippery slopes, ever deeper into His Presence, until that is all there really is.